Forget the Aggravation of Complicated Design Software

Design, Build and Decorate Your New Home on Your Kitchen Table

Computers are great, but when it comes to planning your new home, you don't want the frustration of complicated home design software getting between you and your dream. Visualize and test your designs using our proven design systems. Really see how your ideas work with our **3-D Home Kit** and **Home Quick Planner**.

HOME QUICK PLANNER

Design and Decorate Your New Home

Our Home Quick Planner comes with 700 pre-cut, reusable peel-and-stick furniture, fixture and architectural symbols that let you design floor plans and make changes instantly. Go ahead! Knock down walls and move cabinets, furniture, appliances, bathroom fixtures, windows and doors—even whole rooms. Includes 1/4-in. scale Floor Plan Grid, stairs, outlets, switches, lights, plus design ideas.

Regularly $22.95 **Special Offer: $19.95**

3-D HOME KIT

"Build" Your New Home

Construct a detailed three-dimensional scale model of your new home. Our kit contains a complete assortment of cardboard building materials—from brick, stone, stucco, clapboards, roofing and decking to windows, doors, skylights, stairs, bathroom fixtures, kitchen cabinets and appliances—to construct a home of up to 3,000 square feet. (For larger homes, order an extra kit.) Includes Floor Plan Grid, interior walls, special Scaled Ruler and Roof Slope Calculator, professional design notes and complete model building instructions.

Regularly $33.95 **Special Offer: $29.95**

To order, call
1-800-235-5700
Monday - Friday 8 a.m. - 8 p.m. Eastern Time

the
Garlinghouse
company

new Home Designs
for 2002
A SABOT PUBLICATION

The Garlinghouse Company Staff

Chief Executive Officer & Publisher
James D. McNair, III

Editorial Director
Steve Culpepper

Managing Editor
Debra Cochran

Art Director
Christopher Berrien

Art Production Staff
Debra Novitch, Andy Russell, Karen LeBoulluec

Design Director
Wade Schmelter

Assistant Design Director
Michael Rinaldi

Marketing Assistant
Louise Ryan

Financial Controller
Doug DiMora

Senior Programmer
Jason Cyr

Accounts Receivable/Payable
Elizabeth Unikewicz

Senior Accountant
Angela West

Office Coordinator
Barbara Neal

Telesales Manager
Frank Shekosky

Telesales Staff
Lisa Barnes, Anne Hawkins,
Carol Patenaude, Robert Rogala
Colleen Sawyer, Alice Sonski, Jeanne Willet

Plans Fulfillment Manager
Wayne Green

Advertising Sales Director
Jerry Stoeckigt
1-800-279-7361

Northeast Regional Ad Sales
Erin White
800-895-3715 ext. 4033

Newsstand Distributor
Curtis Circulation Company, 730 River Road
New Milford, New Jersey 07646
Phone: (201) 634-7400
Fax: (201) 634-7499

Circulation Consultant
Michael A. Gerardo Associates

SABOT
PUBLISHING, INC.

James D. Causey	PRESIDENT & CEO
William T. Berry	CHIEF FINANCIAL OFFICER
Patricia B. Fox	VP CIRCULATION, PRODUCTION & OPERATIONS
Sarah M. Hill	VP MARKETING & PROMOTION
Susan A. McConnell-Remes	MARKETING MANAGER
Jennifer L. Phelps	ASSISTANT CIRCULATION MANAGER
Brenda S. Compton	CONTROLLER
Beth C. Wilkerson	SENIOR ACCOUNTANT
Julie M. Plourde	HUMAN RESOURCES SPECIALIST
Patrice B. Fishel	ACCOUNTS PAYABLE SPECIALIST
Teena F. Smith	OFFICE MANAGER

Contents

Cover Designs
Andy Russell

www.familyhomeplans.com

All Website
Credit Card
Transactions
Are Secure With
VeriSign Encryption

We Welcome Your Feedback! Email us at: editor@garlinghouse.com

Hot New Designs

We are pleased to bring you this exciting feature; a special section presenting the newest home designs from our talented network of designers. These innovative floor plans are on the cutting edge of today's market, offering the ultimate in convenience, style and luxurious detailing.

BL		See Order Pages and Index for In
Units	Single	
Price Code	E	
Total Finished	2,441 sq. ft.	
Main Finished	2,441 sq. ft.	
Garage Unfinished	477 sq. ft.	
Dimensions	74'x64'	
Foundation	Slab	
Bedrooms	4	
Full Baths	3	
Half Baths	1	
Main Ceiling	10'-12'	
Primary Roof Pitch	6:12	
Max Ridge Height	21'	
Exterior Walls	2x4	

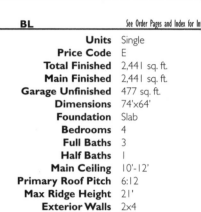

MAIN FLOOR

Design 63061

BL

See Order Pages and Index for Info

Units	Single
Price Code	F
Total Finished	2,636 sq. ft.
Main Finished	2,636 sq. ft.
Garage Unfinished	536 sq. ft.
Dimensions	68'8''x76'
Foundation	Slab
Bedrooms	4
Full Baths	3
Main Ceiling	11'
Primary Roof Pitch	6:12
Max Ridge Height	23'5''
Roof Framing	Truss

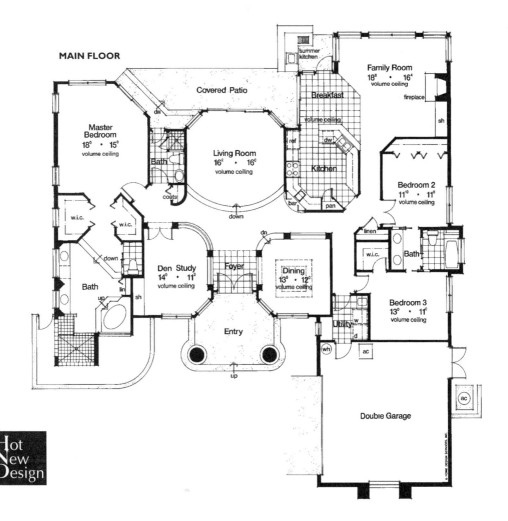

MAIN FLOOR

Master Bedroom 18⁰ · 15⁰ volume ceiling

Covered Patio

summer kitchen

Family Room 18⁸ · 16⁴ volume ceiling

fireplace

Bath

Living Room 16² · 16⁰ volume ceiling

Breakfast volume ceiling

Kitchen

ref

dw

Bedroom 2 11¹⁰ · 11⁰ volume ceiling

w.i.c.

coats

bar

pan

w.i.c.

linen

w.i.c.

Bath

down

Bath

lin

Den Study 14⁰ · 11² volume ceiling

Foyer

Dining 13⁰ · 12⁰ volume ceiling

Bedroom 3 13⁰ · 11⁰ volume ceiling

up

sh

Entry

Utility

wh

ac

ac

Double Garage

Hot New Design

Design 64123

BL

See Order Pages and Index for Info

Units	Single
Price Code	G
Total Finished	1,848 sq. ft.
Main Finished	1,848 sq. ft.
Garage Unfinished	571 sq. ft.
Deck Unfinished	254 sq. ft.
Porch Unfinished	217 sq. ft.
Dimensions	58'x60'
Foundation	Slab
Bedrooms	3
Full Baths	2
Primary Roof Pitch	9:12
Max Ridge Height	30'6''
Exterior Walls	2x6

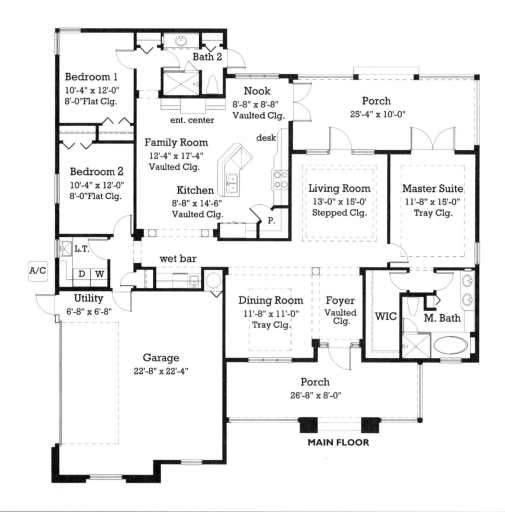

MAIN FLOOR

Design 64124

BL

See Order Pages and Index for Info

Units	Single
Price Code	G
Total Finished	1,848 sq. ft.
Main Finished	1,848 sq. ft.
Garage Unfinished	571 sq. ft.
Deck Unfinished	217 sq. ft.
Porch Unfinished	254 sq. ft.
Dimensions	58'x59'6''
Foundation	Slab
Bedrooms	3
Full Baths	2
Primary Roof Pitch	9:12
Max Ridge Height	30'6'
Exterior Walls	2x6

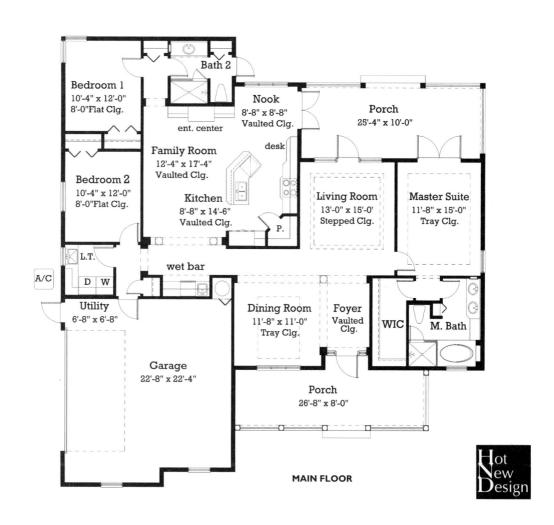

Bedroom 1
10'-4" x 12'-0"
8'-0"Flat Clg.

Bath 2

ent. center

Nook
8'-8" x 8'-8"
Vaulted Clg.

Porch
25'-4" x 10'-0"

Family Room
12'-4" x 17'-4"
Vaulted Clg.

desk

Bedroom 2
10'-4" x 12'-0"
8'-0"Flat Clg.

Kitchen
8'-8" x 14'-6"
Vaulted Clg.

Living Room
13'-0" x 15'-0'
Stepped Clg.

Master Suite
11'-8" x 15'-0"
Tray Clg.

L.T.

A/C   D   W

wet bar

Utility
6'-8" x 6'-8"

Dining Room
11'-8" x 11'-0"
Tray Clg.

Foyer
Vaulted Clg.

WIC   **M. Bath**

Garage
22'-8" x 22'-4"

Porch
26'-8" x 8'-0"

MAIN FLOOR

Hot New Design

Design 64126

BL

See Order Pages and Index for Info

Units	Single
Price Code	H
Total Finished	2,477 sq. ft.
Main Finished	2,477 sq. ft.
Lower Unfinished	1,742 sq. ft.
Dimensions	70'x72'
Foundation	Basement
	Slab
Bedrooms	3
Full Baths	2
Primary Roof Pitch	9:12
Max Ridge Height	29'
Exterior Walls	2x6

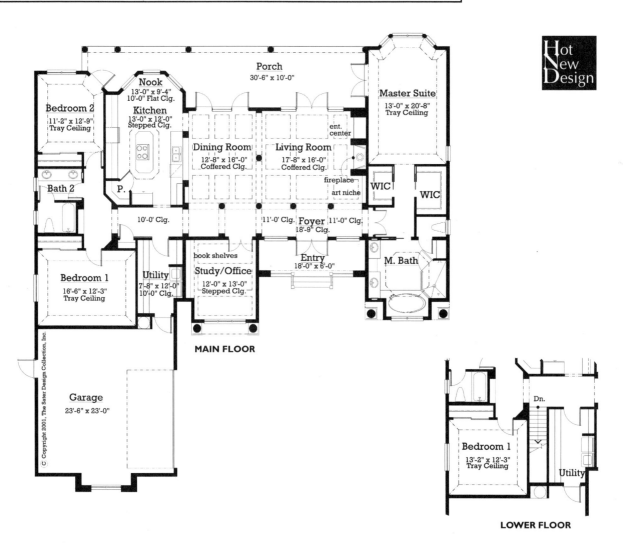

Hot New Design

MAIN FLOOR

Porch
30'-6" x 10'-0"

Nook
13'-0" x 9'-4"
10'-0" Flat Clg.

Kitchen
13'-0" x 12'-0"
Stepped Clg.

Bedroom 2
11'-2" x 12'-9"
Tray Ceiling

Bath 2

P.

Dining Room
12'-8" x 16'-0"
Coffered Clg.

Living Room
17'-8" x 16'-0"
Coffered Clg.

ent. center

fireplace

art niche

Master Suite
13'-0" x 20'-8"
Tray Ceiling

WIC

WIC

10'-0' Clg.

11'-0' Clg.

Foyer
18'-9" Clg.

11'-0" Clg.

M. Bath

book shelves

Study/Office
12'-0" x 13'-0"
Stepped Clg.

Entry
18'-0" x 6'-0"

Bedroom 1
16'-6" x 12'-3"
Tray Ceiling

Utility
7'-8" x 12'-0"
10'-0" Clg.

© Copyright 2001, The Sater Design Collection, Inc.

Garage
23'-6" x 23'-0"

LOWER FLOOR

Dn.

Bedroom 1
13'-2" x 12'-3"
Tray Ceiling

Utility

8

Design 64127

BL

See Order Pages and Index for Info

Units	Single
Price Code	H
Total Finished	2,502 sq. ft.
Main Finished	2,502 sq. ft.
Garage Unfinished	612 sq. ft.
Deck Unfinished	108 sq. ft.
Porch Unfinished	397 sq. ft.
Dimensions	70'x72'
Foundation	Basement
	Slab
Bedrooms	3
Full Baths	2
Primary Roof Pitch	9:12
Max Ridge Height	27'4''
Exterior Walls	2x6

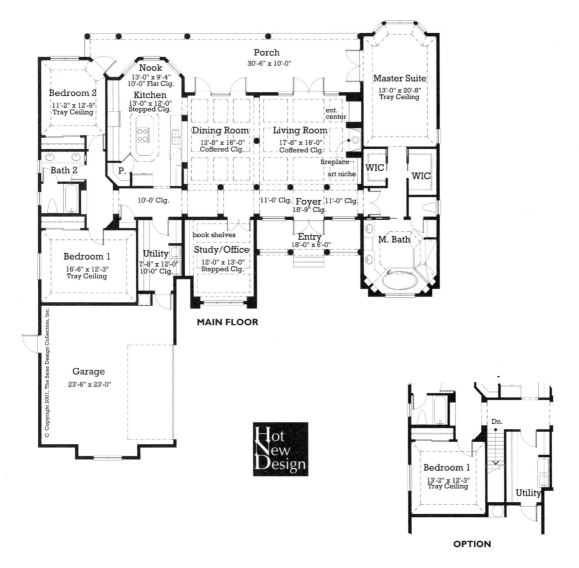

MAIN FLOOR

OPTION

Design 64128

BL

See Order Pages and Index for Info

Units	Single
Price Code	H
Total Finished	2,334 sq. ft.
First Finished	1,716 sq. ft.
Second Finished	618 sq. ft.
Deck Unfinished	210 sq. ft.
Porch Unfinished	128 sq. ft.
Dimensions	47'x50'
Foundation	Slab
Bedrooms	3
Full Baths	3
Primary Roof Pitch	9:12
Max Ridge Height	29'2''
Exterior Walls	2×6

FIRST FLOOR

Master Suite
15'-0" x 13'-8"
Stepped Clg.

Porch
16'-0" x 8'-0"
Vaulted Clg.

Breakfast
12'-0' x 9'-10"
9'-4" Flat Clg.

WIC

WIC

built-ins

Great Room
15'-10" x 15'-4"
Vaulted Clg.

fireplace

Kitchen
12'-6" x 11'-8"

M. Bath

CL.

Dining
11'-8" x 13'-10"
Tray Clg.

Utility
5'-6"x9'-4"

L.

Foyer

Bath 2

L.

bench

Study/Office
13'-0" x 11'-6"
Coffered Clg.

Porch
31'-0" x 6'-0'
9'-4" Flat Clg.

Hot New Design

SECOND FLOOR

Bedroom 1
11'-0' x 13'-0"
8'-0' Flat Clg.

Bath 3

open to below

WIC

desk

desk

Dn.

Dn.

L.

open to
below

WIC

open to
below

Bedroom 2
11'-0' x 13'-6"
8'-0' Flat Clg.

Equip.

plant
shelf

plant
shelf

Design 64139

BL

See Order Pages and Index for Info

Units	Single
Price Code	J
Total Finished	3,098 sq. ft.
First Finished	2,146 sq. ft.
Second Finished	952 sq. ft.
Basement Unfinished	929 sq. ft.
Garage Unfinished	1,004 sq. ft.
Deck Unfinished	426 sq. ft.
Porch Unfinished	426 sq. ft.
Dimensions	52'x65'4''
Foundation	Crawl space
Bedrooms	3
Full Baths	3
Half Baths	1
Max Ridge Height	39'
Exterior Walls	2x6

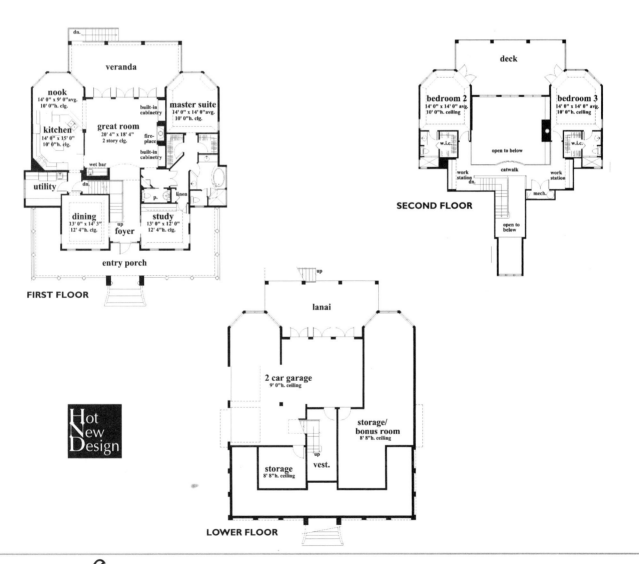

Design 65615

See Order Pages and Index for Info

Units	Single
Price Code	L
Total Finished	5,474 sq. ft.
First Finished	4,193 sq. ft.
Second Finished	1,281 sq. ft.
Dimensions	94'x71'
Foundation	Crawl space
	Slab
Bedrooms	4
Full Baths	4
Half Baths	2
First Ceiling	12'
Second Ceiling	10'
Primary Roof Pitch	8:12

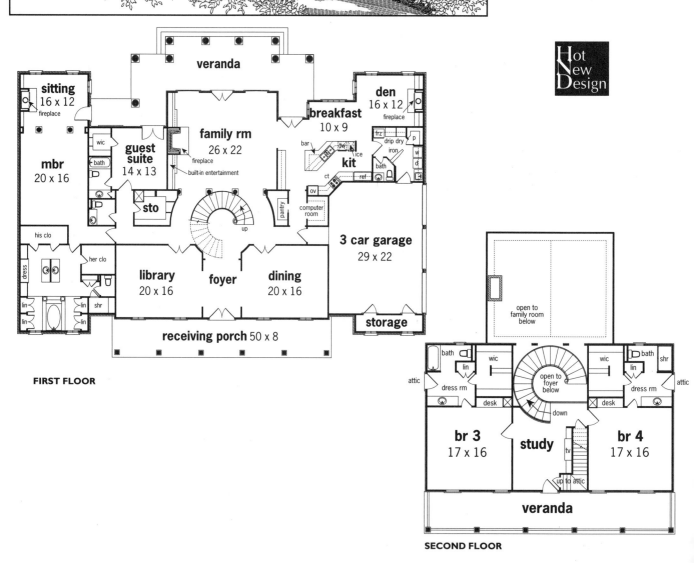

FIRST FLOOR

SECOND FLOOR

Hot New Design

Design 65616

BL

See Order Pages and Index for Info

Units	Single
Price Code	B
Total Finished	1,704 sq. ft.
First Finished	1,704 sq. ft.
Dimensions	71'x50'
Foundation	Crawl space
	Slab
Bedrooms	3
Full Baths	2
Half Baths	1
First Ceiling	8-10
Primary Roof Pitch	12:12

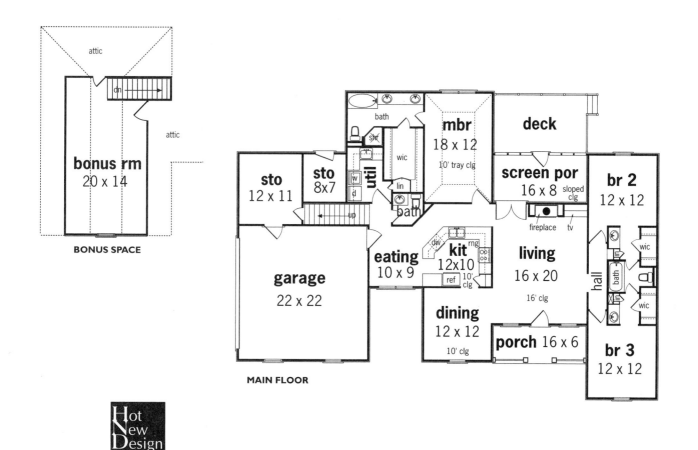

bonus rm 20 x 14

attic

dn

BONUS SPACE

bath

mbr 18 x 12
10' tray clg

deck

wic

screen por 16 x 8 sloped clg

br 2 12 x 12

sto 12 x 11

sto 8x7

util

lin

bath

fireplace   tv

wic

garage 22 x 22

up

eating 10 x 9

dw

kit 12x10
10' clg

rng

ref

living 16 x 20
16' clg

hall

bath

wic

dining 12 x 12
10' clg

porch 16 x 6

br 3 12 x 12

MAIN FLOOR

Hot New Design

Design **69008**

BL   See Order Pages and Index for Info

Units	Single
Price Code	K
Total Finished	3,850 sq. ft.
First Finished	2,306 sq. ft.
Second Finished	1,544 sq. ft.
Dimensions	80'8''x51'8''
Foundation	Basement
Bedrooms	5
Full Baths	3
Half Baths	1

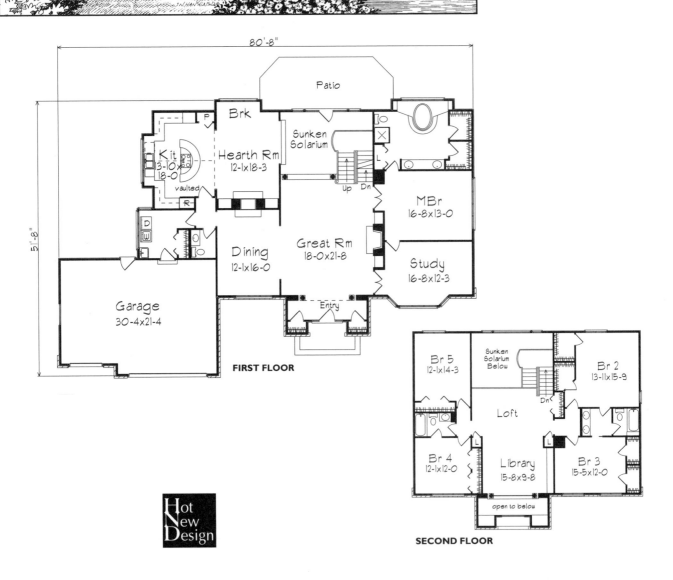

FIRST FLOOR

80'-8"

51'-8"

Patio

Brk

Kit
13-10x18-0
vaulted

Hearth Rm
12-1x18-3

Sunken
Solarium

Up   Dn

MBr
16-8x13-0

Dining
12-1x16-0

Great Rm
18-0x21-8

Study
16-8x12-3

Garage
30-4x21-4

Entry

SECOND FLOOR

Br 5
12-1x14-3

Sunken
Solarium
Below

Br 2
13-11x15-9

Loft

Dn

Br 4
12-1x12-0

Library
15-8x9-8

Br 3
15-5x12-0

open to below

Hot New Design

Design 94288

BL   See Order Pages and Index for Info

Units	Single
Price Code	H
Total Finished	2,374 sq. ft.
First Finished	1,510 sq. ft.
Second Finished	864 sq. ft.
Basement Unfinished	1,290 sq. ft.
Deck Unfinished	275 sq. ft.
Porch Unfinished	275 sq. ft.
Dimensions	44'x49'
Foundation	Basement
Bedrooms	3
Full Baths	3
Half Baths	1
Primary Roof Pitch	10:12
Max Ridge Height	43'4"
Roof Framing	Truss
Exterior Walls	2x6

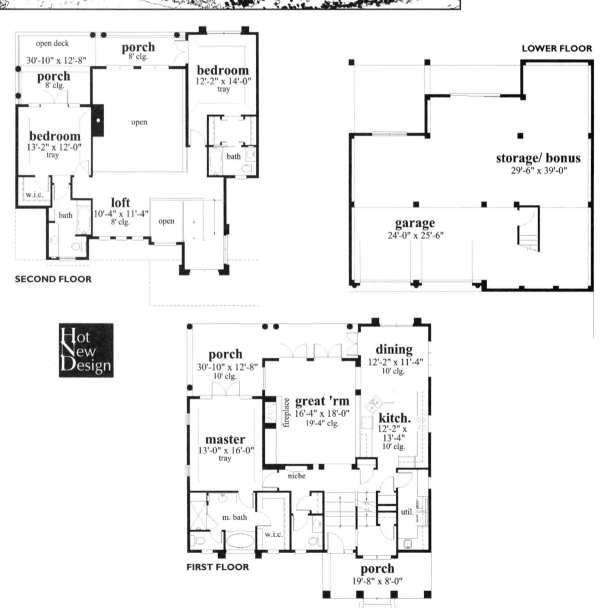

SECOND FLOOR

open deck
30'-10" x 12'-8"

porch
8' clg.

porch
8' clg.

bedroom
12'-2" x 14'-0"
tray

open

bath

bedroom
13'-2" x 12'-0"
tray

w.i.c.

bath

loft
10'-4" x 11'-4"
8' clg.

open

LOWER FLOOR

storage/ bonus
29'-6" x 39'-0"

garage
24'-0" x 25'-6"

Hot New Design

FIRST FLOOR

porch
30'-10" x 12'-8"
10' clg.

dining
12'-2" x 11'-4"
10' clg.

great 'rm
16'-4" x 18'-0"
19'-4" clg.

fireplace

kitch.
12'-2" x
13'-4"
10' clg.

master
13'-0" x 16'-0"
tray

niche

m. bath

w.i.c.

util.

porch
19'-8" x 8'-0"

15

Design 94289

BL

See Order Pages and Index for Info

Units	Single
Price Code	H
Total Finished	2,374 sq. ft.
First Finished	1,510 sq. ft.
Second Finished	864 sq. ft.
Basement Unfinished	1,290 sq. ft.
Dimensions	44'x49'
Foundation	Basement
Bedrooms	3
Full Baths	3
Half Baths	1
Primary Roof Pitch	10:12
Max Ridge Height	43'4''
Roof Framing	Truss
Exterior Walls	2x6

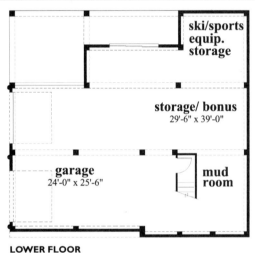

ski/sports equip. storage

storage/ bonus
29'-6" x 39'-0"

garage
24'-0" x 25'-6"

mud room

LOWER FLOOR

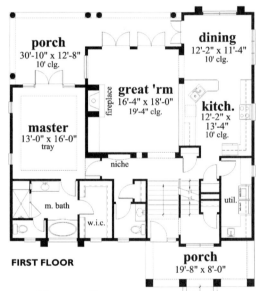

porch
30'-10" x 12'-8"
10' clg.

dining
12'-2" x 11'-4"
10' clg.

great 'rm
16'-4" x 18'-0"
19'-4" clg.

fireplace

kitch.
12'-2" x 13'-4"
10' clg.

master
13'-0" x 16'-0"
tray

niche

m. bath

w.i.c.

util.

FIRST FLOOR

porch
19'-8" x 8'-0"

Hot New Design

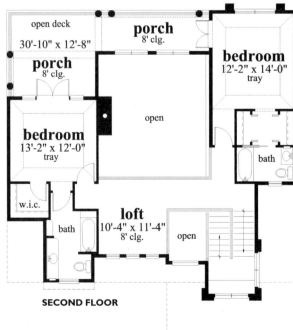

open deck
30'-10" x 12'-8"

porch
8' clg.

porch
8' clg.

bedroom
12'-2" x 14'-0"
tray

open

bedroom
13'-2" x 12'-0"
tray

bath

w.i.c.

bath

loft
10'-4" x 11'-4"
8' clg.

open

SECOND FLOOR

Design 94295

BL

See Order Pages and Index for Info

Units	Single
Price Code	I
Total Finished	2,513 sq. ft.
First Finished	1,542 sq. ft.
Second Finished	971 sq. ft.
Bonus Unfinished	747 sq. ft.
Garage Unfinished	663 sq. ft.
Deck Unfinished	264 sq. ft.
Porch Unfinished	330 sq. ft.
Dimensions	46'x51'
Foundation	Basement
Bedrooms	3
Full Baths	3
Primary Roof Pitch	10:12
Max Ridge Height	39'4"
Roof Framing	Truss
Exterior Walls	2x6

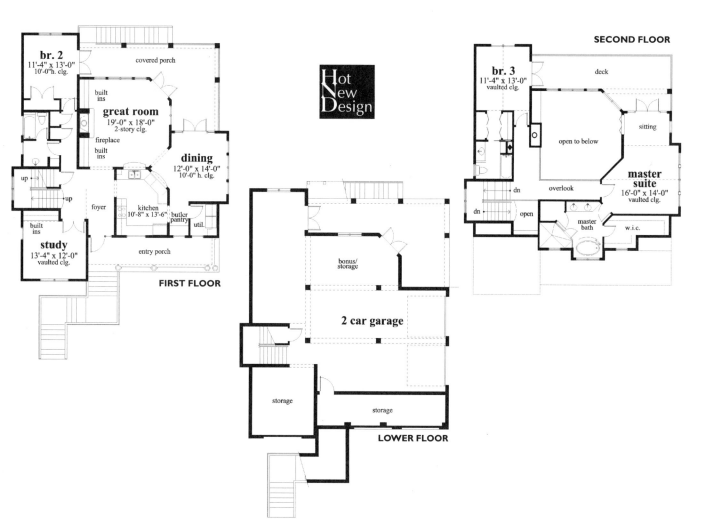

Hot New Design

FIRST FLOOR

- **br. 2** 11'-4" x 13'-0" 10'-0"h. clg.
- covered porch
- built ins
- **great room** 19'-0" x 18'-0" 2-story clg.
- fireplace
- built ins
- **dining** 12'-0" x 14'-0" 10'-0" h. clg.
- up
- up
- foyer
- kitchen 10'-8" x 13'-6"
- butler pantry
- util.
- built ins
- **study** 13'-4" x 12'-0" vaulted clg.
- entry porch

LOWER FLOOR

- bonus/storage
- **2 car garage**
- storage
- storage

SECOND FLOOR

- **br. 3** 11'-4" x 13'-0" vaulted clg.
- deck
- open to below
- sitting
- overlook
- dn
- dn
- open
- **master suite** 16'-0" x 14'-0" vaulted clg.
- master bath
- w.i.c.

Design 97313

BL   See Order Pages and Index for Info

Units	Single
Price Code	G
Total Finished	2,875 sq. ft.
First Finished	2,079 sq. ft.
Second Finished	796 sq. ft.
Porch Unfinished	234 sq. ft.
Dimensions	63'×68'
Foundation	Basement
Bedrooms	4
Full Baths	2
Half Baths	1
First Ceiling	9'-1/8''
Second Ceiling	8'-1/8''
Primary Roof Pitch	12:12
Secondary Roof Pitch	4:12
Max Ridge Height	33'2''
Roof Framing	Truss
Exterior Walls	2x6

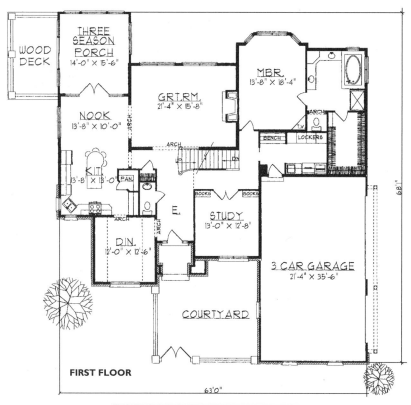

FIRST FLOOR

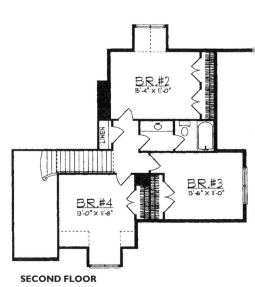

SECOND FLOOR

REAR ELEVATION

Design 97314

See Order Pages and Index for Info

Units	Single
Price Code	L
Total Finished	5,211 sq. ft.
First Finished	3,336 sq. ft.
Lower Finished	1,875 sq. ft.
Basement Unfinished	1,470 sq. ft.
Garage Unfinished	1,377 sq. ft.
Deck Unfinished	237 sq. ft.
Dimensions	119'0''x57'0''
Foundation	Basement
Bedrooms	4
Full Baths	1
Half Baths	1
3/4 Baths	2
Primary Roof Pitch	10:12
Secondary Roof Pitch	12:12
Max Ridge Height	33'4''
Roof Framing	Truss
Exterior Walls	2x6

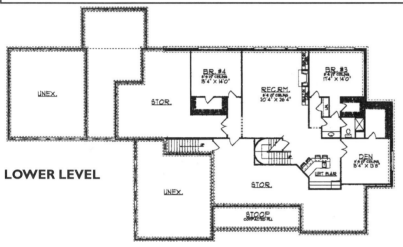

LOWER LEVEL

UPPER LEVEL

Design 97315

Units	Single
Price Code	L
Total Finished	5,639 sq. ft.
Main Finished	2,812 sq. ft.
Lower Finished	2,827 sq. ft.
Garage Unfinished	1,136 sq. ft.
Deck Unfinished	113 sq. ft.
Porch Unfinished	182 sq. ft.
Dimensions	95'x62'
Foundation	Basement
Bedrooms	4
Full Baths	3
Half Baths	1
First Ceiling	10'-1/8
Primary Roof Pitch	6:12
Max Ridge Height	25'4''
Roof Framing	Truss
Exterior Walls	2x6

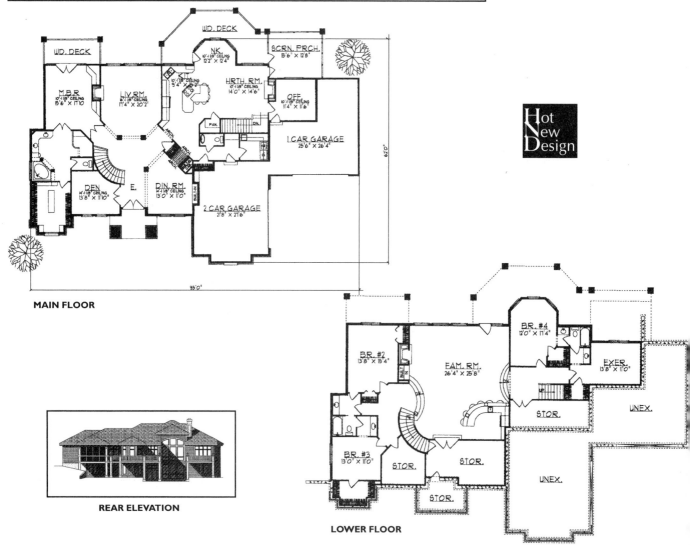

Hot New Design

MAIN FLOOR

REAR ELEVATION

LOWER FLOOR

20

Design 97316

See Order Pages and Index for Info

Units	Single
Price Code	L
Total Finished	6,604 sq. ft.
Main Finished	4,654 sq. ft.
Lower Finished	1,934 sq. ft.
Upper Finished	1,950 sq. ft.
Porch Unfinished	364 sq. ft.
Dimensions	122'4"x97'0"
Bedrooms	4
Full Baths	5
Half Baths	1
First Ceiling	10' 1 1/8
Second Ceiling	9' 1'1/8"
Primary Roof Pitch	10:12
Secondary Roof Pitch	10:12
Max Ridge Height	37'4"
Roof Framing	Truss
Exterior Walls	2x6

UPPER LEVEL

MAIN FLOOR

Hot New Design

LOWER LEVEL

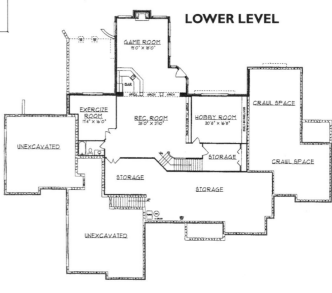

Design 97771

BL

See Order Pages and Index for Info

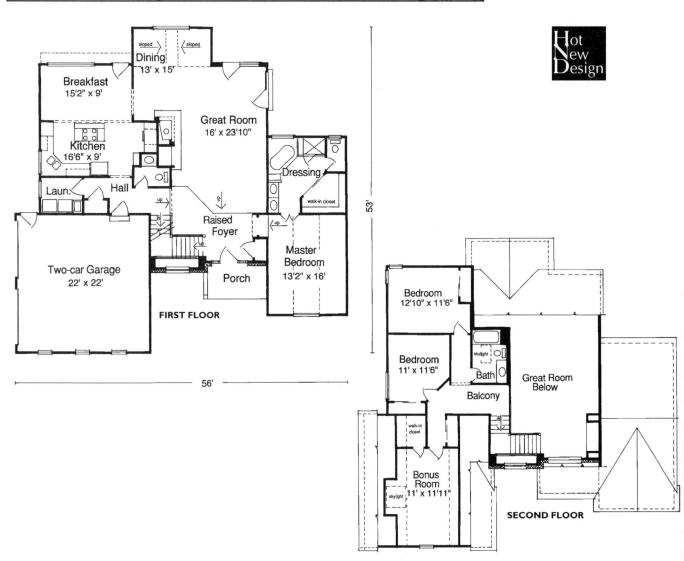

Units	Single
Price Code	D
Total Finished	2,156 sq. ft.
First Finished	1,605 sq. ft.
Second Finished	551 sq. ft.
Bonus Unfinished	249 sq. ft.
Basement Unfinished	1,605 sq. ft.
Garage Unfinished	473 sq. ft.
Porch Unfinished	55 sq. ft.
Dimensions	56'x53'
Foundation	Basement
Bedrooms	3
Full Baths	2
Half Baths	1
First Ceiling	8'
Second Ceiling	8'
Primary Roof Pitch	9:12
Secondary Roof Pitch	9:12
Max Ridge Height	26'
Roof Framing	Truss
Exterior Walls	2x4

Hot New Design

FIRST FLOOR

Breakfast 15'2" x 9'

Dining 13' x 15'

Great Room 16' x 23'10"

Kitchen 16'6" x 9'

Laun.

Hall

Dressing

walk-in closet

Raised Foyer

Master Bedroom 13'2" x 16'

Porch

Two-car Garage 22' x 22'

56'

53'

SECOND FLOOR

Bedroom 12'10" x 11'6"

Bedroom 11' x 11'6"

Bath

skylight

Balcony

Great Room Below

walk-in closet

Bonus Room 11' x 11'11"

skylight

Design 91002

BL/ML/ZIP   See Order Pages and Index for Info

Units	Single
Price Code	A
Total Finished	1,096 sq. ft.
First Finished	808 sq. ft.
Second Finished	288 sq. ft.
Dimensions	24'x32'
Foundation	Crawl space
Bedrooms	2
Full Baths	1
3/4 Baths	1
Primary Roof Pitch	7:12
Max Ridge Height	25'
Roof Framing	Stick
Exterior Walls	2x6

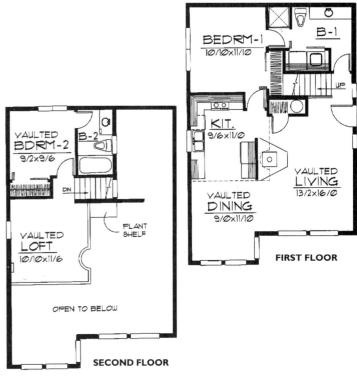

VAULTED BDRM-2
9/2x9/6

B-2

DN

VAULTED LOFT
10/10x11/6

PLANT SHELF

OPEN TO BELOW

SECOND FLOOR

BEDRM-1
10/10x11/10

B-1

KIT.
9/6x11/0

UP

VAULTED LIVING
13/2x16/0

VAULTED DINING
9/0x11/10

FIRST FLOOR

Design 34003

BL/ML/ZIP/RRR   See Order Pages and Index for Info

Units	Single
Price Code	A
Total Finished	1,146 sq. ft.
Main Finished	1,146 sq. ft.
Dimensions	44'x28'
Foundation	Basement
	Crawl space
	Slab
Bedrooms	3
Full Baths	2
First Ceiling	8'
Primary Roof Pitch	5:12
Max Ridge Height	16'
Roof Framing	Stick
Exterior Walls	2x4,2x6

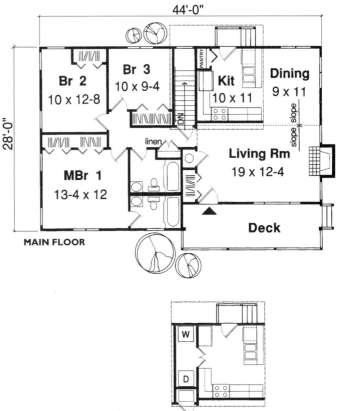

44'-0"

28'-0"

Br 2
10 x 12-8

Br 3
10 x 9-4

PANTRY

Kit
10 x 11

Dining
9 x 11

slope · slope

DN

linen

Living Rm
19 x 12-4

MBr 1
13-4 x 12

Deck

MAIN FLOOR

W

D

SLAB/CRAWLSPACE OPTION

Design 61004

BL

See Order Pages and Index for Info

Units	Single
Price Code	A
Total Finished	1,194 sq. ft.
First Finished	862 sq. ft.
Second Finished	332 sq. ft.
Dimensions	42'x36'2''
Foundation	Slab
Bedrooms	2
Full Baths	2

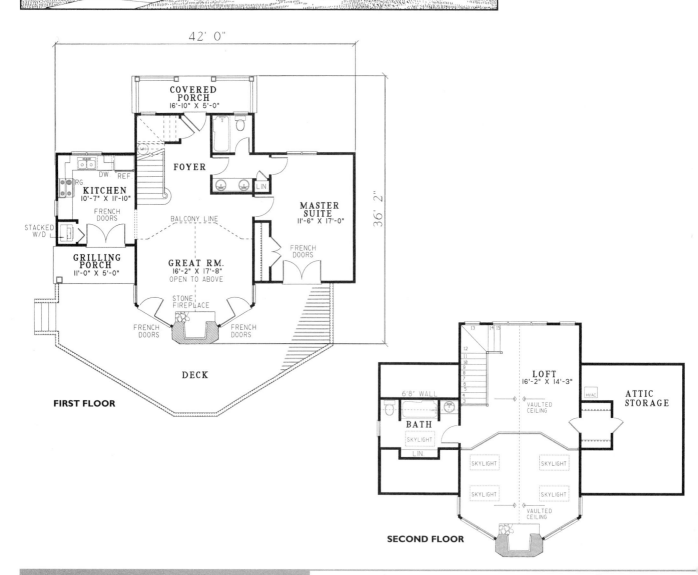

FIRST FLOOR

42' 0"

36' 2"

COVERED PORCH
16'-10" X 5'-0"

FOYER

KITCHEN
10'-7" X 11'-10"

DW   REF.

RG

STACKED W/D

FRENCH DOORS

GRILLING PORCH
11'-0" X 5'-0"

BALCONY LINE

MASTER SUITE
11'-6" X 17'-0"

FRENCH DOORS

LIN

GREAT RM.
16'-2" X 17'-8"
OPEN TO ABOVE

STONE FIREPLACE

FRENCH DOORS

FRENCH DOORS

DECK

SECOND FLOOR

LOFT
16'-2" X 14'-3"

ATTIC STORAGE

HVAC

VAULTED CEILING

BATH
SKYLIGHT
LIN.

6'8" WALL

SKYLIGHT

SKYLIGHT

SKYLIGHT

SKYLIGHT

VAULTED CEILING

Design 92502

BL/ML See Order Pages and Index for Info

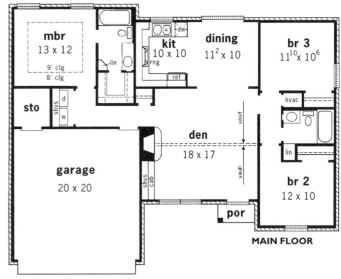

Units	Single
Price Code	A
Total Finished	1,237 sq. ft.
Main Finished	1,237 sq. ft.
Garage Unfinished	436 sq. ft.
Dimensions	50'x38'
Foundation	Crawl space
	Slab
Bedrooms	3
Full Baths	2
First Ceiling	8'
Primary Roof Pitch	8:12
Max Ridge Height	18'6''
Roof Framing	Stick
Exterior Walls	2x4

MAIN FLOOR

mbr 13 x 12 — 9' clg / 8' clg

sto

garage 20 x 20

kit 10 x 10 — rng / ref

dining 11²x 10

den 18 x 17

br 3 11¹⁰x 10⁶

br 2 12 x 10

hvac

por

Design 96484

BL/ML/RRR/ZIP See Order Pages and Index for Info

© Donald A. Gardner Architects, Inc.

Units	Single
Price Code	C
Total Finished	1,246 sq. ft.
Main Finished	1,246 sq. ft.
Garage Unfinished	420 sq. ft.
Dimensions	60'x48'
Foundation	Crawl space
Bedrooms	3
Full Baths	2
First Ceiling	8'
Primary Roof Pitch	9:12
Secondary Roof Pitch	10:12
Max Ridge Height	24'
Exterior Walls	2x4

MAIN FLOOR

DECK

skylight

GARAGE 19-4 x 20-4

SCREEN PORCH 10-0 x 12-0

KIT. 10-0 x 11-0

walk-in closet

MASTER BED RM. 14-0 x 11-8 (cathedral ceiling)

UTIL.

master bath

DINING 12-4 x 9-4

GREAT RM. 15-8 x 15-0 fireplace

(cathedral ceiling)

BED RM. 13-4 x 10-0

bath

PORCH

BED RM./ STUDY 11-0 x 11-4 (cathedral ceiling)

10-0

48-0

60-0

© Donald A. Gardner Architects, Inc.

Design 99806

BL/ML/RRR   See Order Pages and Index for Info

© Donald A. Gardner Architects, Inc.

Units	Single
Price Code	C
Total Finished	1,246 sq. ft.
Main Finished	1,246 sq. ft.
Garage Unfinished	420 sq. ft.
Dimensions	60'x60'
Foundation	Crawl space
Bedrooms	3
Full Baths	2
First Ceiling	8'
Primary Roof Pitch	10:12
Max Ridge Height	22'
Roof Framing	Stick
Exterior Walls	2x4

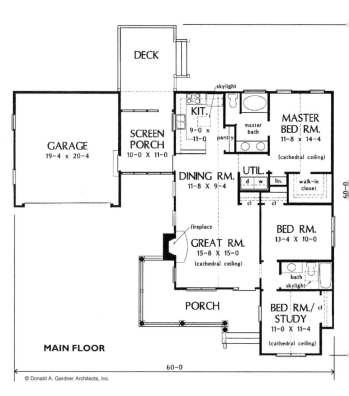

MAIN FLOOR

© Donald A. Gardner Architects, Inc.

Design 92559

BL/ML   See Order Pages and Index for Info

Units	Single
Price Code	A
Total Finished	1,265 sq. ft.
Main Finished	1,265 sq. ft.
Garage Unfinished	523 sq. ft.
Dimensions	64'10"x38'5"
Foundation	Crawl space
	Slab
Bedrooms	3
Full Baths	2
Primary Roof Pitch	9:12
Secondary Roof Pitch	4:12
Max Ridge Height	20'
Roof Framing	Stick
Exterior Walls	2x4

MAIN FLOOR

Design 82045

BL

See Order Pages and Index for Info

Units	Single
Price Code	A
Total Finished	1,289 sq. ft.
Main Finished	1,289 sq. ft.
Garage Unfinished	342 sq. ft.
Porch Unfinished	198 sq. ft.
Dimensions	45'6''×56'10''
Foundation	Basement
	Crawl space
	Slab
Bedrooms	3
Full Baths	2
Main Ceiling	9'
Roof Framing	Stick
Exterior Walls	2x4

45' 6"

56' 10"

GARAGE
17'-8" X 19'-4"

MAIN FLOOR

LAU.
6'-6" X 6'-10"

D W

DINING
9'-4" X 11'-0"

GRILLING PORCH
6'-0" X 13'-0"

PAN.

REF.

KIT.
11'-0" X 12'-0"

RG.

DW

BEDROOM 2
10'-4" X 10'-6"

GREAT RM.
16'-2" X 15'-6"
10' BOXED CEILING

GAS FIREPLACE

WH

BATH

LIN.

FOYER
4'-8" X 10'-2"

BEDROOM 3 / OFFICE
10'-4" X 10'-6"

MASTER SUITE
11'-2" X 12'-0"
10' BOXED CEILING

COVERED PORCH
15'-8" X 6'-6"
8" COLUMNS

Weather Shield
Windows & Doors
www.weathershield.com

WEATHER SHIELD
WINDOWS & DOORS
MEDFORD WI ®

Weather Shield Windows and Doors offers project planning guides
for your remodeling or new home project. FREE.
Specify "Remodeling" or "New Home" Planning Guide by calling

1-800-477-6808

Design 96710

BL/ML

See Order Pages and Index for Info

Units	Single
Price Code	C
Total Finished	1,309 sq. ft.
Main Finished	1,309 sq. ft.
Garage Unfinished	462 sq. ft.
Deck Unfinished	296 sq. ft.
Porch Unfinished	82 sq. ft.
Dimensions	66'4"x36'6"
Foundation	Crawl space
Bedrooms	3
Full Baths	2
Main Ceiling	9'
Primary Roof Pitch	10:12
Secondary Roof Pitch	12:12
Max Ridge Height	23'8"
Exterior Walls	2x4

© Donald A. Gardner Architects, Inc.

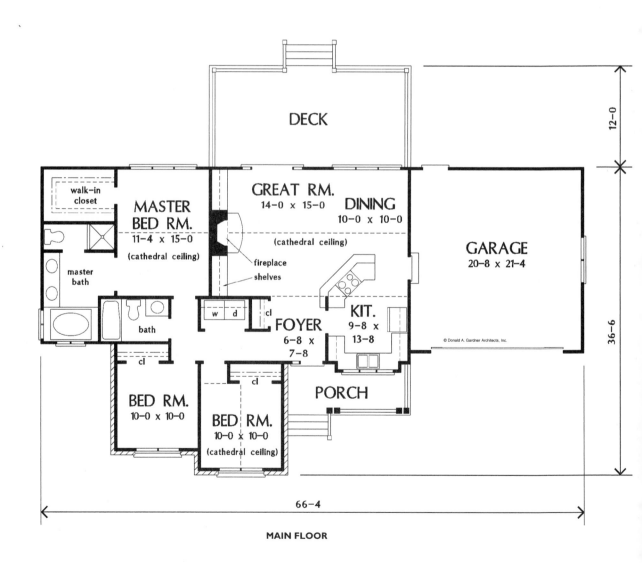

MAIN FLOOR

Design 24700   BL/ML/ZIP   See Order Pages and Index for Info

Units	Single
Price Code	A
Total Finished	1,312 sq. ft.
Main Finished	1,312 sq. ft.
Basement Unfinished	1,293 sq. ft.
Garage Unfinished	459 sq. ft.
Deck Unfinished	185 sq. ft.
Porch Unfinished	84 sq. ft.
Dimensions	50'x40'
Foundation	Basement
	Crawl space
	Slab
Bedrooms	3
Full Baths	2
First Ceiling	8'
Primary Roof Pitch	6:12
Max Ridge Height	20'
Roof Framing	Stick
Exterior Walls	2x6

MAIN FLOOR

Design 97731   BL   See Order Pages and Index for Info

Units	Single
Price Code	A
Total Finished	1,315 sq. ft.
Main Finished	1,315 sq. ft.
Basement Unfinished	1,315 sq. ft.
Garage Unfinished	488 sq. ft.
Porch Unfinished	75 sq. ft.
Dimensions	50'x54'8''
Foundation	Basement
Bedrooms	3
Full Baths	2
First Ceiling	8'
Primary Roof Pitch	6:12
Secondary Roof Pitch	6:12
Max Ridge Height	18'
Roof Framing	Truss
Exterior Walls	2x4

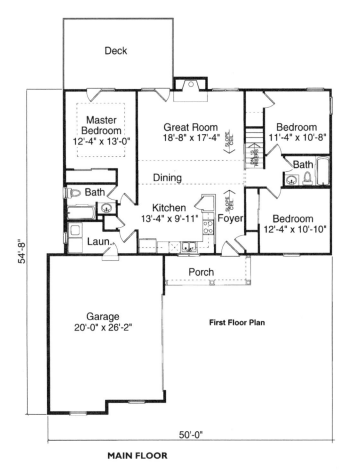

First Floor Plan

MAIN FLOOR

Design 93265

BL/ML/ZIP   See Order Pages and Index for Info

Units	Single
Price Code	A
Total Finished	1,325 sq. ft.
Main Finished	1,269 sq. ft.
Basement Unfinished	382 sq. ft.
Garage Unfinished	598 sq. ft.
Dimensions	45'×36'
Foundation	Basement
Bedrooms	3
Full Baths	2
Primary Roof Pitch	7:12
Secondary Roof Pitch	6.5:12
Max Ridge Height	16'
Roof Framing	Stick/Truss
Exterior Walls	2×4

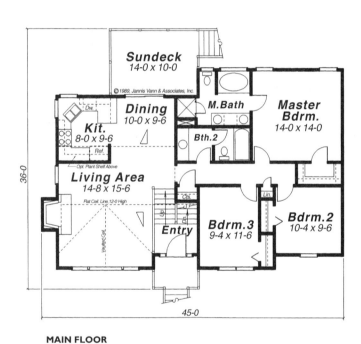

MAIN FLOOR

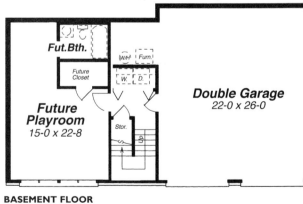

BASEMENT FLOOR

Design 34600

BL/ML/ZIP/RRR See Order Pages and Index for Info

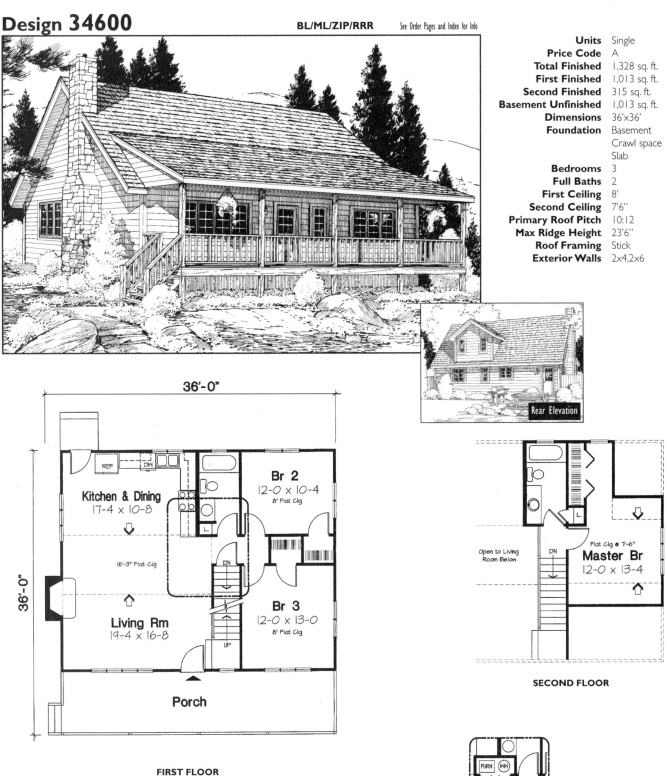

Units	Single
Price Code	A
Total Finished	1,328 sq. ft.
First Finished	1,013 sq. ft.
Second Finished	315 sq. ft.
Basement Unfinished	1,013 sq. ft.
Dimensions	36'x36'
Foundation	Basement Crawl space Slab
Bedrooms	3
Full Baths	2
First Ceiling	8'
Second Ceiling	7'6"
Primary Roof Pitch	10:12
Max Ridge Height	23'6"
Roof Framing	Stick
Exterior Walls	2x4,2x6

Rear Elevation

36'-0"

36'-0"

Kitchen & Dining
17-4 x 10-8

16'-3" Flat Clg

REF   DW

Br 2
12-0 x 10-4
8' Flat Clg

L

DN

Living Rm
19-4 x 16-8

Br 3
12-0 x 13-0
8' Flat Clg

UP

Porch

FIRST FLOOR

Open to Living
Room Below

DN

L

Flat Clg @ 7'-6"

Master Br
12-0 x 13-4

SECOND FLOOR

FURN   WH

Crawl
Space
Access

OPTION

31

Design 93453   BL

See Order Pages and Index for Info

Units	Single
Price Code	A
Total Finished	1,333 sq. ft.
Main Finished	1,333 sq. ft.
Garage Unfinished	520 sq. ft.
Dimensions	55'6"x64'3"
Foundation	Crawlspace
	Slab
Bedrooms	3
Full Baths	2
Main Ceiling	8'
Primary Roof Pitch	7:12
Secondary Roof Pitch	3:12
Max Ridge Height	19'5"
Roof Framing	Stick
Exterior Walls	2x4

MAIN FLOOR

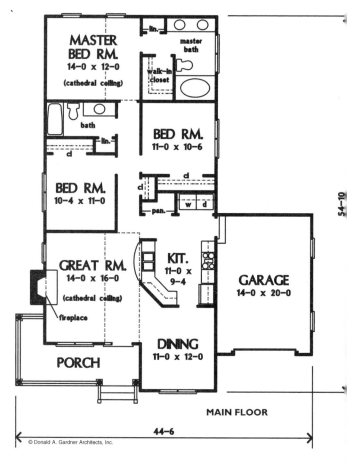

Storage 20 x 6   8' Clg.

Carport 20 x 20   8' Clg.

Master 15 x 13   9' Recessed Clg.

10/6 x 8

Rear Porch 22 x 4

Dining 10 x 13   8' Clg.

Kitchen 9/9 x 13

B.R. #3 10 x 12   8' Clg.

B.R. #2 10 x 11   8' Clg.

Family Room 17 x 14/7   9' Clg.

Porch 40/6 x 6   8' Clg.

Design 98047   BL/ML

See Order Pages and Index for Info

© Donald A. Gardner Architects, Inc.

Units	Single
Price Code	C
Total Finished	1,338 sq. ft.
Main Finished	1,338 sq. ft.
Garage Unfinished	296 sq. ft.
Porch Unfinished	129 sq. ft.
Dimensions	44'6"x54'10"
Foundation	Crawlspace
Bedrooms	3
Full Baths	2
Main Ceiling	8'
Primary Roof Pitch	10:12
Secondary Roof Pitch	8.5:12
Max Ridge Height	20'10"
Roof Framing	Stick
Exterior Walls	2x4

MASTER BED RM. 14-0 x 12-0 (cathedral ceiling)

master bath

walk-in closet

bath

BED RM. 11-0 x 10-6

BED RM. 10-4 x 11-0

pan.

GREAT RM. 14-0 x 16-0 (cathedral ceiling)

fireplace

KIT. 11-0 x 9-4

GARAGE 14-0 x 20-0

PORCH

DINING 11-0 x 12-0

MAIN FLOOR

54-10

44-6

© Donald A. Gardner Architects, Inc.

Design 20156

BL/ML/ZIP/RRR See Order Pages and Index for Info

Units	Single
Price Code	A
Total Finished	1,359 sq. ft.
Main Finished	1,359 sq. ft.
Basement Unfinished	1,359 sq. ft.
Garage Unfinished	501 sq. ft.
Dimensions	58'x34'4''
Foundation	Basement
	Crawl space
	Slab
Bedrooms	3
Full Baths	2
First Ceiling	8'
Primary Roof Pitch	6:12
Secondary Roof Pitch	12:12
Max Ridge Height	18'6''
Roof Framing	Stick
Exterior Walls	2x4, 2x6

58'-0"

Deck

Dining
11-0 x 11-2

Br #2
10-10 x 11-10

Den/Br #3
10-0 x 11-10

Optional Door Location

Kit
10-0 x 11-2

Ldry

Decor. Ceiling

Solid Wall w/ Opt. Door Location

Plant Ledge

34'-4"

DN

Decor. Ceiling

Lin.

Living Rm
14-10 x 17-0
10' clg

Garage
20-4 x 21-8

MBr #1
11-7 x 13-0

Decor. Ceiling

Seat

MAIN FLOOR

REAR ELEVATION

Design 97224

BL See Order Pages and Index for Info

Units	Single
Price Code	A
Total Finished	1,363 sq. ft.
Main Finished	1,363 sq. ft.
Basement Unfinished	715 sq. ft.
Garage Unfinished	677 sq. ft.
Dimensions	47'x35'4''
Foundation	Basement
Bedrooms	3
Full Baths	2
First Ceiling	9'
Primary Roof Pitch	12:12
Max Ridge Height	22'4''
Roof Framing	Stick
Exterior Walls	2x4

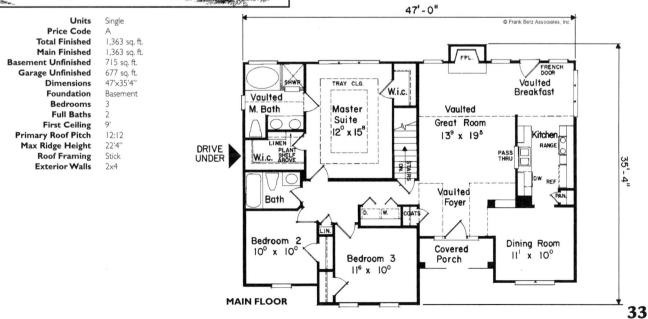

47'-0"

© Frank Betz Associates, Inc.

FPL.

SHWR

TRAY CLG.

Vaulted
M. Bath

W.i.c.

Vaulted

FRENCH DOOR

Vaulted
Breakfast

Master
Suite
12⁰ x 15⁸

Vaulted
Great Room
13⁹ x 19⁵

Kitchen
RANGE

W.i.c.

LINEN
PLANT SHELF ABOVE

DRIVE UNDER

STAIRS
DN

PASS THRU

D.W.

REF

PAN.

Bath

Vaulted
Foyer

D. W.
COATS

LIN.

Bedroom 2
10⁰ x 10⁰

Bedroom 3
11⁶ x 10⁰

Covered
Porch

Dining Room
11' x 10⁰

35'-4"

MAIN FLOOR

Design 99830

BL/ML/ZIP/RRR See Order Pages and Index for Info

© Donald A. Gardner Architects, Inc.

Units	Single
Price Code	C
Total Finished	1,372 sq. ft.
Main Finished	1,372 sq. ft.
Garage Unfinished	537 sq. ft.
Porch Unfinished	120 sq. ft.
Dimensions	46'x61'10"
Foundation	Crawl space
Bedrooms	3
Full Baths	2
Main Ceiling	8'
Primary Roof Pitch	8:12
Secondary Roof Pitch	12:12
Max Ridge Height	21'2"
Roof Framing	Stick
Exterior Walls	2x4

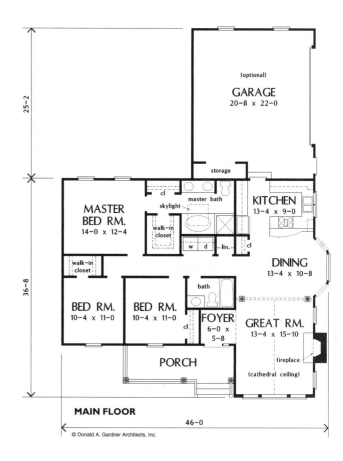

MAIN FLOOR

© Donald A. Gardner Architects, Inc.

Design 98411

BL/ML See Order Pages and Index for Info

Units	Single
Price Code	A
Total Finished	1,373 sq. ft.
Main Finished	1,373 sq. ft.
Basement Unfinished	1,386 sq. ft.
Dimensions	50'4"x45'
Foundation	Basement
	Crawl space
Bedrooms	3
Full Baths	2
Main Ceiling	9'
Primary Roof Pitch	8:12
Max Ridge Height	23'6"
Roof Framing	Stick
Exterior Walls	2x4,2x6

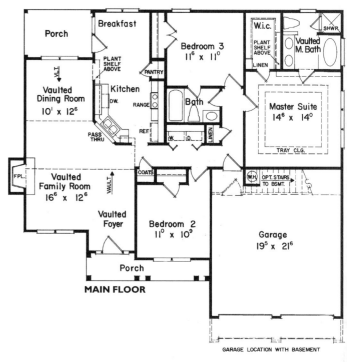

MAIN FLOOR

GARAGE LOCATION WITH BASEMENT

Design 93279

BL/ML/ZIP

See Order Pages and Index for Info

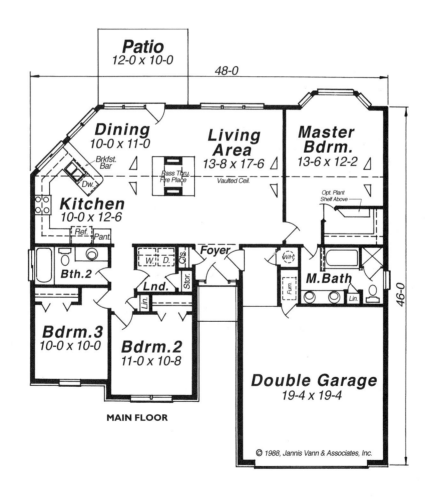

Units	Single
Price Code	A
Total Finished	1,388 sq. ft.
Main Finished	1,388 sq. ft.
Garage Unfinished	400 sq. ft.
Dimensions	48'x46'
Foundation	Crawl space
	Slab
Bedrooms	3
Full Baths	2
Main Ceiling	8'
Primary Roof Pitch	7:12
Secondary Roof Pitch	8:12
Max Ridge Height	18'
Roof Framing	Truss
Exterior Walls	2x4

Patio
12-0 x 10-0

48-0

Dining
10-0 x 11-0

Brkfst.
Bar

Dw.

Living Area
13-8 x 17-6

Pass Thru.
Fire Place

Vaulted Ceil.

Master Bdrm.
13-6 x 12-2

Opt. Plant
Shelf Above

Kitchen
10-0 x 12-6

Ref. Pant.

Foyer

W/H

M.Bath

Lin.

Bth.2

W. D. Cls.

Fum.

Lin.

Lnd. Stor.

46-0

Bdrm.3
10-0 x 10-0

Bdrm.2
11-0 x 10-8

Double Garage
19-4 x 19-4

MAIN FLOOR

© 1988, Jannis Vann & Associates, Inc.

Design 98970 BL

See Order Pages and Index for Info

Units	Single
Price Code	A
Total Finished	1,410 sq. ft.
Main Finished	1,396 sq. ft.
Lower Finished	14 sq. ft.
Garage Unfinished	646 sq. ft.
Deck Unfinished	120 sq. ft.
Dimensions	50'4"x31'
Foundation	Basement
Bedrooms	3
Full Baths	2
First Ceiling	8'
Primary Roof Pitch	7:12
Max Ridge Height	26'
Roof Framing	Stick
Exterior Walls	2x4

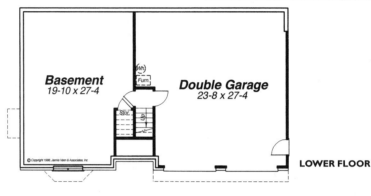

Sundeck 12-0 x 10-0

Dining 10-2 x 11-10

Kit. 10-0 x 11-6

Master Bdrm. 13-6 x 13-6

Bath 2

Living Area 17-0 x 15-6

Bdrm.3 9-2 x 12-0

Bdrm.2 11-6 x 11-0

Entry

31-0

50-4

MAIN FLOOR

Basement 19-10 x 27-4

Double Garage 23-8 x 27-4

© Copyright 1998 Jannis Vann & Associates, Inc.

LOWER FLOOR

Design 97113 BL

See Order Pages and Index for Info

Units	Single
Price Code	A
Total Finished	1,416 sq. ft.
Main Finished	1,416 sq. ft.
Basement Unfinished	1,416 sq. ft.
Dimensions	48'x55'4"
Foundation	Basement
Bedrooms	3
Full Baths	2
Primary Roof Pitch	8:12
Secondary Roof Pitch	8:12
Max Ridge Height	21'8"
Roof Framing	Truss
Exterior Walls	2x6

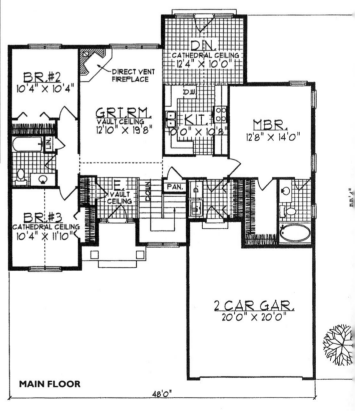

BR. #2 10'4" X 10'4"

DIRECT VENT FIREPLACE

DIN. CATHEDRAL CEILING 12'4" X 10'0"

GRT. RM. VAULT CEILING 12'10" X 19'8"

KIT. 10'0" X 10'8"

MBR. 12'8" X 14'0"

BR. #3 CATHEDRAL CEILING 10'4" X 11'10"

VAULT CEILING

PAN.

2 CAR GAR. 20'0" X 20'0"

MAIN FLOOR

48'0"

Design 90990

BL/ML See Order Pages and Index for Info

Units	Single
Price Code	A
Total Finished	1,423 sq. ft.
Main Finished	1,423 sq. ft.
Basement Unfinished	1,423 sq. ft.
Garage Unfinished	399 sq. ft.
Dimensions	54'x49'
Foundation	Basement
Bedrooms	3
Full Baths	1
3/4 Baths	1
Exterior Walls	2x6

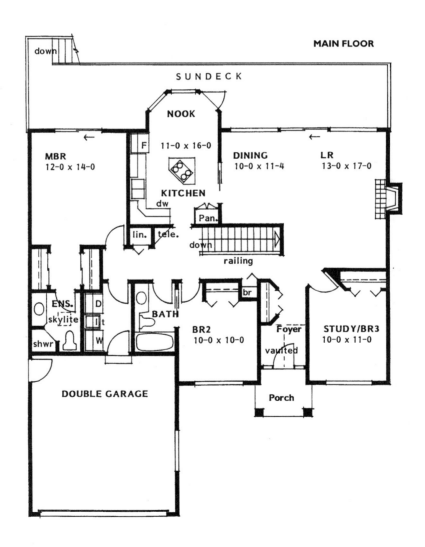

MAIN FLOOR

SUNDECK

NOOK
11-0 x 16-0

KITCHEN
dw

MBR
12-0 x 14-0

DINING
10-0 x 11-4

LR
13-0 x 17-0

Pan.

down
railing

lin. tele.

ENS.
skylite
shwr

D
l t
W

BATH

BR2
10-0 x 10-0

br

Foyer
vaulted

STUDY/BR3
10-0 x 11-0

DOUBLE GARAGE

Porch

down

Design 98415

BL/ML/ZIP   See Order Pages and Index for Info

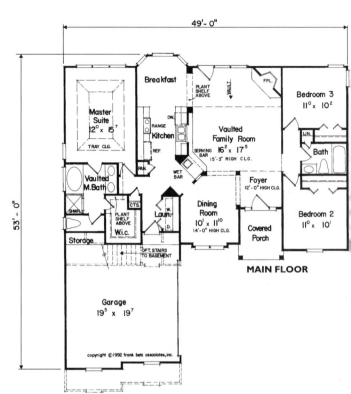

Units	Single
Price Code	A
Total Finished	1,429 sq. ft.
Main Finished	1,429 sq. ft.
Basement Unfinished	1,472 sq. ft.
Garage Unfinished	438 sq. ft.
Dimensions	49'x53'
Foundation	Basement
	Crawl space
	Slab
Bedrooms	3
Full Baths	2
Main Ceiling	8'
Primary Roof Pitch	10:12
Max Ridge Height	23'
Roof Framing	Stick
Exterior Walls	2x4

Design 97274

BL/ML   See Order Pages and Index for Info

Units	Single
Price Code	A
Total Finished	1,432 sq. ft.
Main Finished	1,432 sq. ft.
Basement Unfinished	1,454 sq. ft.
Garage Unfinished	440 sq. ft.
Dimensions	49'x52'4"
Foundation	Basement
	Crawl space
Bedrooms	3
Full Baths	2
Primary Roof Pitch	10:12
Max Ridge Height	24'2"
Roof Framing	Stick
Exterior Walls	2x4

Design 96509

BL/ML   See Order Pages and Index for Info

Units	Single
Price Code	A
Total Finished	1,438 sq. ft.
Main Finished	1,438 sq. ft.
Garage Unfinished	486 sq. ft.
Deck Unfinished	282 sq. ft.
Porch Unfinished	126 sq. ft.
Dimensions	54'x57'
Foundation	Crawl space
	Slab
Bedrooms	3
Full Baths	2
Primary Roof Pitch	7:12
Secondary Roof Pitch	3:12
Max Ridge Height	19'
Roof Framing	Stick
Exterior Walls	2x4

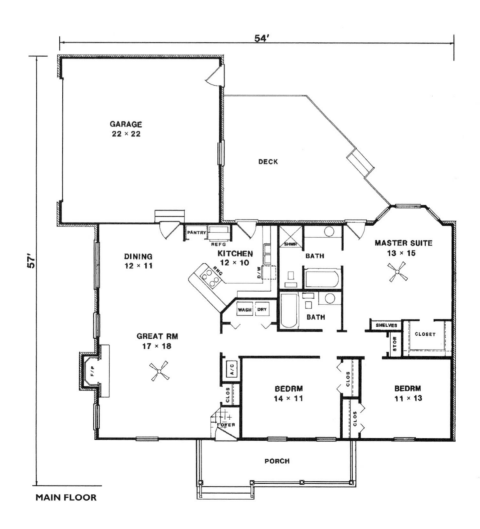

MAIN FLOOR

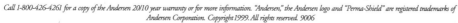

Design 92685 BL

See Order Pages and Index for Info

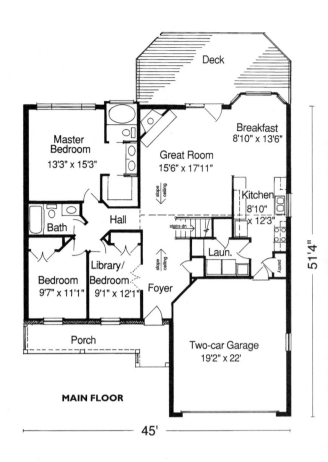

Units	Single
Price Code	A
Total Finished	1,442 sq. ft.
Main Finished	1,442 sq. ft.
Basement Unfinished	1,442 sq. ft.
Garage Unfinished	421 sq. ft.
Deck Unfinished	288 sq. ft.
Porch Unfinished	137 sq. ft.
Dimensions	45'x51'4"
Foundation	Basement
Bedrooms	3
Full Baths	2
Main Ceiling	8'
Primary Roof Pitch	8:12
Secondary Roof Pitch	1212
Max Ridge Height	24'
Roof Framing	Truss
Exterior Walls	2x4

MAIN FLOOR

45'

Design 24706 BL/ML/ZIP

See Order Pages and Index for Info

Units	Single
Price Code	A
Total Finished	1,470 sq. ft.
First Finished	1,035 sq. ft.
Second Finished	435 sq. ft.
Basement Unfinished	1,018 sq. ft.
Deck Unfinished	240 sq. ft.
Porch Unfinished	192 sq. ft.
Dimensions	35'x42'
Foundation	Basement
	Crawlspace
	Slab
Bedrooms	3
Full Baths	2
First Ceiling	8'
Second Ceiling	8'
Primary Roof Pitch	12:12
Secondary Roof Pitch	8:12
Max Ridge Height	27'
Roof Framing	Stick
Exterior Walls	2x4
	2x6

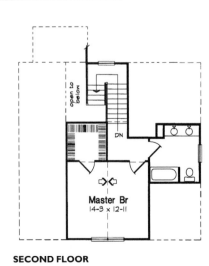

SECOND FLOOR

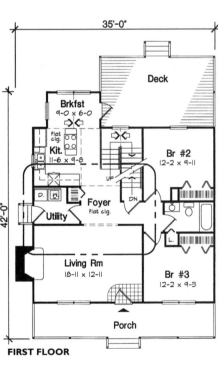

FIRST FLOOR

ALTERNATE FOUNDATION PLAN

Design 93165 **BL**

See Order Pages and Index for Info

Units	Single
Price Code	A
Total Finished	1,472 sq. ft.
Main Finished	1,472 sq. ft.
Basement Unfinished	1,472 sq. ft.
Garage Unfinished	424 sq. ft.
Dimensions	48'x56'4''
Foundation	Basement
Bedrooms	3
Full Baths	2
Primary Roof Pitch	8:12
Secondary Roof Pitch	8:12
Max Ridge Height	19'8''
Roof Framing	Stick
Exterior Walls	2x6

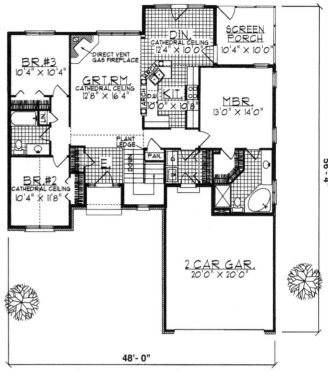

MAIN FLOOR

Design 93416 **BL**

See Order Pages and Index for Info

Units	Single
Price Code	A
Total Finished	1,475 sq. ft.
Main Finished	1,475 sq. ft.
Garage Unfinished	455 sq. ft.
Porch Unfinished	234 sq. ft.
Dimensions	43'x43'
Foundation	Crawl space
	Slab
Bedrooms	3
Full Baths	2
Primary Roof Pitch	8:12
Secondary Roof Pitch	4:12
Max Ridge Height	24'
Roof Framing	Stick
Exterior Walls	2x4

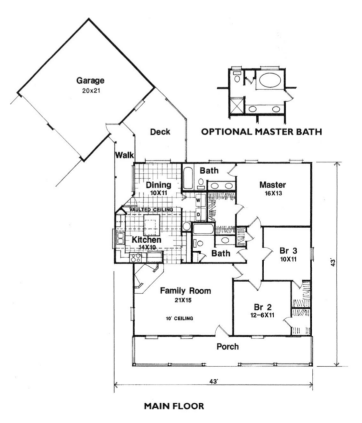

MAIN FLOOR

Design 65001 BL/ML

See Order Pages and Index for Info

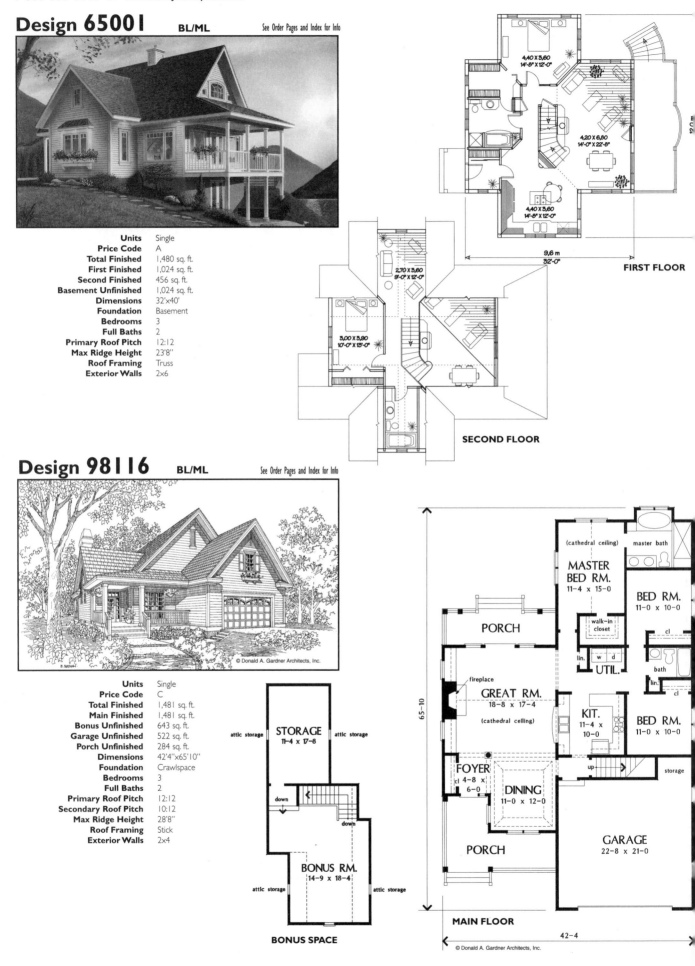

Units	Single
Price Code	A
Total Finished	1,480 sq. ft.
First Finished	1,024 sq. ft.
Second Finished	456 sq. ft.
Basement Unfinished	1,024 sq. ft.
Dimensions	32'x40'
Foundation	Basement
Bedrooms	3
Full Baths	2
Primary Roof Pitch	12:12
Max Ridge Height	23'8"
Roof Framing	Truss
Exterior Walls	2x6

FIRST FLOOR

SECOND FLOOR

Design 98116 BL/ML

See Order Pages and Index for Info

© Donald A. Gardner Architects, Inc.

Units	Single
Price Code	C
Total Finished	1,481 sq. ft.
Main Finished	1,481 sq. ft.
Bonus Unfinished	643 sq. ft.
Garage Unfinished	522 sq. ft.
Porch Unfinished	284 sq. ft.
Dimensions	42'4"x65'10"
Foundation	Crawlspace
Bedrooms	3
Full Baths	2
Primary Roof Pitch	12:12
Secondary Roof Pitch	10:12
Max Ridge Height	28'8"
Roof Framing	Stick
Exterior Walls	2x4

STORAGE
11-4 x 17-8
attic storage   attic storage

down

down

BONUS RM.
14-9 x 18-4
attic storage   attic storage

BONUS SPACE

MAIN FLOOR

© Donald A. Gardner Architects, Inc.

Design 98441 BL

See Order Pages and Index for Info

Units	Single
Price Code	B
Total Finished	1,502 sq. ft.
Main Finished	1,502 sq. ft.
Basement Unfinished	1,555 sq. ft.
Garage Unfinished	448 sq. ft.
Dimensions	51'x50'6"
Foundation	Basement
	Crawl space
Bedrooms	3
Full Baths	2
Primary Roof Pitch	10:12
Max Ridge Height	24'9"
Roof Framing	Stick
Exterior Walls	2x4

BASEMENT OPTION

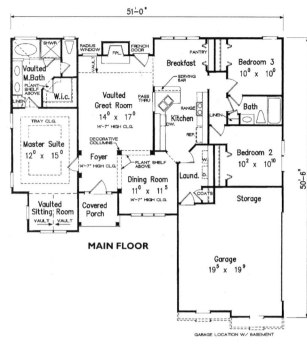

MAIN FLOOR

Design 96458 BL/ML/RRR

See Order Pages and Index for Info

Units	Single
Price Code	D
Total Finished	1,512 sq. ft.
Main Finished	1,512 sq. ft.
Garage Unfinished	455 sq. ft.
Dimensions	64'4"x44'4"
Foundation	Crawl space
Bedrooms	3
Full Baths	2
First Ceiling	8'
Primary Roof Pitch	12:12
Secondary Roof Pitch	9.5:12
Max Ridge Height	22'8"
Roof Framing	Stick
Exterior Walls	2x4

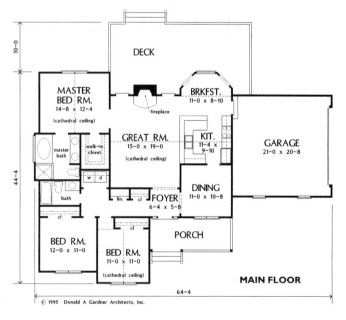

MAIN FLOOR

© 1995 Donald A Gardner Architects, Inc.

Design 98004 BL/ML/RRR

See Order Pages and Index for Info

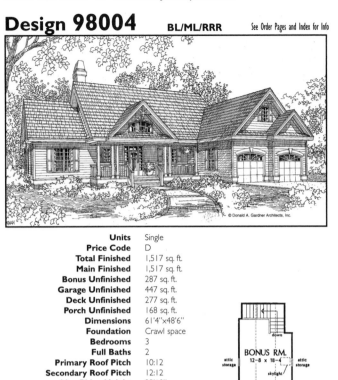

© Donald A. Gardner Architects, Inc.

Units	Single
Price Code	D
Total Finished	1,517 sq. ft.
Main Finished	1,517 sq. ft.
Bonus Unfinished	287 sq. ft.
Garage Unfinished	447 sq. ft.
Deck Unfinished	277 sq. ft.
Porch Unfinished	168 sq. ft.
Dimensions	61'4"x48'6"
Foundation	Crawl space
Bedrooms	3
Full Baths	2
Primary Roof Pitch	10:12
Secondary Roof Pitch	12:12
Max Ridge Height	23'10"
Roof Framing	Stick
Exterior Walls	2x4

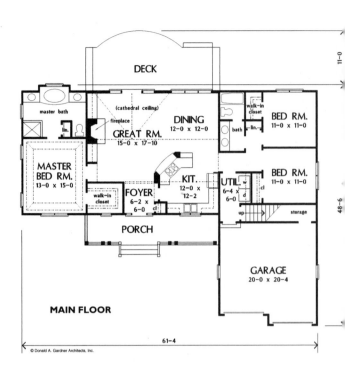

MAIN FLOOR

DECK

master bath

GREAT RM. 15-0 x 17-10

(cathedral ceiling)

fireplace

DINING 12-0 x 12-0

walk-in closet

BED RM. 11-0 x 11-0

bath

MASTER BED RM. 13-0 x 15-0

walk-in closet

FOYER 6-2 x 6-0

KIT. 12-0 x 12-2

UTIL. 6-4 x 6-0

BED RM. 11-0 x 11-0

up

storage

PORCH

GARAGE 20-0 x 20-4

61-4

11-0

48-6

© Donald A. Gardner Architects, Inc.

BONUS RM. 12-8 x 18-4

attic storage

attic storage

down

skylight

BONUS SPACE

Design 94315 BL

See Order Pages and Index for Info

Units	Single
Price Code	B
Total Finished	1,550 sq. ft.
First Finished	736 sq. ft.
Second Finished	814 sq. ft.
Basement Unfinished	746 sq. ft.
Garage Unfinished	400 sq. ft.
Deck Unfinished	96 sq. ft.
Porch Unfinished	72 sq. ft.
Dimensions	42'x34'
Foundation	Basement
Bedrooms	4
Full Baths	2
Half Baths	1
First Ceiling	8'
Second Ceiling	8'
Primary Roof Pitch	7:12
Max Ridge Height	26'6"
Roof Framing	Truss
Exterior Walls	2x4

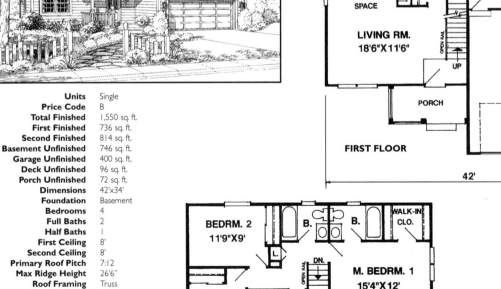

PATIO

W. D.

UTIL.

LAV.

FAMILY RM. 15'4"X12'4"

Opt. Fireplace

KITCH. 11'6"X8'6"

DINING SPACE

PANT.

DN.

LIVING RM. 18'6"X11'6"

OPEN RAIL

UP

GARAGE 19'4"X21'

PORCH

FIRST FLOOR

34'

42'

BEDRM. 2 11'9"X9'

B.

B.

WALK-IN CLO.

L.

DN.

M. BEDRM. 1 15'4"X12'

OPEN RAIL

BEDRM. 3 9'X11'9"

BEDRM. 4 9'X12'9"

SECOND FLOOR

Design 99863 BL/ML/RRR See Order Pages and Index for Info

© Donald A. Gardner Architects, Inc.

Units	Single
Price Code	D
Total Finished	1,557 sq. ft.
First Finished	1,057 sq. ft.
Second Finished	500 sq. ft.
Bonus Unfinished	378 sq. ft.
Garage Unfinished	578 sq. ft.
Dimensions	59'4"x50'
Foundation	Crawl space
Bedrooms	3
Full Baths	2
First Ceiling	9'
Second Ceiling	8'
Primary Roof Pitch	10:12
Secondary Roof Pitch	12:12
Max Ridge Height	25'
Roof Framing	Stick
Exterior Walls	2x4

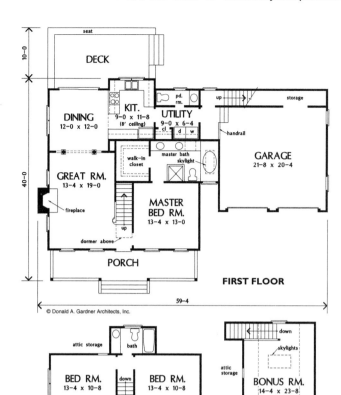

FIRST FLOOR

© Donald A. Gardner Architects, Inc.

SECOND FLOOR

BONUS SPACE

Design 96417 BL/ML/ZIP/RRR See Order Pages and Index for Info

© 1995 Donald A. Gardner Architects, Inc.

Units	Single
Price Code	D
Total Finished	1,561 sq. ft.
Main Finished	1,561 sq. ft.
Garage Unfinished	446 sq. ft.
Dimensions	60'10"x51'6"
Foundation	Crawl space
Bedrooms	3
Full Baths	2
Main Ceiling	9'
Primary Roof Pitch	9:12
Secondary Roof Pitch	12:12
Max Ridge Height	24'10"
Roof Framing	Stick
Exterior Walls	2x4

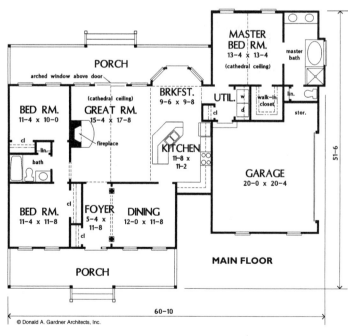

MAIN FLOOR

© Donald A. Gardner Architects, Inc.

Design 97615 BL/ML

See Order Pages and Index for Info

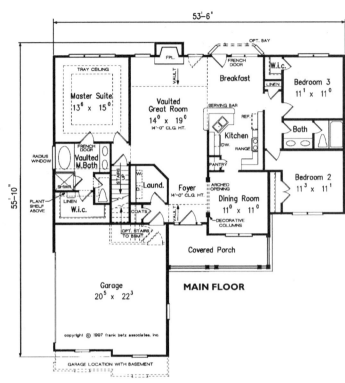

Units	Single
Price Code	B
Total Finished	1,571 sq. ft.
Main Finished	1,571 sq. ft.
Bonus Unfinished	334 sq. ft.
Basement Unfinished	1,642 sq. ft.
Garage Unfinished	483 sq. ft.
Dimensions	53'6"x55'10"
Foundation	Basement
Bedrooms	3
Full Baths	2
Primary Roof Pitch	10:12
Max Ridge Height	23'6"
Roof Framing	Stick
Exterior Walls	2x4

MAIN FLOOR

copyright © 1997 frank betz associates, inc.

GARAGE LOCATION WITH BASEMENT

Design 99802 BL/ML/ZIP/RRR

See Order Pages and Index for Info

© Donald A. Gardner Architects, Inc.

Units	Single
Price Code	D
Total Finished	1,576 sq. ft.
Main Finished	1,576 sq. ft.
Garage Unfinished	465 sq. ft.
Dimensions	60'6"x47'3"
Foundation	Crawl space
Bedrooms	3
Full Baths	2
Primary Roof Pitch	12:12
Max Ridge Height	21'9"
Roof Framing	Stick
Exterior Walls	2x4

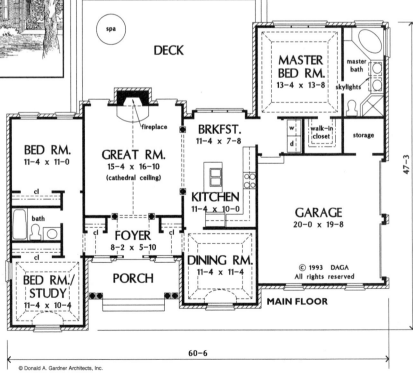

MAIN FLOOR

© 1993 DAGA All rights reserved

© Donald A. Gardner Architects, Inc.

Design 97762

BL   See Order Pages and Index for Info

Units	Single
Price Code	B
Total Finished	1,594 sq. ft.
First Finished	1,594 sq. ft.
Basement Unfinished	1,954 sq. ft.
Garage Unfinished	512 sq. ft.
Deck Unfinished	328 sq. ft.
Porch Unfinished	125 sq. ft.
Dimensions	52'8"x55'5"
Foundation	Basement
Bedrooms	3
Full Baths	2
First Ceiling	8'
Vaulted Ceiling	10'
Primary Roof Pitch	8:12
Max Ridge Height	23'6"
Roof Framing	Truss
Exterior Walls	2x4

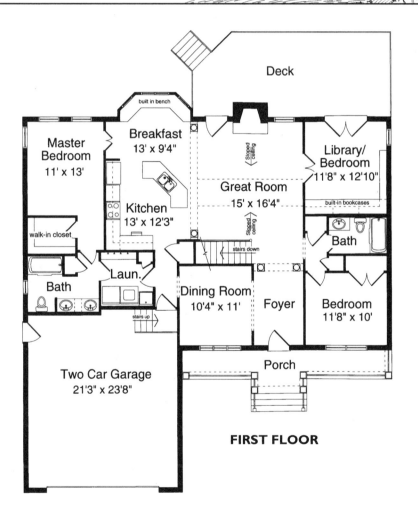

FIRST FLOOR

Deck

Breakfast 13' x 9'4"
built in bench

Master Bedroom 11' x 13'

Kitchen 13' x 12'3"

walk-in closet

Bath

Laun.

Two Car Garage 21'3" x 23'8"

stairs up

Dining Room 10'4" x 11'

Great Room 15' x 16'4"
Sloped ceiling

stairs down

Library/ Bedroom 11'8" x 12'10"
built-in bookcases

Bath

Foyer

Bedroom 11'8" x 10'

Porch

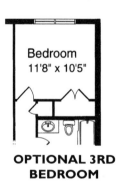

Bedroom 11'8" x 10'5"

OPTIONAL 3RD BEDROOM

Design 97235 BL

See Order Pages and Index for Info

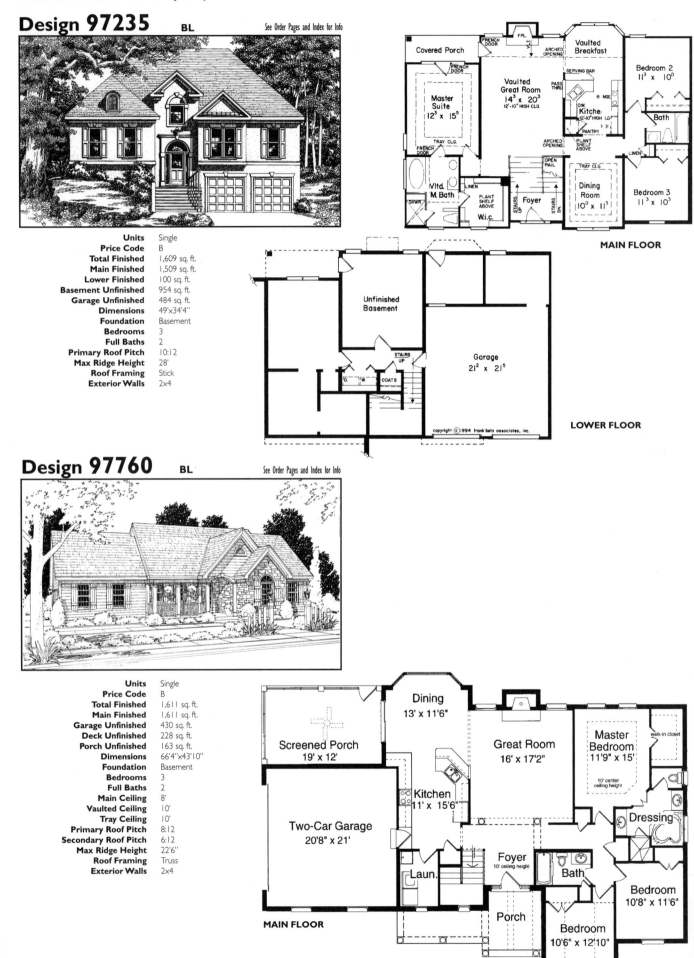

Units	Single
Price Code	B
Total Finished	1,609 sq. ft.
Main Finished	1,509 sq. ft.
Lower Finished	100 sq. ft.
Basement Unfinished	954 sq. ft.
Garage Unfinished	484 sq. ft.
Dimensions	49'x34'4''
Foundation	Basement
Bedrooms	3
Full Baths	2
Primary Roof Pitch	10:12
Max Ridge Height	28'
Roof Framing	Stick
Exterior Walls	2x4

MAIN FLOOR

LOWER FLOOR

copyright © 1994 frank betz associates, inc.

Design 97760 BL

See Order Pages and Index for Info

Units	Single
Price Code	B
Total Finished	1,611 sq. ft.
Main Finished	1,611 sq. ft.
Garage Unfinished	430 sq. ft.
Deck Unfinished	228 sq. ft.
Porch Unfinished	163 sq. ft.
Dimensions	66'4''x43'10''
Foundation	Basement
Bedrooms	3
Full Baths	2
Main Ceiling	8'
Vaulted Ceiling	10'
Tray Ceiling	10'
Primary Roof Pitch	8:12
Secondary Roof Pitch	6:12
Max Ridge Height	22'6''
Roof Framing	Truss
Exterior Walls	2x4

MAIN FLOOR

Design 92255

BL See Order Pages and Index for Info

Units	Single
Price Code	B
Total Finished	1,624 sq. ft.
First Finished	854 sq. ft.
Second Finished	770 sq. ft.
Basement Unfinished	854 sq. ft.
Garage Unfinished	437 sq. ft.
Deck Unfinished	102 sq. ft.
Porch Unfinished	36 sq. ft.
Dimensions	50'x36'1"
Foundation	Basement
	Crawl space
	Slab
Bedrooms	3
Full Baths	2
Half Baths	1
First Ceiling	8'
Primary Roof Pitch	12:8
Max Ridge Height	24'
Roof Framing	Truss
Exterior Walls	2x4

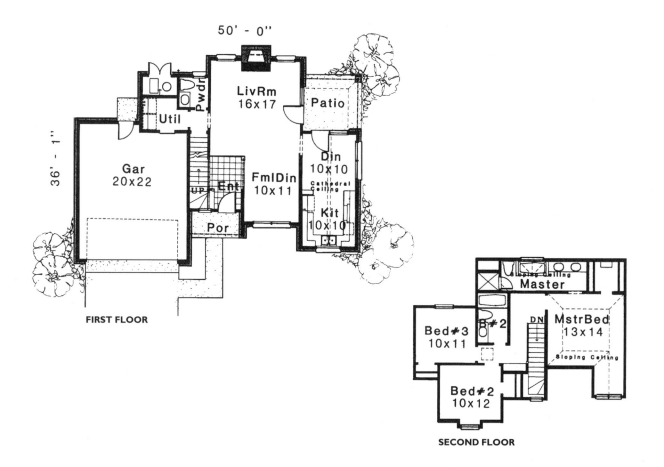

FIRST FLOOR

SECOND FLOOR

Design 24701

BL/ML/ZIP   See Order Pages and Index for Info

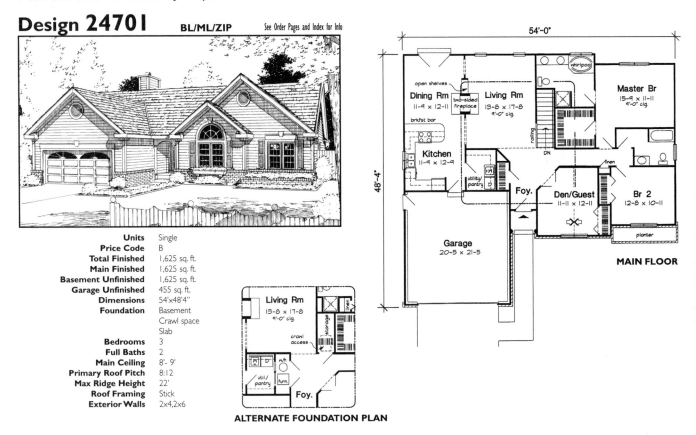

Units	Single
Price Code	B
Total Finished	1,625 sq. ft.
Main Finished	1,625 sq. ft.
Basement Unfinished	1,625 sq. ft.
Garage Unfinished	455 sq. ft.
Dimensions	54'x48'4''
Foundation	Basement
	Crawl space
	Slab
Bedrooms	3
Full Baths	2
Main Ceiling	8'- 9'
Primary Roof Pitch	8:12
Max Ridge Height	22'
Roof Framing	Stick
Exterior Walls	2x4,2x6

ALTERNATE FOUNDATION PLAN

MAIN FLOOR

Design 96463

BL/ML/RRR   See Order Pages and Index for Info

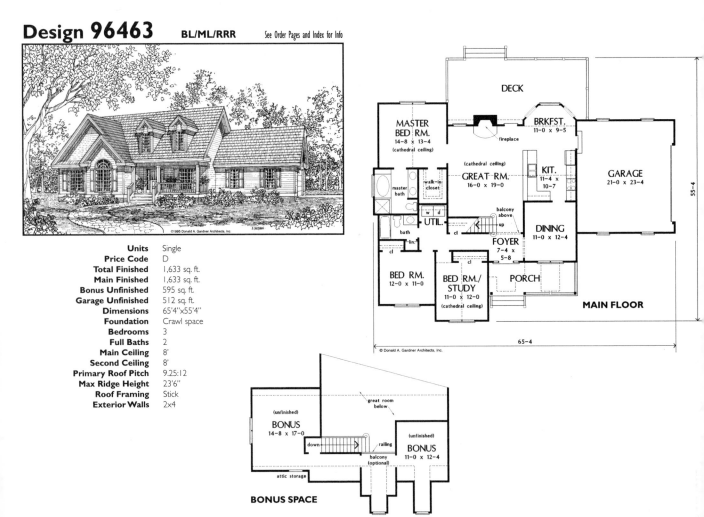

Units	Single
Price Code	D
Total Finished	1,633 sq. ft.
Main Finished	1,633 sq. ft.
Bonus Unfinished	595 sq. ft.
Garage Unfinished	512 sq. ft.
Dimensions	65'4''x55'4''
Foundation	Crawl space
Bedrooms	3
Full Baths	2
Main Ceiling	8'
Second Ceiling	8'
Primary Roof Pitch	9.25:12
Max Ridge Height	23'6''
Roof Framing	Stick
Exterior Walls	2x4

MAIN FLOOR

BONUS SPACE

Design 96513

BL/ML/ZIP See Order Pages and Index for Info

Units	Single
Price Code	B
Total Finished	1,648 sq. ft.
Main Finished	1,648 sq. ft.
Garage Unfinished	479 sq. ft.
Dimensions	68'x50'
Foundation	Crawl space / Slab
Bedrooms	3
Full Baths	2
Half Baths	1
Main Ceiling	9'
Primary Roof Pitch	11:12
Secondary Roof Pitch	8:12
Max Ridge Height	20'
Roof Framing	Stick
Exterior Walls	2x4

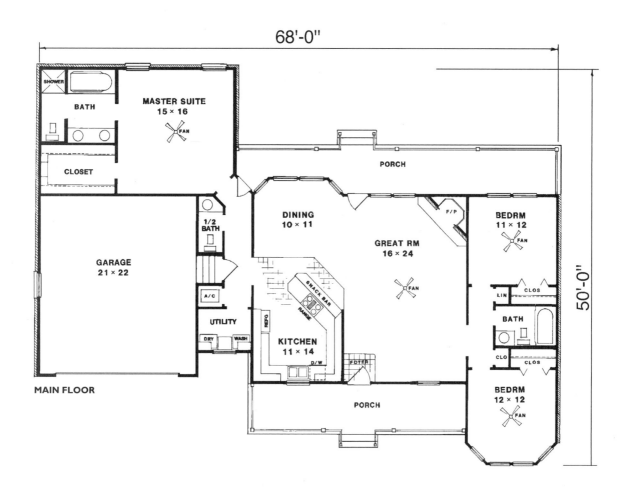

68'-0" **50'-0"**

MAIN FLOOR

MASTER SUITE 15 × 16 · BATH · CLOSET · SHOWER · GARAGE 21 × 22 · 1/2 BATH · A/C · UTILITY · DRY · WASH · KITCHEN 11 × 14 · DINING 10 × 11 · GREAT RM 16 × 24 · SNACK BAR · FLAME · REFG · D/W · FOYER · PORCH · F/P · BEDRM 11 × 12 · BATH · LIN · CLOS · BEDRM 12 × 12

Design 94938

BL/ML See Order Pages and Index for Info

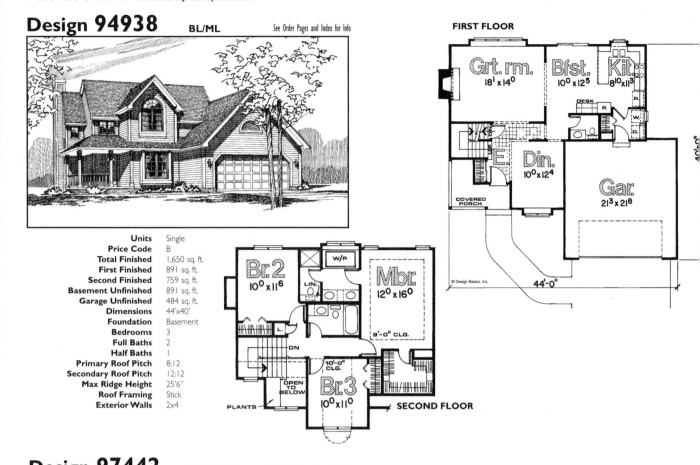

FIRST FLOOR

Grt. rm. 18' x 14'0"
Bfst. 10'0 x 12'5
Kit. 8'10 x 11'3
Din. 10'0 x 12'4
Gar. 21'3 x 21'8
COVERED PORCH
© Design Basics, Inc.
44'-0"

Units	Single
Price Code	B
Total Finished	1,650 sq. ft.
First Finished	891 sq. ft.
Second Finished	759 sq. ft.
Basement Unfinished	891 sq. ft.
Garage Unfinished	484 sq. ft.
Dimensions	44'x40'
Foundation	Basement
Bedrooms	3
Full Baths	2
Half Baths	1
Primary Roof Pitch	8:12
Secondary Roof Pitch	12:12
Max Ridge Height	25'6"
Roof Framing	Stick
Exterior Walls	2x4

Br. 2 10'0 x 11'6
w/p
LIN.
Mbr. 12'0 x 16'0
9'-0" CLG.
L.
DN
10'-0" CLG.
OPEN TO BELOW
Br. 3 10'0 x 11'0
PLANTS
SECOND FLOOR

Design 97442

BL/ML/RRR See Order Pages and Index for Info

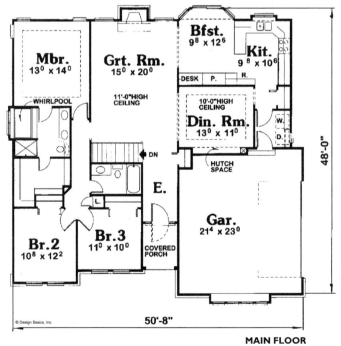

Units	Single
Price Code	B
Total Finished	1,650 sq. ft.
Main Finished	1,650 sq. ft.
Garage Unfinished	529 sq. ft.
Dimensions	50'8"x48'
Foundation	Basement
Bedrooms	3
Full Baths	2
Main Ceiling	9'
Primary Roof Pitch	6:12
Secondary Roof Pitch	6:12
Max Ridge Height	20'6"
Roof Framing	Stick
Exterior Walls	2x4

Mbr. 13'0 x 14'0
WHIRLPOOL
Grt. Rm. 15'0 x 20'0
11'-0" HIGH CEILING
Bfst. 9'8 x 12'6
Kit. 9'8 x 10'6
DESK P. R.
Din. Rm. 13'0 x 11'0
10'-0" HIGH CEILING
DN
HUTCH SPACE
E.
Br. 2 10'8 x 12'2
Br. 3 11'0 x 10'0
L.
COVERED PORCH
Gar. 21'4 x 23'0
48'-0"
50'-8"
© Design Basics, Inc.
MAIN FLOOR

Design 96506 BL/ML/ZIP

See Order Pages and Index for Info

Units	Single
Price Code	B
Total Finished	1,654 sq. ft.
Main Finished	1,654 sq. ft.
Garage Unfinished	480 sq. ft.
Dimensions	68'x46'
Foundation	Crawl space
	Slab
Bedrooms	3
Full Baths	2
Half Baths	1
First Ceiling	9'
Primary Roof Pitch	9:12
Max Ridge Height	21
Roof Framing	Stick
Exterior Walls	2x4

MAIN FLOOR

Design 94923 BL/ML

See Order Pages and Index for Info

Units	Single
Price Code	B
Total Finished	1,666 sq. ft.
Main Finished	1,666 sq. ft.
Basement Unfinished	1,666 sq. ft.
Garage Unfinished	496 sq. ft.
Dimensions	55'4"x48'
Foundation	Basement
Bedrooms	3
Full Baths	2
Primary Roof Pitch	8:12
Secondary Roof Pitch	8:12
Max Ridge Height	22'9"
Roof Framing	Stick
Exterior Walls	2x4

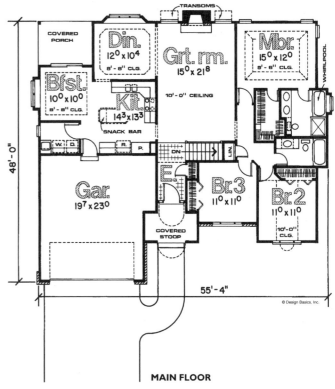

MAIN FLOOR

© Design Basics, Inc.

Design 93219

BL/ML/ZIP See Order Pages and Index for Info

Units	Single
Price Code	B
Total Finished	1,668 sq. ft.
First Finished	1,057 sq. ft.
Second Finished	611 sq. ft.
Basement Unfinished	511 sq. ft.
Garage Unfinished	546 sq. ft.
Dimensions	40'4"x38'
Foundation	Basement
Bedrooms	3
Full Baths	2
Half Baths	1
First Ceiling	8'
Second Ceiling	8'
Primary Roof Pitch	12:12
Secondary Roof Pitch	5:12
Max Ridge Height	23'
Roof Framing	Stick
Exterior Walls	2x4

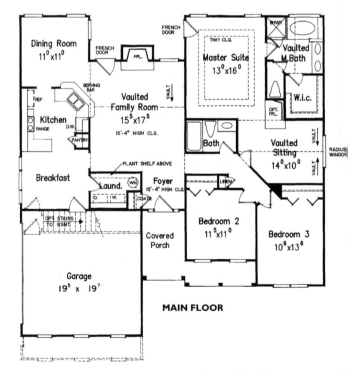

FIRST FLOOR

SECOND FLOOR

Design 98423

BL/ML/ZIP See Order Pages and Index for Info

Units	Single
Price Code	B
Total Finished	1,671 sq. ft.
Main Finished	1,671 sq. ft.
Basement Unfinished	1,685 sq. ft.
Garage Unfinished	400 sq. ft.
Dimensions	50'x51'
Foundation	Basement
	Crawlspace
	Slab
Bedrooms	3
Full Baths	2
Main Ceiling	9'
Primary Roof Pitch	9:12
Max Ridge Height	22'6"
Roof Framing	Stick
Exterior Walls	2x4

MAIN FLOOR

Design 99914 BL/ML

See Order Pages and Index for Info

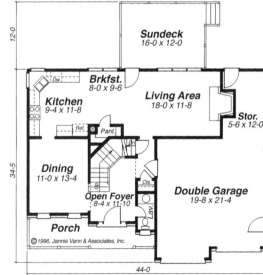

FIRST FLOOR

Labels in first floor plan: BR 2 12-0x13-0, Pantry, frzr, Mud Rm/Utility, clos., W D, Bath, Porch, FOYER, up, stor, KITCHEN 12-4x12-0, dw, LR 15-0x18-6, DINING 12-0x12-0/9-9, Gas FP, Patio door, SUNDECK

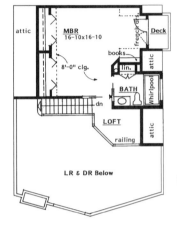

SECOND FLOOR

Labels in second floor plan: attic, MBR 16-10x16-10, freezer, Deck, books, 8'-0" clg., lin., attic, BATH, Whirlpool, dn, LOFT, railing, attic, LR & DR Below

Units	Single
Price Code	B
Total Finished	1,677 sq. ft.
First Finished	1,064 sq. ft.
Second Finished	613 sq. ft.
Deck Unfinished	474 sq. ft.
Porch Unfinished	32 sq. ft.
Dimensions	28'x40'
Foundation	Basement
	Crawl space
Bedrooms	2
Full Baths	2
First Ceiling	8'
Second Ceiling	8'
Vaulted Ceiling	22'
Primary Roof Pitch	12:12
Max Ridge Height	26'6"
Roof Framing	Stick
Exterior Walls	2x6

Design 93298 BL

See Order Pages and Index for Info

Units	Single
Price Code	B
Total Finished	1,683 sq. ft.
First Finished	797 sq. ft.
Second Finished	886 sq. ft.
Basement Unfinished	797 sq. ft.
Garage Unfinished	414 sq. ft.
Deck Unfinished	192 sq. ft.
Porch Unfinished	118 sq. ft.
Dimensions	44'x34'5"
Foundation	Basement
	Crawl space
	Slab
Bedrooms	3
Full Baths	2
Half Baths	1
Primary Roof Pitch	10:12
Secondary Roof Pitch	12:12
Max Ridge Height	29'
Roof Framing	Stick
Exterior Walls	2x4

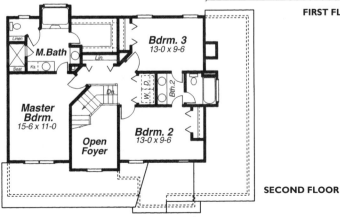

First floor labels: 12-0, Sundeck 16-0 x 12-0, Dw, Brkfst. 8-0 x 9-6, Living Area 18-0 x 11-8, Stor. 5-6 x 12-0, Kitchen 9-4 x 11-8, Ref., Pant., Dining 11-0 x 13-4, 34-5, Open Foyer 8-4 x 11-10, Lav., Double Garage 19-8 x 21-4, Porch, © 1996, Jannis Vann & Associates, Inc., 44-0

FIRST FLOOR

Second floor labels: Linen, M.Bath, Seat, Ks., Lin., Bdrm. 3 13-0 x 9-6, W.D., Bth 2, Master Bdrm. 15-6 x 11-0, Dn., Open Foyer, Bdrm. 2 13-0 x 9-6

SECOND FLOOR

Design 97254

BL

See Order Pages and Index for Info

Units	Single
Price Code	B
Total Finished	1,692 sq. ft.
Main Finished	1,692 sq. ft.
Bonus Unfinished	358 sq. ft.
Basement Unfinished	1,705 sq. ft.
Garage Unfinished	472 sq. ft.
Dimensions	54'x56'6''
Foundation	Basement
	Crawl space
Bedrooms	3
Full Baths	2
Primary Roof Pitch	10:12
Max Ridge Height	27'
Roof Framing	Stick
Exterior Walls	2x4

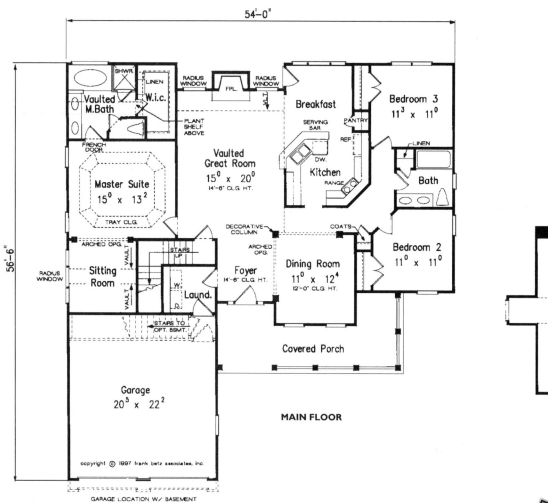

MAIN FLOOR

copyright © 1997 frank betz associates, inc.

GARAGE LOCATION W/ BASEMENT

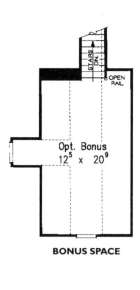

BONUS SPACE

Design 19422

BL/ML/ZIP

See Order Pages and Index for Info

Photography supplied by the Meredith Corporation

Units	Single
Price Code	B
Total Finished	1,695 sq. ft.
Main Finished	1,290 sq. ft.
Second Finished	405 sq. ft.
Garage Unfinished	513 sq. ft.
Porch Unfinished	152 sq. ft.
Dimensions	50'8"x61'8"
Foundation	Basement
	Crawl space
Bedrooms	2
Full Baths	2
Main Ceiling	9'
Second Ceiling	8'
Primary Roof Pitch	10:12
Max Ridge Height	29'
Roof Framing	Stick/Truss
Exterior Walls	2x4

SECOND FLOOR

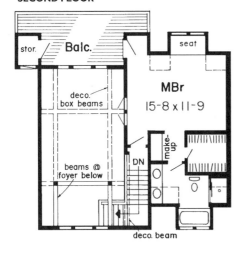

FIRST FLOOR

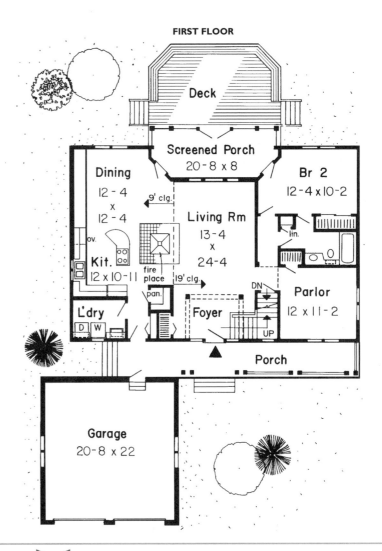

Design 99811

BL/ML/ZIP/RRR   See Order Pages and Index for Info

Units	Single
Price Code	D
Total Finished	1,699 sq. ft.
Main Finished	1,699 sq. ft.
Bonus Unfinished	336 sq. ft.
Garage Unfinished	498 sq. ft.
Dimensions	64'6"x49'8"
Foundation	Crawl space
Bedrooms	3
Full Baths	2
First Ceiling	8'
Primary Roof Pitch	12:12
Max Ridge Height	21'8"
Roof Framing	Stick
Exterior Walls	2x4

© Donald A. Gardner Architects, Inc.

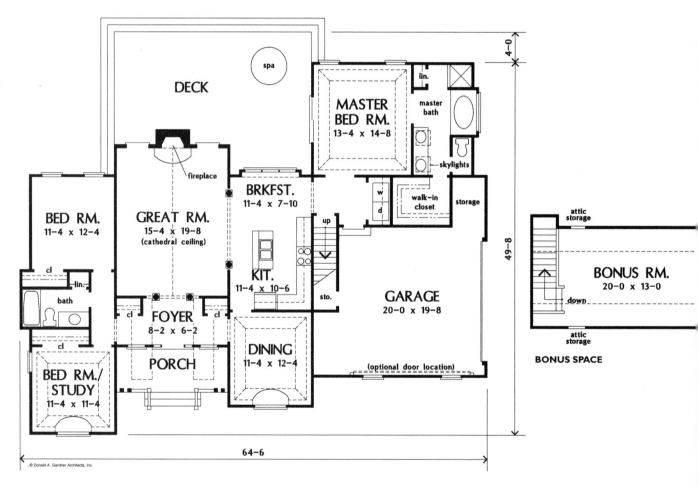

MAIN FLOOR

DECK

spa

MASTER BED RM. 13-4 x 14-8

lin.

master bath

skylights

fireplace

BRKFST. 11-4 x 7-10

w d

walk-in closet

storage

GREAT RM. 15-4 x 19-8 (cathedral ceiling)

BED RM. 11-4 x 12-4

cl

lin.

bath

up

KIT. 11-4 x 10-6

cl

cl

FOYER 8-2 x 6-2

sto.

GARAGE 20-0 x 19-8

cl

BED RM./ STUDY 11-4 x 11-4

PORCH

DINING 11-4 x 12-4

(optional door location)

64-6

4-0

49-8

© Donald A. Gardner Architects, Inc.

BONUS SPACE

attic storage

BONUS RM. 20-0 x 13-0

down

attic storage

Merillat®

Visit us at www.merillat.com

Design 99066

BL   See Order Pages and Index for Info

Units	Single
Price Code	B
Total Finished	1,703 sq. ft.
First Finished	848 sq. ft.
Second Finished	855 sq. ft.
Basement Unfinished	848 sq. ft.
Garage Unfinished	220 sq. ft.
Deck Unfinished	192 sq. ft.
Dimensions	29'10"x39'
Foundation	Basement
Bedrooms	3
Full Baths	2
Half Baths	1
First Ceiling	8'
Second Ceiling	8'
Primary Roof Pitch	9:12
Max Ridge Height	30'
Roof Framing	Stick
Exterior Walls	2x4

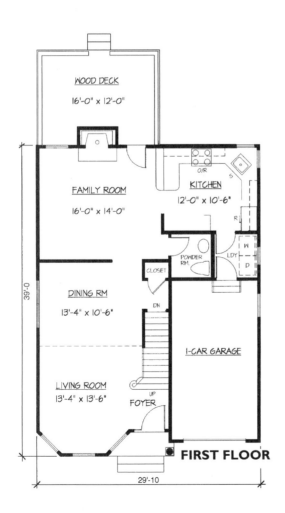

FIRST FLOOR

WOOD DECK
16'-0" x 12'-0"

FAMILY ROOM
16'-0" x 14'-0"

KITCHEN
12'-0" x 10'-6"

POWDER RM.

CLOSET

LDY

DINING RM
13'-4" x 10'-6"

DN

1-CAR GARAGE

LIVING ROOM
13'-4" x 13'-6"

UP

FOYER

39'-0"

29'-10"

SECOND FLOOR

WALK-IN CLOSET

MASTER BATH

MASTER BEDROOM
12'-2" x 14'-0"

WALK-IN CLOSET

BEDROOM
10'-2" x 11'-0"

CLOSET

PN

LINEN

CLOSET

OPEN TO LIVING ROOM BELOW

BEDROOM
11'-2" x 10'-0"

Design 98456 BL/ML

See Order Pages and Index for Info

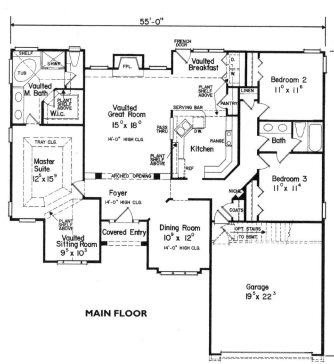

Units	Single
Price Code	B
Total Finished	1,715 sq. ft.
Main Finished	1,715 sq. ft.
Basement Unfinished	1,715 sq. ft.
Garage Unfinished	450 sq. ft.
Dimensions	55'x51'6"
Foundation	Basement
	Crawl space
	Slab
Bedrooms	3
Full Baths	2
Main Ceiling	9'1"
Primary Roof Pitch	12:12
Max Ridge Height	25'
Roof Framing	Stick
Exterior Walls	2x4

MAIN FLOOR

Design 98087 BL/ML

See Order Pages and Index for Info

© Donald A. Gardner Architects, Inc.

Units	Single
Price Code	D
Total Finished	1,733 sq. ft.
Main Finished	1,733 sq. ft.
Dimensions	65'8"x49'8"
Foundation	Crawl space
Bedrooms	3
Full Baths	2
Main Ceiling	9'
Primary Roof Pitch	9:12
Secondary Roof Pitch	12:12
Max Ridge Height	25'9.5"
Roof Framing	Stick
Exterior Walls	2x4

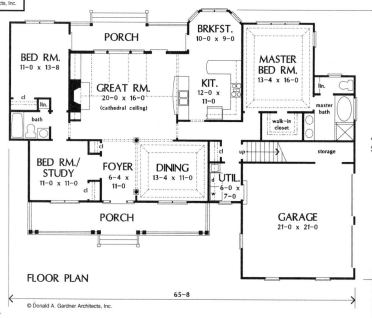

FLOOR PLAN

© Donald A. Gardner Architects, Inc.

650 Home Plans FREE!

Thanks for buying this Garlinghouse magazine and giving us a chance to better understand your needs and desires. To receive your FREE copy of 650 Best Selling Home Plans book, please:

1. Fill out the questionnaire.
2. Cut out the bar code on the front of this magazine and affix it to the questionaire.
3. Enclose a check for $3.50 to cover postage and handling. Your book will be shipped book rate and will arrive in about 1-3 weeks.
4. Mail your questionnaire, bar code and check for postage to:
   Publisher
   Garlinghouse Inc.
   174 Oakwood Drive
   Glastonbury, CT 06033

FREE! FREE! FREE!

✂

Name: _____

Address: _____

City: _____ **State:** _____ **Zip:** _____

Daytime telephone number: ( ) _____

FREE 650 — Affix Bar Code Here

Where did you buy this magazine?
❑ Newsstand
❑ Grocery store
❑ Pharmacy/Conv Store
❑ Lumberyard
❑ Bookstore
❑ Other

When are you planning to build?
❑ Within 6 months
❑ 6 months to 12 months
❑ 1 to 2 years
❑ More than 2 years
❑ Undecided

What style are you most interested in?
❑ Farmhouse or country style
❑ Colonial
❑ Rustic cottage or cabin
❑ Victorian
❑ Eurostyle
❑ Traditional
❑ Other _____
_____
_____

What is the approximate size of the home?
❑ Under 1,000 square feet
❑ 1,000 to 2,000
❑ 2,000 to 3,000
❑ 3,000 to 4,000
❑ Over 4,000

What type of home?
❑ One level
❑ Two story with all bedrooms on second floor
❑ Two story with one or two bedrooms on first floor
❑ Other _____
_____

Please provide any other comments.
Please tell us anything else about the dream house you'd like to build. Let us know if you have special floor plan requirements (i.e. you want a great room but no living room) or specific property features (i.e. you have a sloped or narrow lot).
_____
_____
_____
_____
_____
_____
_____

Design 96469

BL/ML/RRR   See Order Pages and Index for Info

© Donald A. Gardner Architects, Inc.   B. NATHAN

Units	Single
Price Code	D
Total Finished	1,746 sq. ft.
First Finished	1,099 sq. ft.
Second Finished	647 sq. ft.
Bonus Unfinished	377 sq. ft.
Garage Unfinished	581 sq. ft.
Dimensions	61'6"x36'4"
Foundation	Crawl space
Bedrooms	3
Full Baths	2
Primary Roof Pitch	11:12
Max Ridge Height	23'10"
Roof Framing	Stick
Exterior Walls	2x4

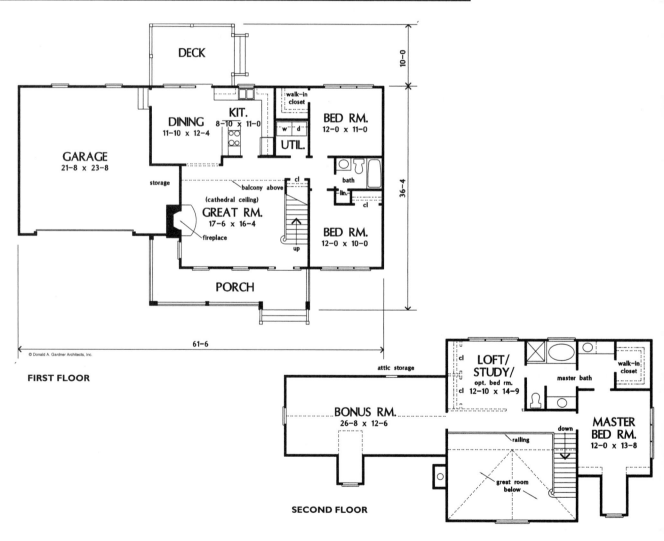

DECK

DINING 11-10 x 12-4

KIT. 8-10 x 11-0

walk-in closet

BED RM. 12-0 x 11-0

UTIL.

w / d

GARAGE 21-8 x 23-8

storage

balcony above

(cathedral ceiling)

GREAT RM. 17-6 x 16-4

fireplace

bath

cl

lin.

cl

BED RM. 12-0 x 10-0

up

PORCH

10-0

36-4

61-6

© Donald A. Gardner Architects, Inc.

FIRST FLOOR

attic storage

LOFT/ STUDY/ opt. bed rm. 12-10 x 14-9

cl

cl

cl

master bath

walk-in closet

BONUS RM. 26-8 x 12-6

railing

great room below

down

MASTER BED RM. 12-0 x 13-8

SECOND FLOOR

Design 94822

BL/ML

See Order Pages and Index for Info

Units	Single
Price Code	B
Total Finished	1,746 sq. ft.
Main Finished	1,746 sq. ft.
Basement Unfinished	1,746 sq. ft.
Deck Unfinished	407 sq. ft.
Dimensions	56'4"x49'
Foundation	Basement
Bedrooms	3
Full Baths	2
Primary Roof Pitch	8:12
Max Ridge Height	23'
Roof Framing	Stick
Exterior Walls	2x4

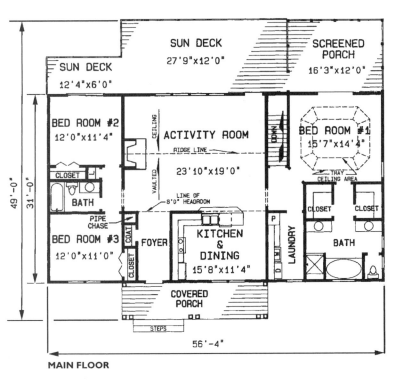

MAIN FLOOR

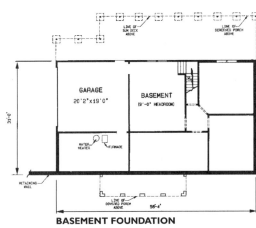

BASEMENT FOUNDATION

Design 92625

BL/ML/ZIP

See Order Pages and Index for Info

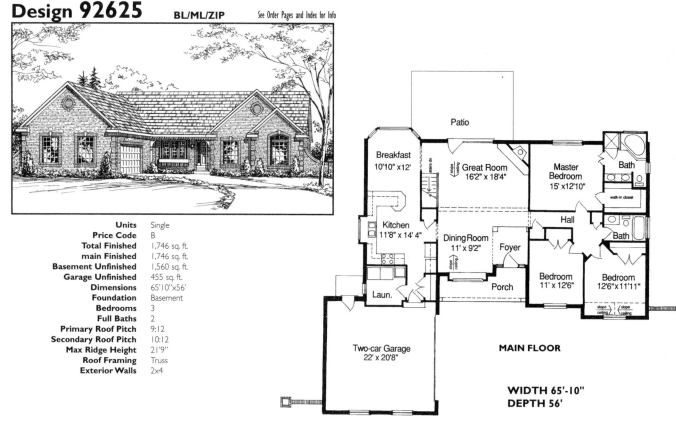

Units	Single
Price Code	B
Total Finished	1,746 sq. ft.
main Finished	1,746 sq. ft.
Basement Unfinished	1,560 sq. ft.
Garage Unfinished	455 sq. ft.
Dimensions	65'10"x56'
Foundation	Basement
Bedrooms	3
Full Baths	2
Primary Roof Pitch	9:12
Secondary Roof Pitch	10:12
Max Ridge Height	21'9"
Roof Framing	Truss
Exterior Walls	2x4

MAIN FLOOR

WIDTH 65'-10"
DEPTH 56'

Design 97757

BL

See Order Pages and Index for Info

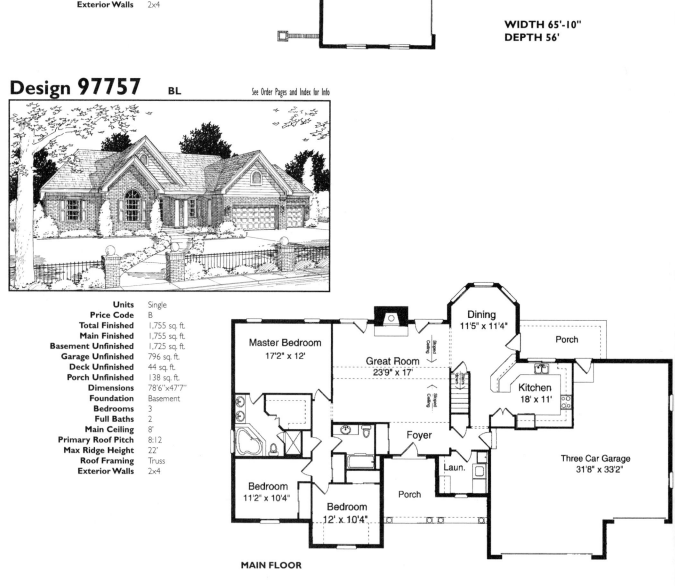

Units	Single
Price Code	B
Total Finished	1,755 sq. ft.
Main Finished	1,755 sq. ft.
Basement Unfinished	1,725 sq. ft.
Garage Unfinished	796 sq. ft.
Deck Unfinished	44 sq. ft.
Porch Unfinished	138 sq. ft.
Dimensions	78'6"x47'7"
Foundation	Basement
Bedrooms	3
Full Baths	2
Main Ceiling	8'
Primary Roof Pitch	8:12
Max Ridge Height	22'
Roof Framing	Truss
Exterior Walls	2x4

MAIN FLOOR

Design 90870 BL See Order Pages and Index for Info

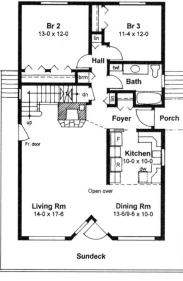

FIRST FLOOR

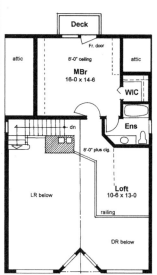

Units	Single
Price Code	C
Total Finished	1,755 sq. ft.
First Finished	1,208 sq. ft.
Second Finished	547 sq. ft.
Basement Unfinished	1,208 sq. ft.
Deck	413 sq. ft.
Porch	32 sq. ft.
Dimensions	36'x50'
Foundation	Basement
Bedrooms	3
Full Baths	2
Primary Roof Pitch	12:12
Secondary Roof Pitch	8:12
Max Ridge Height	31'
Roof Framing	Stick/Truss
Exterior Walls	2x6

SECOND FLOOR

Deck
attic
8'-0" ceiling
attic
MBr
16-0 x 14-6
Fr. door
WIC
dn
Ens
8'-0" plus clg.
LR below
Loft
10-6 x 13-0
railing
DR below

Br 2
13-0 x 12-0
Br 3
11-4 x 12-0
lin
Hall
brm
Bath
twl
up
dn
Foyer
Porch
Fr. door
Kitchen
10-0 x 10-0
F
R
dw
Open over
Living Rm
14-0 x 17-6
Dining Rm
13-6/9-6 x 10-0
Sundeck

Design 93133 BL/ML/ZIP/RRR See Order Pages and Index for Info

Units	Single
Price Code	C
Total Finished	1,761 sq. ft.
Main Finished	1,761 sq. ft.
Basement Unfinished	1,761 sq. ft.
Garage Unfinished	658 sq. ft.
Dimensions	67'8''x42'8''
Foundation	Basement
Bedrooms	3
Full Baths	2
First Ceiling	8'
Vaulted Ceiling	14'
Primary Roof Pitch	8:12
Secondary Roof Pitch	8:12
Max Ridge Height	22'
Roof Framing	Truss
Exterior Walls	2x6

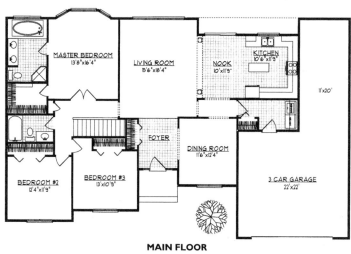

MASTER BEDROOM
13'8"x16'4"
LIVING ROOM
15'6"x18'4"
NOOK
10'x11'9"
KITCHEN
10'6"x11'9"
11'x20'
FOYER
DINING ROOM
11'6"x12'4"
BEDROOM #2
12'4"x11'9"
BEDROOM #3
13'x10'9"
3 CAR GARAGE
22'x22'

MAIN FLOOR

Design 98931 BL

See Order Pages and Index for Info

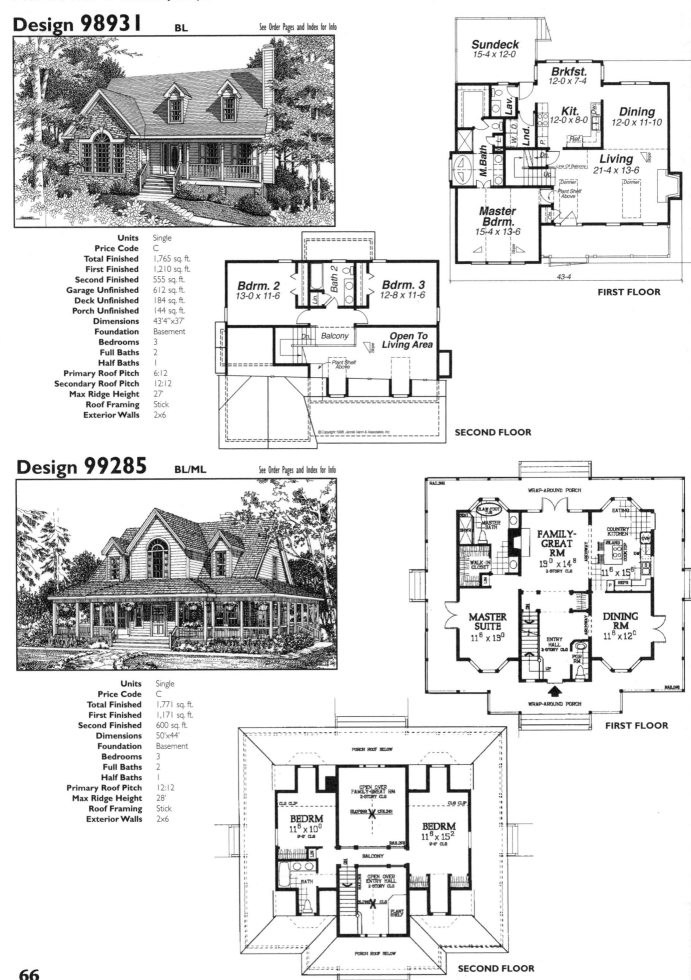

Sundeck 15-4 x 12-0

Brkfst. 12-0 x 7-4

Kit. 12-0 x 8-0

Dining 12-0 x 11-10

Lav.

W.D.

Lnd.

Ref.

M.Bath

Living 21-4 x 13-6

Slope

Dormer

Dn.

Up

Line Of Balcony

Plant Shelf Above

Master Bdrm. 15-4 x 13-6

Slope

Dormer

43-4

FIRST FLOOR

Units	Single
Price Code	C
Total Finished	1,765 sq. ft.
First Finished	1,210 sq. ft.
Second Finished	555 sq. ft.
Garage Unfinished	612 sq. ft.
Deck Unfinished	184 sq. ft.
Porch Unfinished	144 sq. ft.
Dimensions	43'4''x37'
Foundation	Basement
Bedrooms	3
Full Baths	2
Half Baths	1
Primary Roof Pitch	6:12
Secondary Roof Pitch	12:12
Max Ridge Height	27'
Roof Framing	Stick
Exterior Walls	2x6

Bdrm. 2 13-0 x 11-6

Lin.

Bath 2

Bdrm. 3 12-8 x 11-6

Dn.

Balcony

Slope

Open To Living Area

Plant Shelf Above

© Copyright 1998, Jannis Vann & Associates, Inc.

SECOND FLOOR

Design 99285 BL/ML

See Order Pages and Index for Info

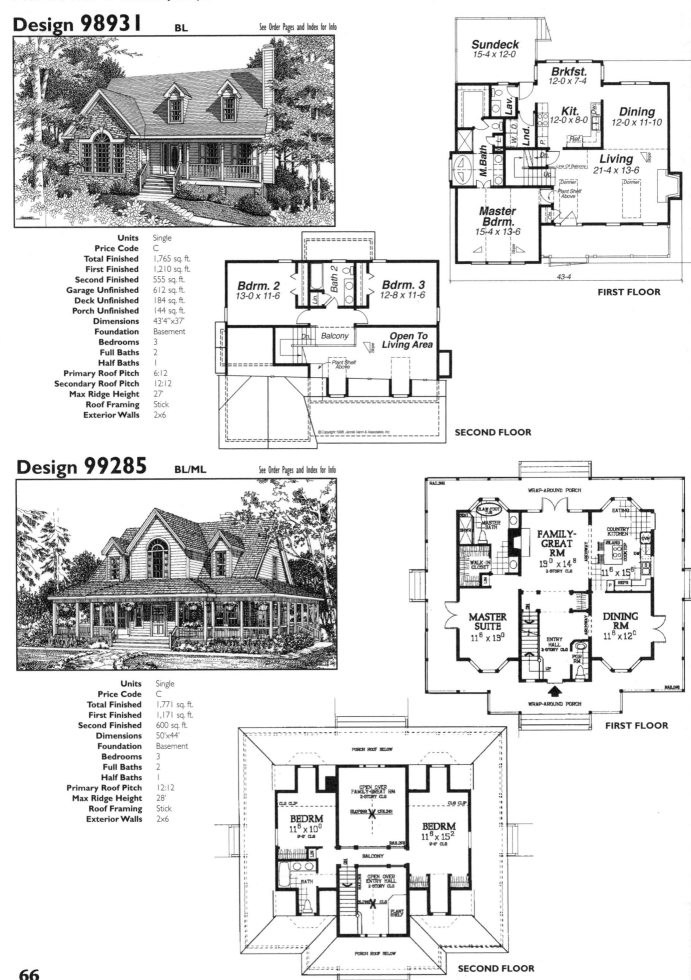

RAILING

WRAP-AROUND PORCH

CLAW-FOOT TUB

SEAT

MASTER BATH

SHWR

WALK-IN CLOSET

LIN.

FAMILY-GREAT RM 13-0 x 14-8 2-STORY CLG

ARCHWAY

EATING

COUNTRY KITCHEN 11-6 x 15-6

ISLAND

OVN

DW

P

REFG

MASTER SUITE 11-6 x 19-0

DN.

UP

ENTRY HALL 2-STORY CLG

ARCHWAY

PDR. RM

DINING RM 11-8 x 12-0

RAILING

WRAP-AROUND PORCH

FIRST FLOOR

Units	Single
Price Code	C
Total Finished	1,771 sq. ft.
First Finished	1,171 sq. ft.
Second Finished	600 sq. ft.
Dimensions	50'x44'
Foundation	Basement
Bedrooms	3
Full Baths	2
Half Baths	1
Primary Roof Pitch	12:12
Max Ridge Height	28'
Roof Framing	Stick
Exterior Walls	2x6

PORCH ROOF BELOW

CLG CLIP

OPEN OVER FAMILY-GREAT RM 2-STORY CLG

SLOPING CEILING

CLG CLIP

BEDRM 11-6 x 10-0 9'-0" CLG

LIN.

RAILING

BEDRM 11-8 x 15-2 9'-0" CLG

BALCONY

BATH

DN.

OPEN OVER ENTRY HALL 2-STORY CLG

SLOPING CLG

PLANT SHELF

PORCH ROOF BELOW

SECOND FLOOR

Design 93261

BL/ML/ZIP

See Order Pages and Index for Info

Units	Single
Price Code	C
Total Finished	1,778 sq. ft.
First Finished	1,778 sq. ft.
Basement Unfinished	1,008 sq. ft.
Garage Unfinished	728 sq. ft.
Dimensions	62'x28'
Foundation	Basement
Bedrooms	3
Full Baths	2
First Ceiling	8'
Vaulted Ceiling	10'4''
Primary Roof Pitch	6:12
Max Ridge Height	26'
Roof Framing	Stick/Truss
Exterior Walls	2x4

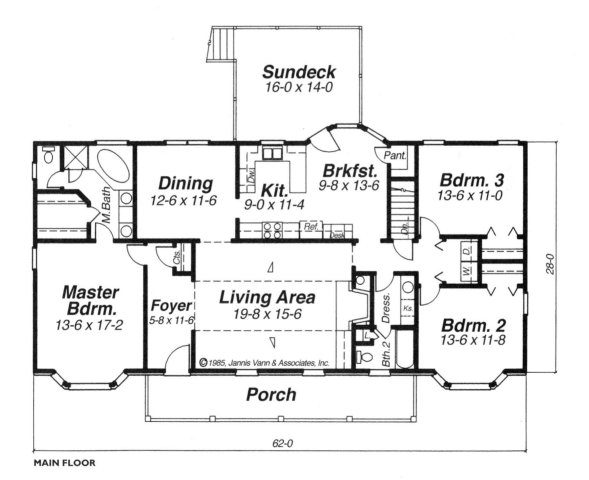

Sundeck
16-0 x 14-0

Pant.

Dining
12-6 x 11-6

Kit.
9-0 x 11-4

Dw.

Brkfst.
9-8 x 13-6

Bdrm. 3
13-6 x 11-0

M.Bath

Ref.

Desk

Dn.

W. D.

28-0

Master Bdrm.
13-6 x 17-2

Cts.

Foyer
5-8 x 11-6

Living Area
19-8 x 15-6

Dress.

Ks.

Bth.2

© 1985, Jannis Vann & Associates, Inc.

Bdrm. 2
13-6 x 11-8

Porch

62-0

MAIN FLOOR

Design 99832

BL/ML/RRR   See Order Pages and Index for Info

© Donald A. Gardner Architects, Inc.

Units	Single
Price Code	E
Total Finished	1,781 sq. ft.
Main Finished	1,781 sq. ft.
Bonus Unfinished	386 sq. ft.
Garage Unfinished	681 sq. ft.
Porch Unfinished	190 sq. ft.
Dimensions	63'11"x55'8"
Foundation	Crawl space
Bedrooms	3
Full Baths	2
First Ceiling	8'
Primary Roof Pitch	9.5:12
Secondary Roof Pitch	12:12
Max Ridge Height	26'2"
Roof Framing	Stick
Exterior Walls	2x4

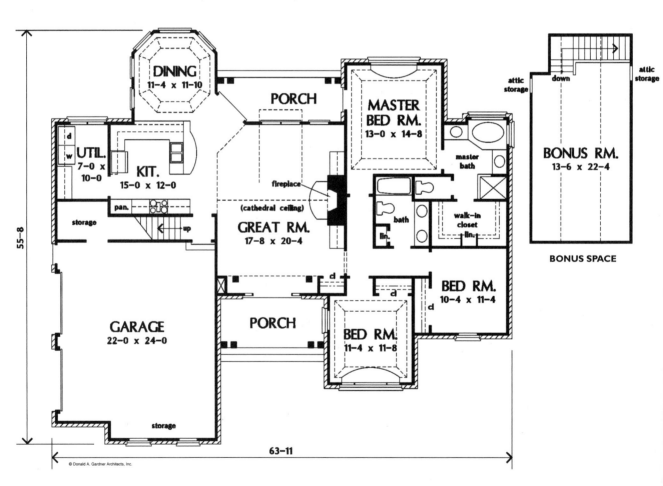

MAIN FLOOR

© Donald A. Gardner Architects, Inc.

Design 92632

BL

See Order Pages and Index for Info

Units	Single
Price Code	C
Total Finished	1,784 sq. ft.
First Finished	934 sq. ft.
Second Finished	850 sq. ft.
Basement Unfinished	831 sq. ft.
Garage Unfinished	229 sq. ft.
Dimensions	37'x37'
Foundation	Basement
Bedrooms	3
Full Baths	2
Half Baths	1
Primary Roof Pitch	8:12
Secondary Roof Pitch	12:12
Max Ridge Height	30'
Roof Framing	Truss
Exterior Walls	2x4

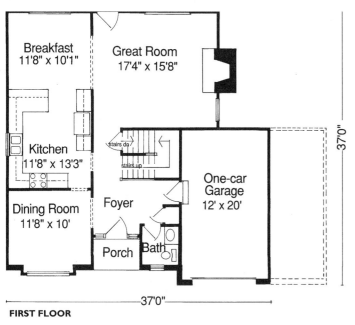

FIRST FLOOR

Breakfast 11'8" x 10'1"

Great Room 17'4" x 15'8"

Kitchen 11'8" x 13'3"

stairs dn

stairs up

One-car Garage 12' x 20'

Dining Room 11'8" x 10'

Foyer

Porch

Bath

37'0"

37'0"

SECOND FLOOR

walk-in closet

Bath

Master Bedroom 12'1" x 15'8"

Bedroom 11'8" x 10'1"

walk-in closet

Bath

Hall

stairs dn

Loft / Opt. Laun.

Bedroom 11'8" x 11'7"

Laun.

OPTIONAL LAUNDRY

Design 24610

BL/ML/ZIP

See Order Pages and Index for Info

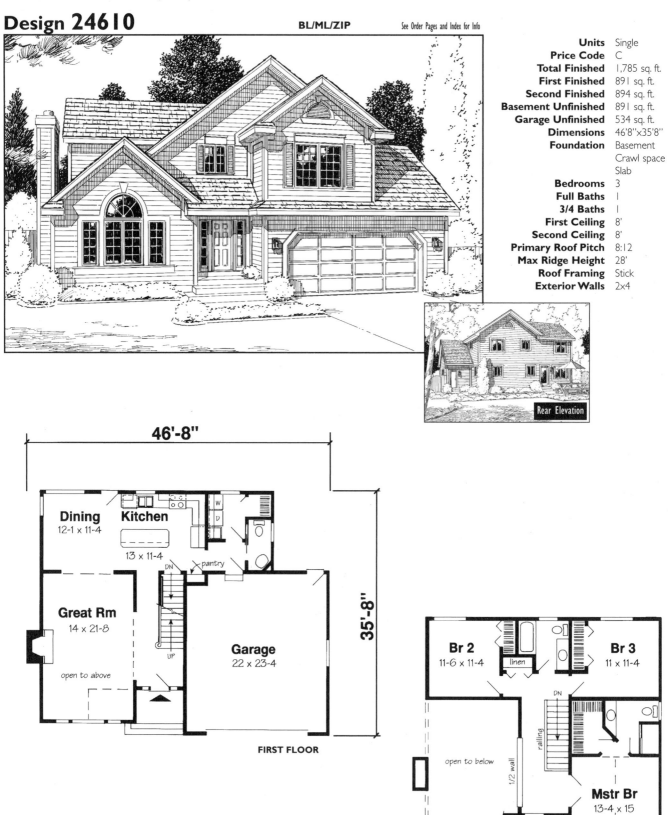

Rear Elevation

Units	Single
Price Code	C
Total Finished	1,785 sq. ft.
First Finished	891 sq. ft.
Second Finished	894 sq. ft.
Basement Unfinished	891 sq. ft.
Garage Unfinished	534 sq. ft.
Dimensions	46'8''x35'8''
Foundation	Basement
	Crawl space
	Slab
Bedrooms	3
Full Baths	1
3/4 Baths	1
First Ceiling	8'
Second Ceiling	8'
Primary Roof Pitch	8:12
Max Ridge Height	28'
Roof Framing	Stick
Exterior Walls	2x4

46'-8"

35'-8"

Dining
12-1 x 11-4

Kitchen
13 x 11-4

DN

pantry

Great Rm
14 x 21-8

open to above

UP

Garage
22 x 23-4

FIRST FLOOR

Br 2
11-6 x 11-4

linen

Br 3
11 x 11-4

DN

railing

open to below

1/2 wall

Mstr Br
13-4 x 15

SECOND FLOOR

Design 99805

BL/ML/ZIP/RRR See Order Pages and Index for Info

© Donald A. Gardner Architects, Inc.

B. NATHAN

Units	Single
Price Code	E
Total Finished	1,787 sq. ft.
First Finished	1,787 sq. ft.
Bonus Unfinished	326 sq. ft.
Garage Unfinished	521 sq. ft.
Dimensions	66'2"x66'8"
Foundation	Crawl space
Bedrooms	3
Full Baths	2
First Ceiling	8'
Primary Roof Pitch	10:12
Secondary Roof Pitch	4:12
Max Ridge Height	24'8"
Roof Framing	Stick
Exterior Walls	2x4

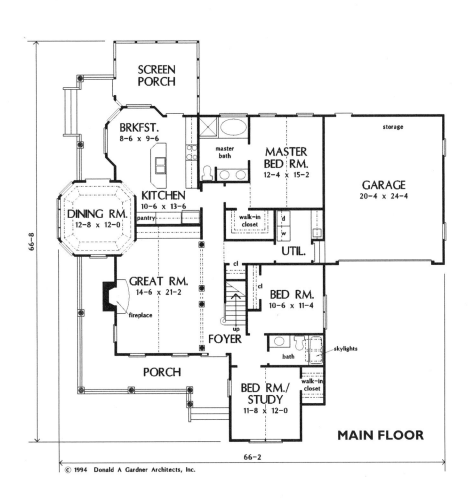

MAIN FLOOR

SCREEN PORCH

BRKFST.
8-6 x 9-6

master bath

MASTER BED RM.
12-4 x 15-2

storage

GARAGE
20-4 x 24-4

KITCHEN
10-6 x 13-6

pantry

DINING RM.
12-8 x 12-0

walk-in closet

d w

UTIL.

GREAT RM.
14-6 x 21-2

fireplace

cl

cl

BED RM.
10-6 x 11-4

up

FOYER

bath

skylights

PORCH

BED RM./ STUDY
11-8 x 12-0

walk-in closet

66-8

66-2

© 1994 Donald A Gardner Architects, Inc.

BONUS SPACE

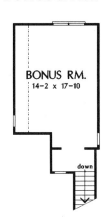

BONUS RM.
14-2 x 17-10

down

Design 99836

BL/ML/ZIP/RRR See Order Pages and Index for Info

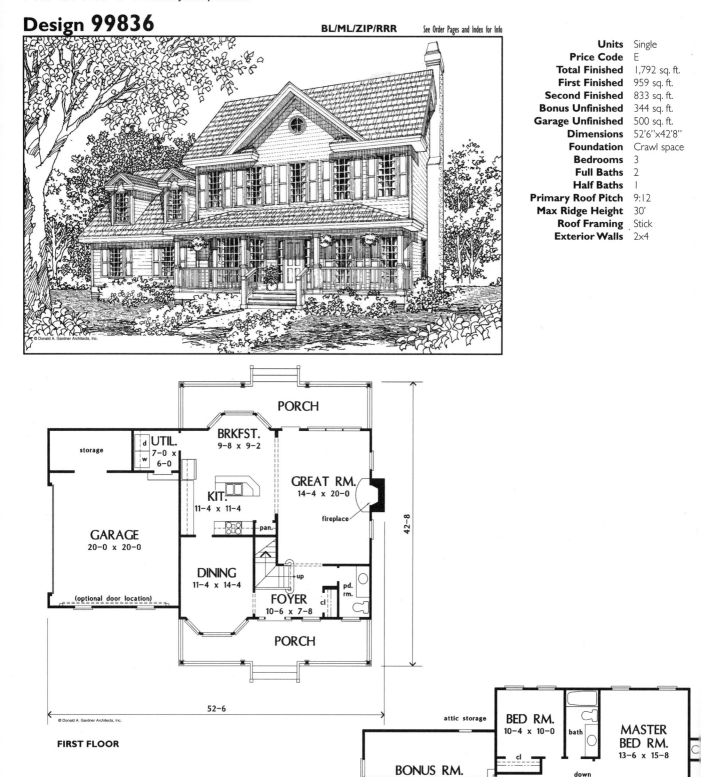

© Donald A. Gardner Architects, Inc.

Units	Single
Price Code	E
Total Finished	1,792 sq. ft.
First Finished	959 sq. ft.
Second Finished	833 sq. ft.
Bonus Unfinished	344 sq. ft.
Garage Unfinished	500 sq. ft.
Dimensions	52'6"x42'8"
Foundation	Crawl space
Bedrooms	3
Full Baths	2
Half Baths	1
Primary Roof Pitch	9:12
Max Ridge Height	30'
Roof Framing	Stick
Exterior Walls	2x4

FIRST FLOOR

PORCH

storage

UTIL. 7-0 x 6-0

BRKFST. 9-8 x 9-2

KIT. 11-4 x 11-4

GREAT RM. 14-4 x 20-0

fireplace

GARAGE 20-0 x 20-0

pan.

DINING 11-4 x 14-4

up

FOYER 10-6 x 7-8

pd. rm.

cl

(optional door location)

52-6

42-8

© Donald A. Gardner Architects, Inc.

PORCH

SECOND FLOOR

attic storage

BED RM. 10-4 x 10-0

bath

cl

MASTER BED RM. 13-6 x 15-8

BONUS RM. 20-0 x 14-2

attic storage

down

BED RM. 11-4 x 11-10

walk-in closet

walk-in closet

master bath

© Donald A. Gardner Architects, Inc.

Merillat. Visit us at www.merillat.com

Design 20198

BL/ML/ZIP   See Order Pages and Index for Info

Units	Single
Price Code	C
Total Finished	1,792 sq. ft.
Main Finished	1,792 sq. ft.
Basement Unfinished	818 sq. ft.
Garage Unfinished	857 sq. ft.
Dimensions	56'x32'
Foundation	Basement
Bedrooms	3
Full Baths	2
Main Ceiling	8'
Primary Roof Pitch	6:12
Secondary Roof Pitch	3:12
Max Ridge Height	25'
Roof Framing	Stick
Exterior Walls	2x4, 2x6

Rear Elevation

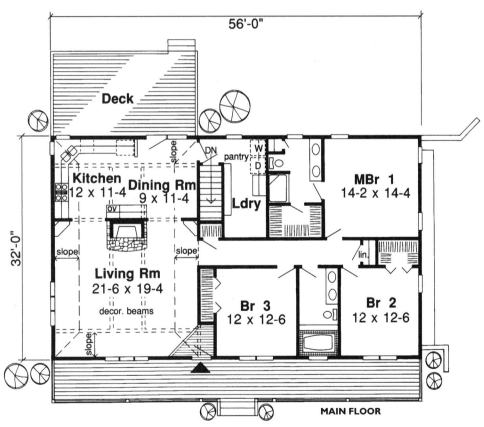

MAIN FLOOR

56'-0"

32'-0"

Deck

Kitchen
12 x 11-4

Dining Rm
9 x 11-4

DN

pantry

W
D

Ldry

MBr 1
14-2 x 14-4

slope

slope

slope

Living Rm
21-6 x 19-4

decor. beams

lin.

Br 3
12 x 12-6

Br 2
12 x 12-6

slope

ov

Design 96453

BL/ML/RRR   See Order Pages and Index for Info

Units	Single
Price Code	E
Total Finished	1,807 sq. ft.
First Finished	1,807 sq. ft.
Bonus Unfinished	419 sq. ft.
Garage Unfinished	669 sq. ft.
Dimensions	70'8''x53'
Foundation	Crawl space
Bedrooms	3
Full Baths	2
First Ceiling	8'
Primary Roof Pitch	12:12
Secondary Roof Pitch	3.5:12
Max Ridge Height	24'4''
Roof Framing	Stick
Exterior Walls	2x4

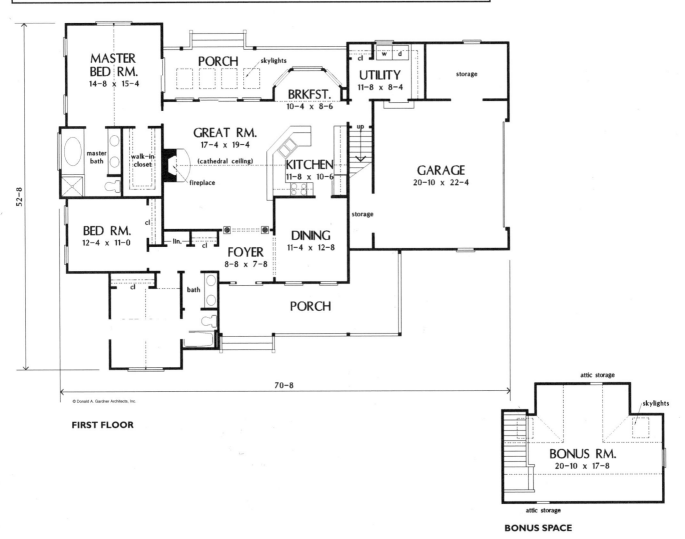

© Donald A. Gardner Architects, Inc.

B. NATHAN

FIRST FLOOR

MASTER BED RM. 14-8 x 15-4
PORCH
skylights
master bath
walk-in closet
fireplace
GREAT RM. 17-4 x 19-4
(cathedral ceiling)
BRKFST. 10-4 x 8-6
KITCHEN 11-8 x 10-6
UTILITY 11-8 x 8-4
cl w d
storage
up
GARAGE 20-10 x 22-4
storage
BED RM. 12-4 x 11-0
cl
lin.
cl
FOYER 8-8 x 7-8
DINING 11-4 x 12-8
storage
cl
bath
PORCH

52-8
70-8

© Donald A. Gardner Architects, Inc.

BONUS SPACE

attic storage
skylights
BONUS RM. 20-10 x 17-8
attic storage

Design 92220

BL/ML/ZIP   See Order Pages and Index for Info

Units	Single
Price Code	C
Total Finished	1,830 sq. ft.
Main Finished	1,830 sq. ft.
Garage Unfinished	759 sq. ft.
Deck Unfinished	315 sq. ft.
Porch Unfinished	390 sq. ft.
Dimensions	75'×52'3''
Foundation	Basement
	Crawl space
	Slab
Bedrooms	3
Full Baths	2
Primary Roof Pitch	9:12
Max Ridge Height	27'3''
Roof Framing	Stick
Exterior Walls	2×4

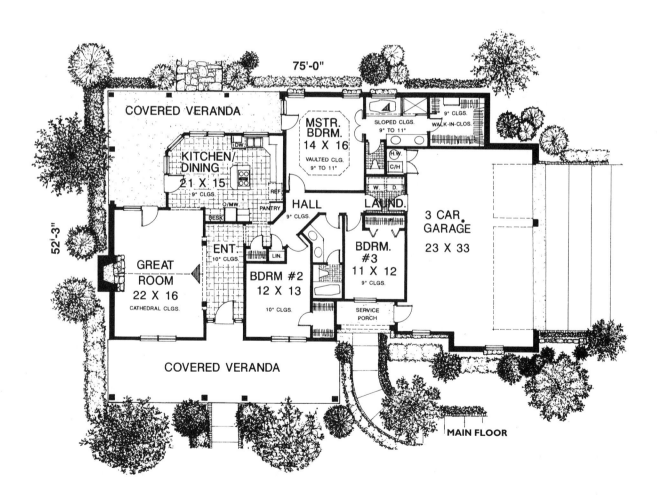

Design 99859

BL/ML/ZIP/RRR See Order Pages and Index for Info

© Donald A. Gardner Architects, Inc.

Units	Single
Price Code	E
Total Finished	1,831 sq. ft.
First Finished	1,289 sq. ft.
Second Finished	542 sq. ft.
Bonus Unfinished	393 sq. ft.
Garage Unfinished	521 sq. ft.
Dimensions	66'4"x40'4"
Foundation	Crawl space
Bedrooms	3
Full Baths	2
Half Baths	1
First Ceiling	9'
Second Ceiling	8'
Primary Roof Pitch	10:12
Secondary Roof Pitch	12:12
Max Ridge Height	25'
Roof Framing	Stick
Exterior Walls	2x4

BONUS RM.
14-4 x 23-8

**BONUS SPACE
ABOVE GARAGE**

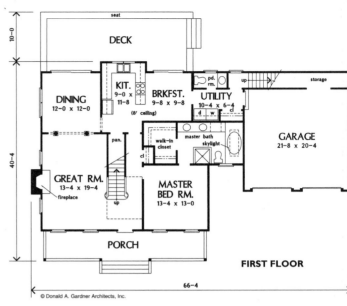

FIRST FLOOR

© Donald A. Gardner Architects, Inc.

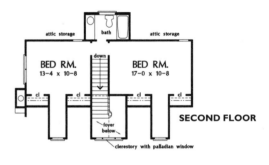

SECOND FLOOR

Design 99808

BL/ML/ZIP/RRR See Order Pages and Index for Info

© Donald A. Gardner Architects, Inc.

Units	Single
Price Code	E
Total Finished	1,832 sq. ft.
First Finished	1,832 sq. ft.
Bonus Unfinished	425 sq. ft.
Garage Unfinished	562 sq. ft.
Dimensions	65'4"x62'
Foundation	Crawl space
Bedrooms	3
Full Baths	2
First Ceiling	8'
Primary Roof Pitch	9:12
Max Ridge Height	25'
Roof Framing	Stick
Exterior Walls	2x4

BONUS RM.
12-8 x 22-4

**BONUS SPACE
ABOVE GARAGE**

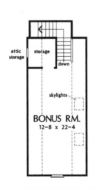

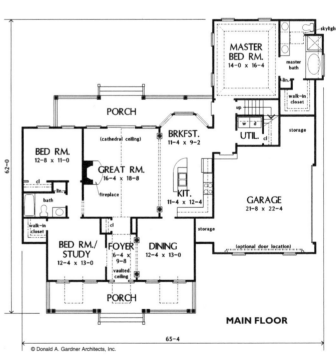

MAIN FLOOR

© Donald A. Gardner Architects, Inc.

Design **96819**

BL/ML

See Order Pages and Index for Info

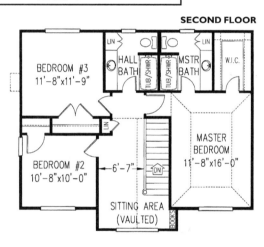

Units	Single
Price Code	C
Total Finished	1,840 sq. ft.
First Finished	1,014 sq. ft.
Second Finished	826 sq. ft.
Garage Unfinished	690 sq. ft.
Dimensions	62'7"x45'
Foundation	Basement
	Crawl space
	Slab
Bedrooms	4
Full Baths	3
First Ceiling	9'
Primary Roof Pitch	9:12
Roof Framing	Stick
Exterior Walls	2x4

SECOND FLOOR

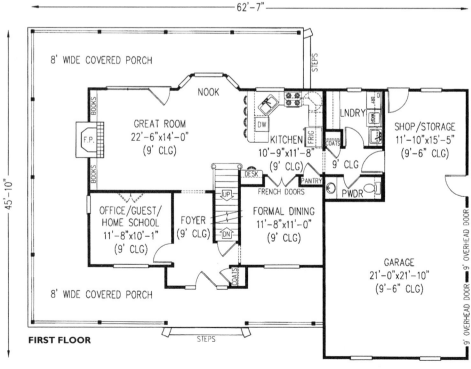

FIRST FLOOR

Design 96457

BL/ML/RRR   See Order Pages and Index for Info

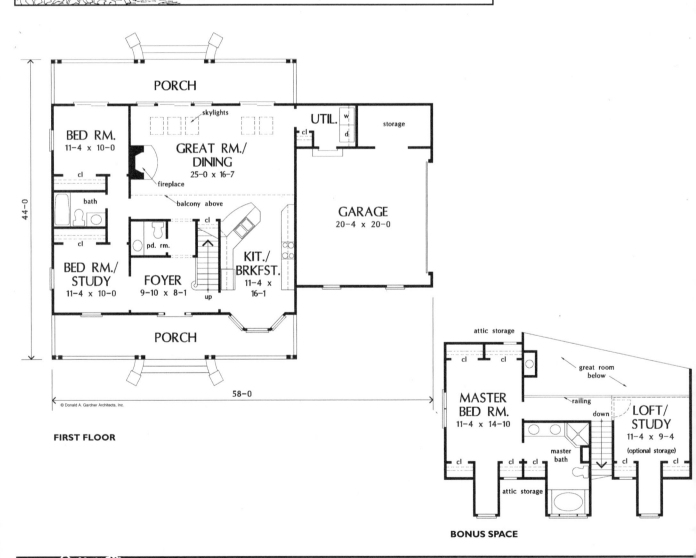

© Donald A. Gardner Architects, Inc.

Units	Single
Price Code	E
Total Finished	1,843 sq. ft.
First Finished	1,234 sq. ft.
Second Finished	609 sq. ft.
Garage Unfinished	496 sq. ft.
Dimensions	58'x44'
Foundation	Crawl space
Bedrooms	3
Full Baths	2
Half Baths	1
First Ceiling	8'
Primary Roof Pitch	12:12
Secondary Roof Pitch	4:12
Max Ridge Height	26'10"
Roof Framing	Stick
Exterior Walls	2x4

FIRST FLOOR

PORCH

BED RM.
11-4 x 10-0

GREAT RM./
DINING
25-0 x 16-7

skylights

fireplace

balcony above

UTIL.

storage

BED RM./
STUDY
11-4 x 10-0

bath

pd. rm.

FOYER
9-10 x 8-1

up

KIT./
BRKFST.
11-4 x
16-1

GARAGE
20-4 x 20-0

PORCH

44-0

58-0

© Donald A. Gardner Architects, Inc.

BONUS SPACE

attic storage

great room
below

MASTER
BED RM.
11-4 x 14-10

railing

down

LOFT/
STUDY
11-4 x 9-4

(optional storage)

master
bath

attic storage

Design 99861

BL/ML/RRR   See Order Pages and Index for Info

© Donald A. Gardner Architects, Inc.

Units	Single
Price Code	E
Total Finished	1,844 sq. ft.
First Finished	1,844 sq. ft.
Garage Unfinished	575 sq. ft.
Dimensions	93'1"x61'10"
Foundation	Crawl space
Bedrooms	3
Full Baths	2
First Ceiling	8'
Primary Roof Pitch	8:12
Max Ridge Height	17'6"
Roof Framing	Stick
Exterior Walls	2x4

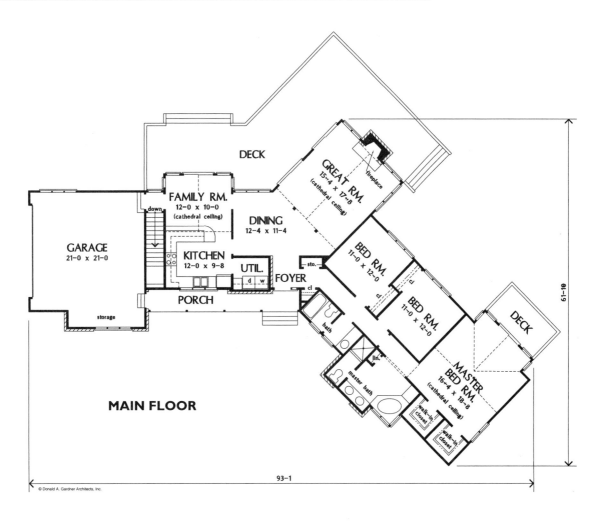

MAIN FLOOR

© Donald A. Gardner Architects, Inc.

Design 98425

BL/ML

See Order Pages and Index for Info

Units	Single
Price Code	C
Total Finished	1,845 sq. ft.
First Finished	1,845 sq. ft.
Bonus Unfinished	409 sq. ft.
Basement Unfinished	1,845 sq. ft.
Garage Unfinished	529 sq. ft.
Dimensions	56'x60'
Foundation	Basement
	Crawl space
Bedrooms	3
Full Baths	2
Half Baths	1
First Ceiling	9'
Primary Roof Pitch	10:12
Max Ridge Height	26'6''
Roof Framing	Stick
Exterior Walls	2x4

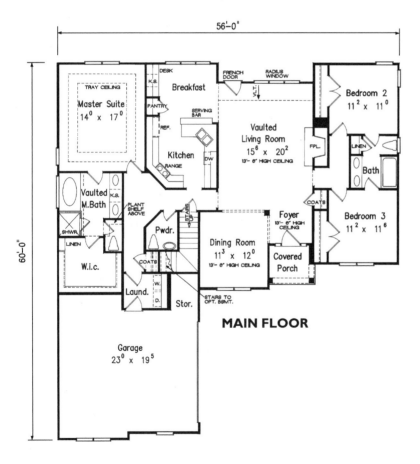

MAIN FLOOR

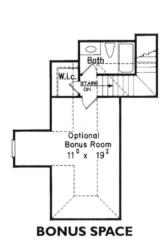

BONUS SPACE

Design 90466

BL/ML

See Order Pages and Index for Info

Units	Single
Price Code	C
Total Finished	1,845 sq. ft.
Main Finished	1,845 sq. ft.
Garage Unfinished	512 sq. ft.
Deck Unfinished	216 sq. ft.
Porch Unfinished	38 sq. ft.
Dimensions	57'2"x54'10"
Foundation	Crawl space
	Slab
Bedrooms	3
Full Baths	2
Half Baths	1
Main Ceiling	8'
Primary Roof Pitch	10:12
Max Ridge Height	23'10"
Roof Framing	Stick
Exterior Walls	2x4

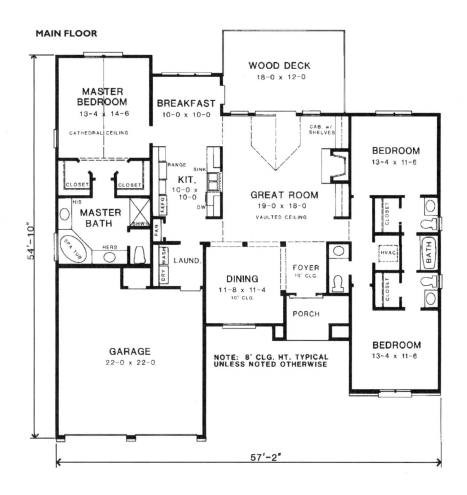

MAIN FLOOR

WOOD DECK
18-0 x 12-0

MASTER BEDROOM
13-4 x 14-6
CATHEDRAL CEILING

BREAKFAST
10-0 x 10-0

CAB. w/ SHELVES

BEDROOM
13-4 x 11-6

CLOSET   CLOSET

RANGE   SINK

KIT.
10-0 x 10-0

HIS

MASTER BATH

SPA TUB   HERS

DRY   WASH   LAUND.

GREAT ROOM
19-0 x 18-0
VAULTED CEILING

CLOSET

HVAC

BATH

54'-10"

DINING
11-8 x 11-4
10' CLG.

FOYER
10' CLG.

CLOSET

PORCH

GARAGE
22-0 x 22-0

NOTE: 8' CLG. HT. TYPICAL
UNLESS NOTED OTHERWISE

BEDROOM
13-4 x 11-6

57'-2"

Design 99491

BL/ML

See Order Pages and Index for Info

Units	Single
Price Code	C
Total Finished	1,846 sq. ft.
First Finished	919 sq. ft.
Second Finished	927 sq. ft.
Garage Unfinished	414 sq. ft.
Dimensions	44'x40'
Foundation	Basement
	Slab
Bedrooms	4
Full Baths	2
Half Baths	1
Primary Roof Pitch	8:12
Secondary Roof Pitch	12:12
Max Ridge Height	26'10"
Roof Framing	Stick
Exterior Walls	2x4

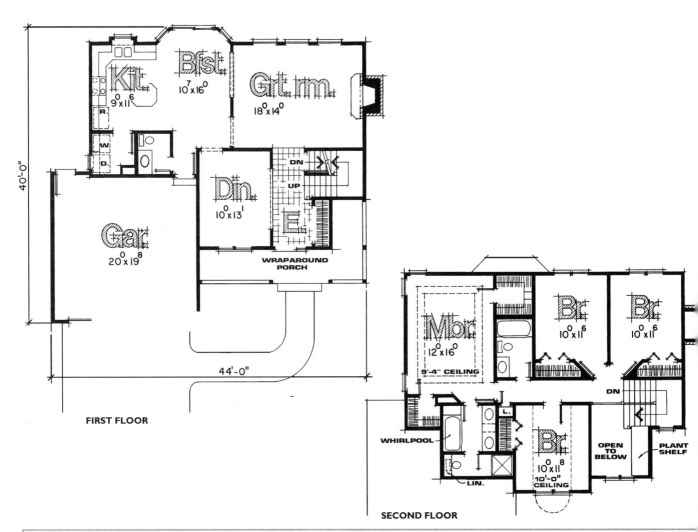

FIRST FLOOR

Kit. 9⁰x11⁰

Bfst. 10⁷x16⁰

Grt. rm. 18⁰x14⁰

Dn. 10⁰x13¹

Gar. 20⁰x19⁸

WRAPAROUND PORCH

40'-0"

44'-0"

SECOND FLOOR

Mbr 12⁰x16⁰
9'-4" CEILING

Br 10⁰x11⁶

Br 10⁰x11⁶

WHIRLPOOL

LIN.

L.

Br 10⁰x11⁸
10'-0" CEILING

DN

OPEN TO BELOW

PLANT SHELF

Design 98408

BL/ML/ZIP   See Order Pages and Index for Info

Units	Single
Price Code	C
Total Finished	1,856 sq. ft.
First Finished	1,856 sq. ft.
Basement Unfinished	1,856 sq. ft.
Garage Unfinished	429 sq. ft.
Dimensions	59'x54'6"
Foundation	Basement
	Crawl space
	Slab
Bedrooms	3
Full Baths	2
First Ceiling	9'
Primary Roof Pitch	8:12
Max Ridge Height	25'6"
Roof Framing	Stick
Exterior Walls	2x4

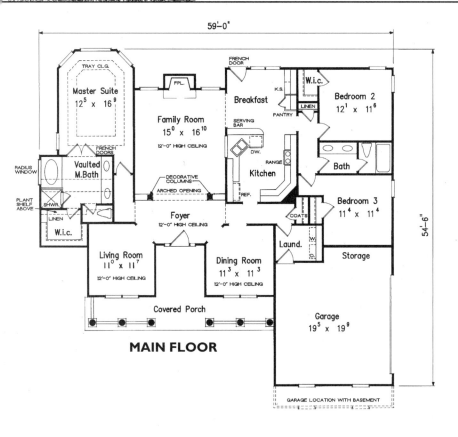

MAIN FLOOR

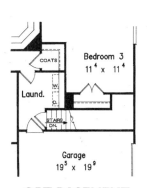

OPT. BASEMENT STAIR LOCATION

Design 99878

BL/ML/ZIP/RRR   See Order Pages and Index for Info

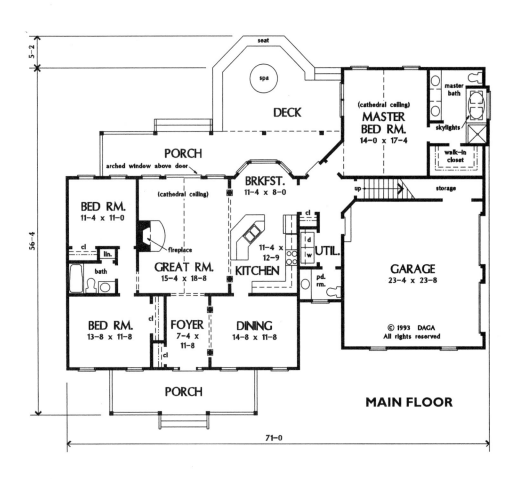

© Donald A. Gardner Architects, Inc.

Units	Single
Price Code	E
Total Finished	1,864 sq. ft.
First Finished	1,864 sq. ft.
Bonus Unfinished	420 sq. ft.
Garage Unfinished	614 sq. ft.
Dimensions	71'x56'4"
Foundation	Crawl space
Bedrooms	3
Full Baths	2
Half Baths	1
First Ceiling	9'
Primary Roof Pitch	8:12
Secondary Roof Pitch	12:12
Max Ridge Height	23'6"
Roof Framing	Stick
Exterior Walls	2x4

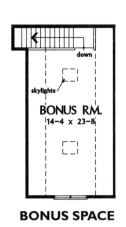

MAIN FLOOR

BONUS SPACE

Design 98966

BL

See Order Pages and Index for Info

Units	Single
Price Code	C
Total Finished	1,864 sq. ft.
Main Finished	1,864 sq. ft.
Garage Unfinished	555 sq. ft.
Deck Unfinished	192 sq. ft.
Porch Unfinished	100 sq. ft.
Dimensions	60'x65'2''
Foundation	Crawl space
	Slab
Bedrooms	3
Full Baths	2
Half Baths	1
Main Ceiling	9'
Primary Roof Pitch	9:12
Max Ridge Height	23'
Roof Framing	Stick
Exterior Walls	2x4

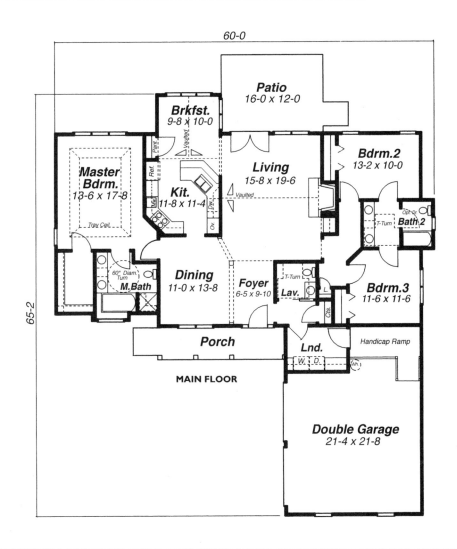

MAIN FLOOR

Design 99807

BL/ML/ZIP/RRR See Order Pages and Index for Info

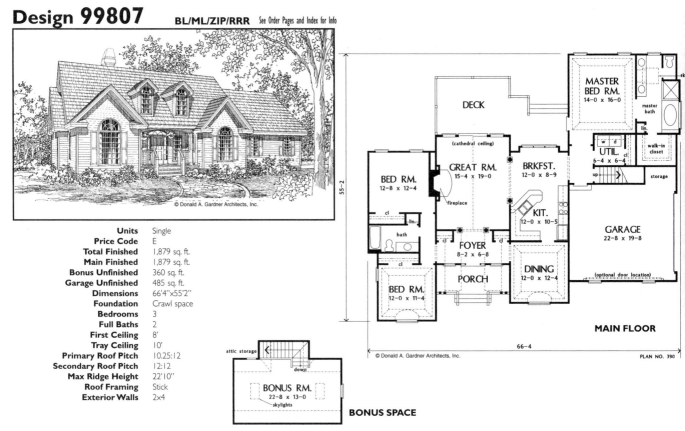

© Donald A. Gardner Architects, Inc.

Units	Single
Price Code	E
Total Finished	1,879 sq. ft.
Main Finished	1,879 sq. ft.
Bonus Unfinished	360 sq. ft.
Garage Unfinished	485 sq. ft.
Dimensions	66'4"x55'2"
Foundation	Crawl space
Bedrooms	3
Full Baths	2
First Ceiling	8'
Tray Ceiling	10'
Primary Roof Pitch	10.25:12
Secondary Roof Pitch	12:12
Max Ridge Height	22'10"
Roof Framing	Stick
Exterior Walls	2x4

MAIN FLOOR

© Donald A. Gardner Architects, Inc.

PLAN NO. 390

BONUS SPACE

Design 92566

BL/ML See Order Pages and Index for Info

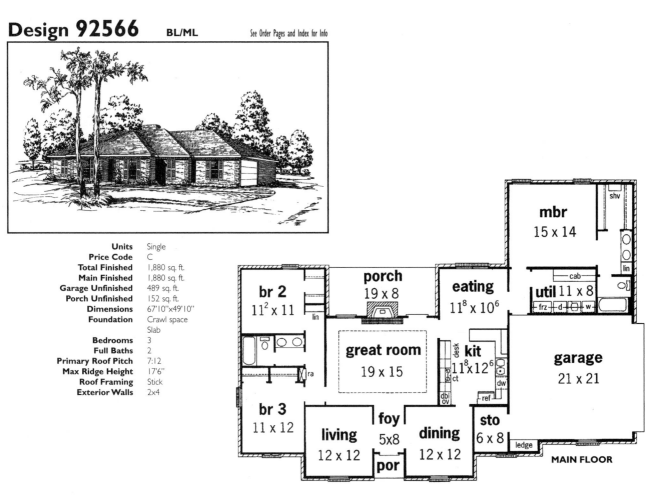

Units	Single
Price Code	C
Total Finished	1,880 sq. ft.
Main Finished	1,880 sq. ft.
Garage Unfinished	489 sq. ft.
Porch Unfinished	152 sq. ft.
Dimensions	67'10"x49'10"
Foundation	Crawl space
	Slab
Bedrooms	3
Full Baths	2
Primary Roof Pitch	7:12
Max Ridge Height	17'6"
Roof Framing	Stick
Exterior Walls	2x4

MAIN FLOOR

Design 98430

BL/ML

See Order Pages and Index for Info

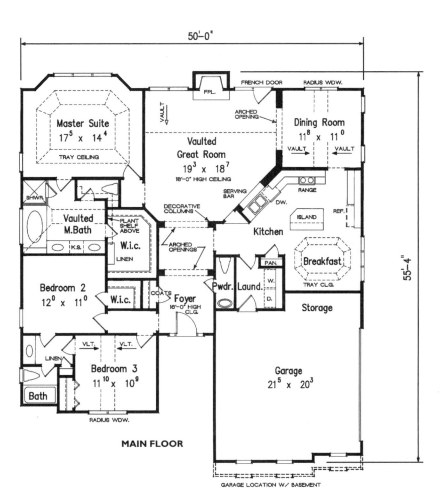

Units	Single
Price Code	C
Total Finished	1,884 sq. ft.
Main Finished	1,884 sq. ft.
Basement Unfinished	1,908 sq. ft.
Garage Unfinished	495 sq. ft.
Dimensions	50'x55'4''
Foundation	Basement
	Crawl space
	Slab
Bedrooms	3
Full Baths	2
Half Baths	1
Main Ceiling	9'
Primary Roof Pitch	10:12
Max Ridge Height	25'
Roof Framing	Stick
Exterior Walls	2x4

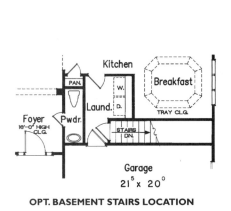

OPT. BASEMENT STAIRS LOCATION

MAIN FLOOR

Design 98575 BL

See Order Pages and Index for Info

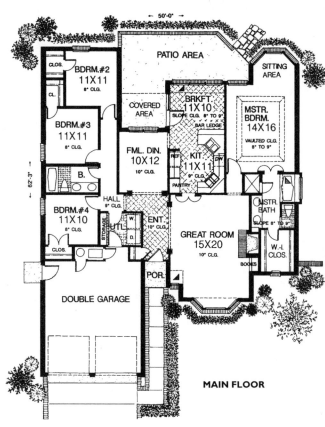

Units	Single
Price Code	C
Total Finished	1,917 sq. ft.
Main Finished	1,917 sq. ft.
Garage Unfinished	440 sq. ft.
Deck Unfinished	275 sq. ft.
Porch Unfinished	32 sq. ft.
Dimensions	50'x62'3''
Foundation	Slab
Bedrooms	4
Full Baths	2
Primary Roof Pitch	10:12
Max Ridge Height	26'2''
Roof Framing	Stick
Exterior Walls	2x4

MAIN FLOOR

Design 93098 BL

See Order Pages and Index for Info

Units	Single
Price Code	C
Total Finished	1,932 sq. ft.
Main Finished	1,932 sq. ft.
Garage Unfinished	552 sq. ft.
Deck Unfinished	225 sq. ft.
Dimensions	65'10''x53'5''
Foundation	Crawlspace / Slab
Bedrooms	3
Full Baths	2
Primary Roof Pitch	8:12
Secondary Roof Pitch	12:12
Max Ridge Height	22'4''
Roof Framing	Stick
Exterior Walls	2x4

MAIN FLOOR

Design 98435

BL/ML

See Order Pages and Index for Info

Units	Single
Price Code	C
Total Finished	1,945 sq. ft.
First Finished	1,945 sq. ft.
Dimensions	56'6''x52'6''
Foundation	Basement
	Crawl space
Bedrooms	4
Full Baths	2
First Ceiling	9'
Primary Roof Pitch	10:12
Max Ridge Height	26'4''
Roof Framing	Stick
Exterior Walls	2x4

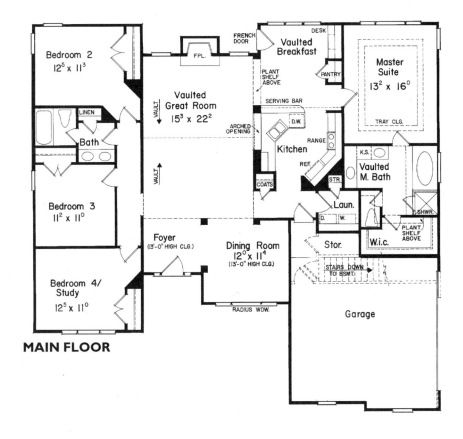

MAIN FLOOR

Bedroom 2
12⁵ x 11³

Vaulted
Great Room
15³ x 22²

FRENCH DOOR

Vaulted Breakfast

DESK

Master Suite
13² x 16⁰

PLANT SHELF ABOVE

PANTRY

SERVING BAR

TRAY CLG.

LINEN

Bath

ARCHED OPENING

D.W.

Kitchen

RANGE

K.S.

Vaulted M. Bath

REF.

STR.

Bedroom 3
11² x 11⁰

COATS

Laun.

SHWR.

PLANT SHELF ABOVE

Foyer
(13'-0" HIGH CLG.)

Dining Room
12⁰ x 11⁴
(13'-0" HIGH CLG.)

Stor.

W.i.c.

Bedroom 4/ Study
12⁵ x 11⁰

RADIUS WDW.

STAIRS DOWN TO BSMT.

Garage

WIDTH 56'-6"
DEPTH 52'-6"

Design 98046 BL/ML

See Order Pages and Index for Info

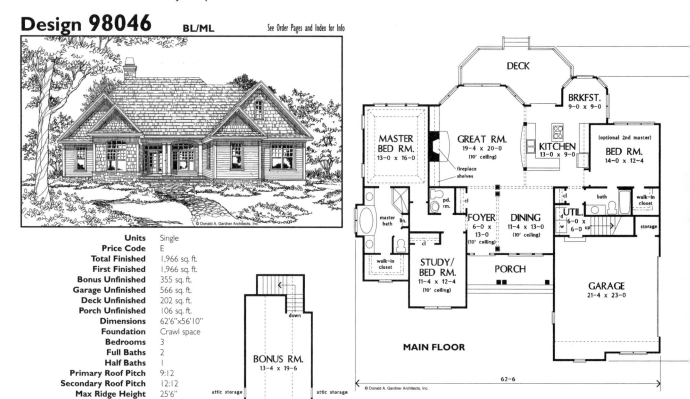

© Donald A. Gardner Architects, Inc.

Units	Single
Price Code	E
Total Finished	1,966 sq. ft.
First Finished	1,966 sq. ft.
Bonus Unfinished	355 sq. ft.
Garage Unfinished	566 sq. ft.
Deck Unfinished	202 sq. ft.
Porch Unfinished	106 sq. ft.
Dimensions	62'6"x56'10"
Foundation	Crawl space
Bedrooms	3
Full Baths	2
Half Baths	1
Primary Roof Pitch	9:12
Secondary Roof Pitch	12:12
Max Ridge Height	25'6"
Roof Framing	Stick
Exterior Walls	2x4

BONUS SPACE

BONUS RM.
13-4 x 19-6

MAIN FLOOR

Design 99803 BL/ML/ZIP/RRR

See Order Pages and Index for Info

© Donald A. Gardner Architects, Inc.

Units	Single
Price Code	E
Total Finished	1,977 sq. ft.
Main Finished	1,977 sq. ft.
Bonus Unfinished	430 sq. ft.
Garage Unfinished	610 sq. ft.
Dimensions	69'8"x59'6"
Foundation	Crawl space
Bedrooms	3
Full Baths	2
Main Ceiling	9'
Vaulted Ceiling	19'
Primary Roof Pitch	12:12
Max Ridge Height	27'
Roof Framing	Stick
Exterior Walls	2x4

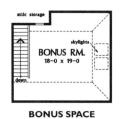

BONUS SPACE

BONUS RM.
18-0 x 19-0

MAIN FLOOR

© Donald A. Gardner Architects, Inc.

Design 97701

BL   See Order Pages and Index for Info

Units	Single
Price Code	C
Total Finished	1,980 sq. ft.
Main Finished	1,980 sq. ft.
Basement Unfinished	1,980 sq. ft.
Garage Unfinished	440 sq. ft.
Dimensions	55'x58'
Foundation	Basement
Bedrooms	3
Full Baths	2
Main Ceiling	8'
Primary Roof Pitch	6:12
Secondary Roof Pitch	8:12
Roof Framing	Truss
Exterior Walls	2x4

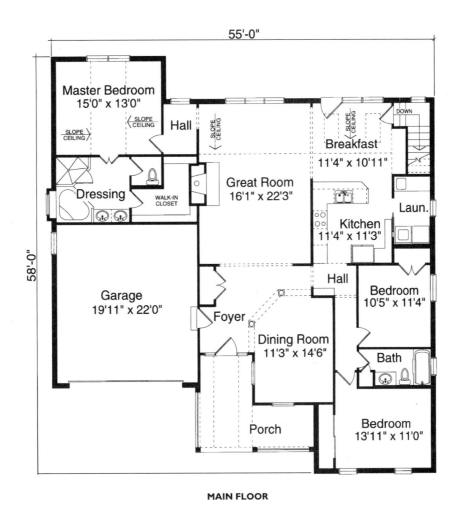

MAIN FLOOR

Weather Shield
Windows & Doors
www.weathershield.com

Weather Shield Windows and Doors offers project planning guides for your remodeling or new home project. **FREE.**
Specify "Remodeling" or "New Home" Planning Guide by calling

1-800-477-6808

Design 82080   BL

See Order Pages and Index for Info

Units	Single
Price Code	C
Total Finished	1,994 sq. ft.
Main Finished	1,994 sq. ft.
Garage Unfinished	417 sq. ft.
Porch Unfinished	118 sq. ft.
Dimensions	65'2"x63'
Foundation	Basement
	Crawlspace
	Slab
Bedrooms	3
Full Baths	2
Primary Roof Pitch	8:12
Roof Framing	Stick
Exterior Walls	2x4

MAIN FLOOR

Design 63049   BL

See Order Pages and Index for Info

Units	Single
Price Code	C
Total Finished	1,997 sq. ft.
Main Finished	1,997 sq. ft.
Bonus Unfinished	310 sq. ft.
Garage Unfinished	502 sq. ft.
Dimensions	64'x57'
Foundation	Basement
Bedrooms	3
Full Baths	2
Main Ceiling	10'
Primary Roof Pitch	7:12
Secondary Roof Pitch	12:12
Max Ridge Height	23'
Roof Framing	Truss
Exterior Walls	2x4

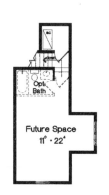

BONUS SPACE

MAIN FLOOR

Design 97151

BL

See Order Pages and Index for Info

Units	Single
Price Code	D
Total Finished	2,007 sq. ft.
First Finished	2,007 sq. ft.
Deck Unfinished	144 sq. ft.
Dimensions	67'x53'
Foundation	Basement
Bedrooms	3
Full Baths	2
Primary Roof Pitch	8:12
Secondary Roof Pitch	8:12
Max Ridge Height	24'
Roof Framing	Truss
Exterior Walls	2x6

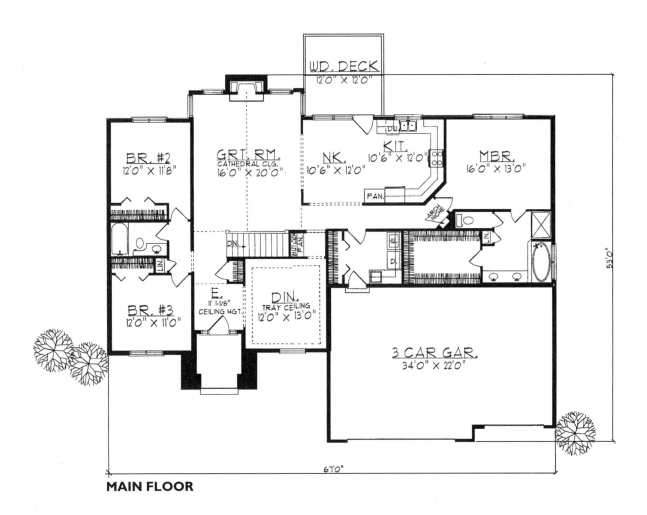

MAIN FLOOR

Design 98964 BL

See Order Pages and Index for Info

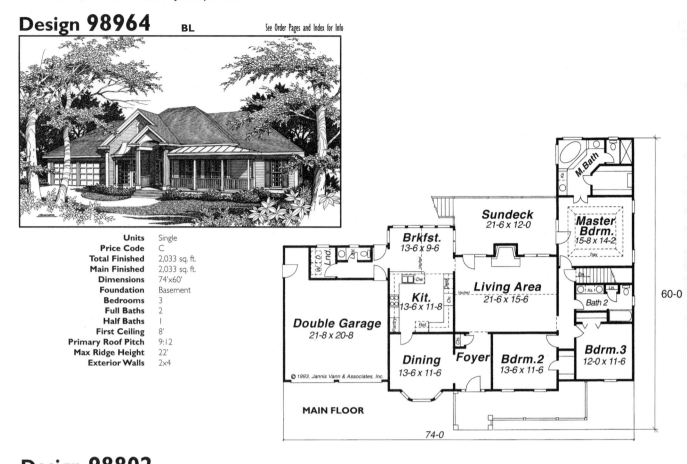

Units	Single
Price Code	C
Total Finished	2,033 sq. ft.
Main Finished	2,033 sq. ft.
Dimensions	74'x60'
Foundation	Basement
Bedrooms	3
Full Baths	2
Half Baths	1
First Ceiling	8'
Primary Roof Pitch	9:12
Max Ridge Height	22'
Exterior Walls	2x4

© 1993, Jannis Vann & Associates, Inc.

Design 98802 BL

See Order Pages and Index for Info

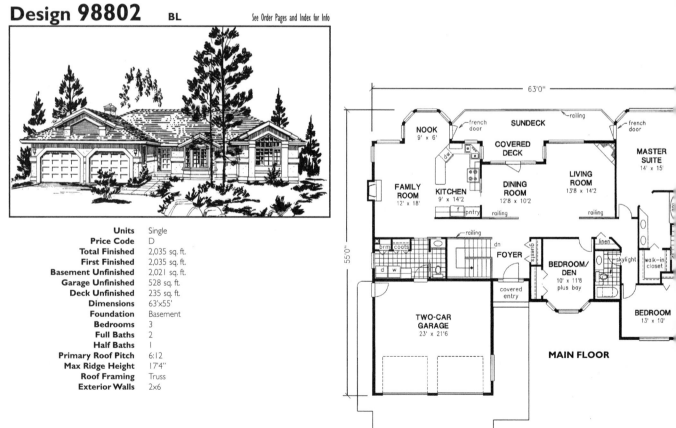

Units	Single
Price Code	D
Total Finished	2,035 sq. ft.
First Finished	2,035 sq. ft.
Basement Unfinished	2,021 sq. ft.
Garage Unfinished	528 sq. ft.
Deck Unfinished	235 sq. ft.
Dimensions	63'x55'
Foundation	Basement
Bedrooms	3
Full Baths	2
Half Baths	1
Primary Roof Pitch	6:12
Max Ridge Height	17'4"
Roof Framing	Truss
Exterior Walls	2x6

Design 98019

BL/ML/RRR   See Order Pages and Index for Info

Units	Single
Price Code	F
Total Finished	2,042 sq. ft.
First Finished	2,042 sq. ft.
Bonus Unfinished	475 sq. ft.
Garage Unfinished	660 sq. ft.
Porch Unfinished	514 sq. ft.
Dimensions	75'11"x56'7"
Foundation	Crawl space
Bedrooms	3
Full Baths	2
Half Baths	1
Primary Roof Pitch	9:12
Secondary Roof Pitch	12:12
Max Ridge Height	25'7"
Roof Framing	Stick
Exterior Walls	2x4

B. NATHAN

© Donald A. Gardner Architects, Inc.

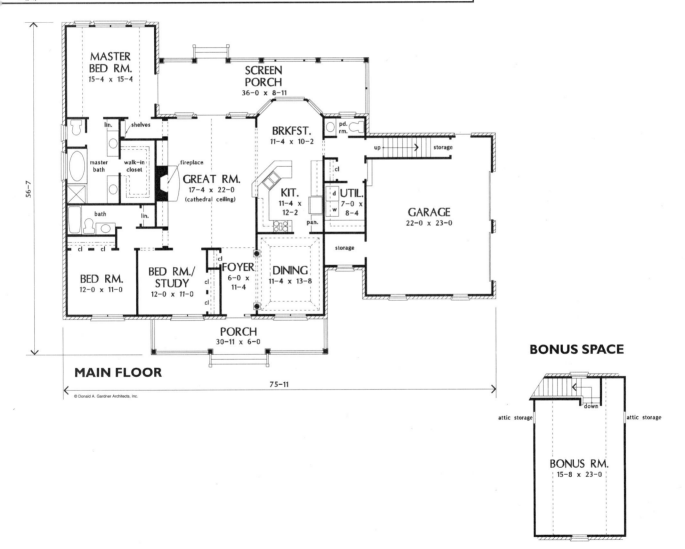

MASTER BED RM.
15-4 x 15-4

SCREEN PORCH
36-0 x 8-11

lin.   shelves

master bath   walk-in closet   fireplace

GREAT RM.
17-4 x 22-0
(cathedral ceiling)

BRKFST.
11-4 x 10-2

pd. rm.

up   storage

KIT.
11-4 x 12-2

cl

UTIL.
7-0 x 8-4

d w

pan.

GARAGE
22-0 x 23-0

bath   lin.

storage

56-7

cl   cl

BED RM.
12-0 x 11-0

BED RM./STUDY
12-0 x 11-0

cl   cl

FOYER
6-0 x 11-4

DINING
11-4 x 13-8

PORCH
30-11 x 6-0

MAIN FLOOR

75-11

© Donald A. Gardner Architects, Inc.

BONUS SPACE

attic storage   down   attic storage

BONUS RM.
15-8 x 23-0

Design 98427 BL/ML

See Order Pages and Index for Info

Units	Single
Price Code	D
Total Finished	2,051 sq. ft.
Main Finished	2,051 sq. ft.
Basement Unfinished	2,051 sq. ft.
Garage Unfinished	441 sq. ft.
Dimensions	56'x60'6''
Foundation	Basement
	Crawl space
	Slab
Bedrooms	3
Full Baths	2
Main Ceiling	9'
Primary Roof Pitch	10:12
Max Ridge Height	27'5''
Roof Framing	Stick
Exterior Walls	2x4

MAIN FLOOR

Design 97622 BL

See Order Pages and Index for Info

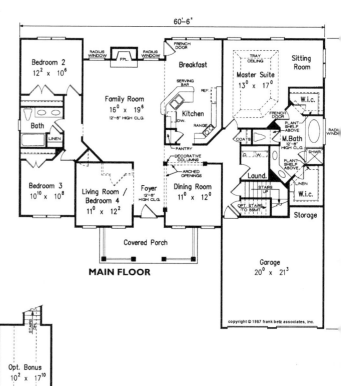

Units	Single
Price Code	D
Total Finished	2,056 sq. ft.
Main Finished	2,056 sq. ft.
Bonus Unfinished	208 sq. ft.
Basement Unfinished	2,056 sq. ft.
Garage Unfinished	454 sq. ft.
Dimensions	60'6''x56'
Foundation	Basement
	Crawl space
Bedrooms	3
Full Baths	2
Main Ceiling	9'
Primary Roof Pitch	8:12
Max Ridge Height	22'8''
Roof Framing	Stick
Exterior Walls	2x4

MAIN FLOOR

OPTIONAL BONUS SPACE

copyright © 1987 frank betz associates, inc.

Design 98048

BL/ML

See Order Pages and Index for Info

Units	Single
Price Code	F
Total Finished	2,082 sq. ft.
Main Finished	2,082 sq. ft.
Bonus Unfinished	466 sq. ft.
Garage Unfinished	606 sq. ft.
Dimensions	47'10"x86'4"
Foundation	Crawl space
Bedrooms	3
Full Baths	2
Primary Roof Pitch	10.75:12
Secondary Roof Pitch	12:12
Max Ridge Height	26'4"
Roof Framing	Stick
Exterior Walls	2x4

© Donald A. Gardner Architects, Inc.

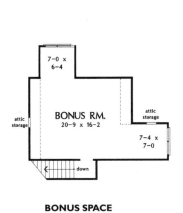

BONUS SPACE

Bonus space labels:
- 7-0 x 6-4
- BONUS RM. 20-9 x 16-2
- attic storage
- 7-4 x 7-0
- down

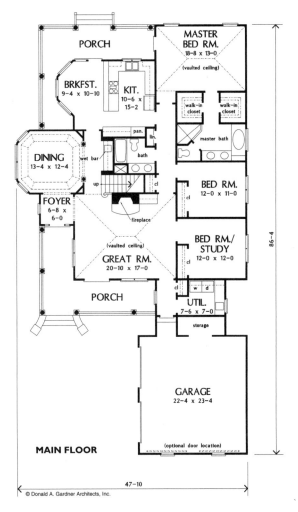

Main floor labels:
- PORCH
- MASTER BED RM. 18-8 x 13-0 (vaulted ceiling)
- BRKFST. 9-4 x 10-10
- KIT. 10-6 x 15-2
- walk-in closet
- walk-in closet
- master bath
- DINING 13-4 x 12-4
- wet bar
- pan.
- lin.
- bath
- BED RM. 12-0 x 11-0
- FOYER 6-8 x 6-0
- up
- cl
- fireplace
- BED RM./STUDY 12-0 x 12-0
- (vaulted ceiling)
- GREAT RM. 20-10 x 17-0
- PORCH
- UTIL. 7-6 x 7-0
- w d
- storage
- GARAGE 22-4 x 23-4
- (optional door location)
- 86-4
- 47-10

MAIN FLOOR

© Donald A. Gardner Architects, Inc.

Design 98967 BL

See Order Pages and Index for Info

Units	Single
Price Code	E
Total Finished	2,089 sq. ft.
Main Finished	2,089 sq. ft.
Garage Unfinished	616 sq. ft.
Deck Unfinished	192 sq. ft.
Porch Unfinished	92 sq. ft.
Dimensions	66'x66'
Foundation	Crawl space
	Slab
Bedrooms	4
Full Baths	2
Half Baths	1
First Ceiling	9'
Primary Roof Pitch	9:12
Max Ridge Height	23'
Roof Framing	Stick
Exterior Walls	2x4

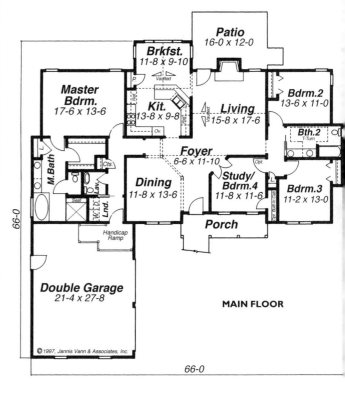

MAIN FLOOR

© 1997, Jannis Vann & Associates, Inc.

Design 91537 BL/ML

See Order Pages and Index for Info

Units	Single
Price Code	D
Total Finished	2,107 sq. ft.
First Finished	1,032 sq. ft.
Second Finished	1,075 sq. ft.
Dimensions	49'x40'
Foundation	Crawl space
Bedrooms	4
Full Baths	2
Half Baths	1
Primary Roof Pitch	7:12
Secondary Roof Pitch	5:12
Max Ridge Height	27'
Roof Framing	Truss
Exterior Walls	2x6

FIRST FLOOR

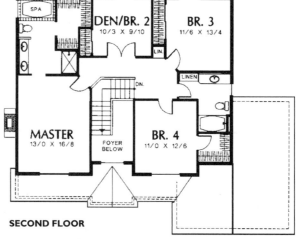

SECOND FLOOR

Design 97100

BL

See Order Pages and Index for Info

Units	Single
Price Code	D
Total Finished	2,120 sq. ft.
First Finished	995 sq. ft.
Second Finished	1,125 sq. ft.
Basement Unfinished	995 sq. ft.
Dimensions	56'4"x35'8"
Foundation	Basement
Bedrooms	4
Full Baths	2
Half Baths	1
Primary Roof Pitch	8:12
Secondary Roof Pitch	10:12
Max Ridge Height	28'4"
Roof Framing	Truss
Exterior Walls	2x6

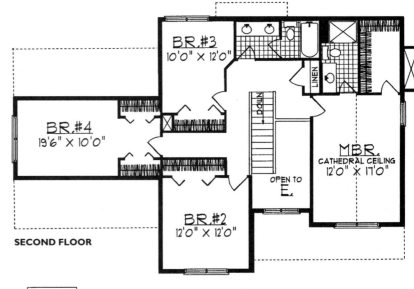

SECOND FLOOR

BR.#3 10'0" X 12'0"

LINEN

BR.#4 19'6" X 10'0"

DOWN

OPEN TO E.

MBR. CATHEDRAL CEILING 12'0" X 17'0"

BR.#2 12'0" X 12'0"

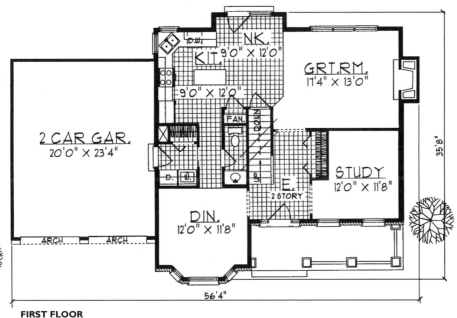

FIRST FLOOR

2 CAR GAR. 20'0" X 23'4"

KIT. 9'0" X 12'0"

NK. 9'0" X 12'0"

GRT.RM. 17'4" X 13'0"

PAN.

DOWN

STUDY 12'0" X 11'8"

E. 2 STORY

DIN. 12'0" X 11'8"

ARCH   ARCH

56'4"

35'8"

Design 97219 BL

See Order Pages and Index for Info

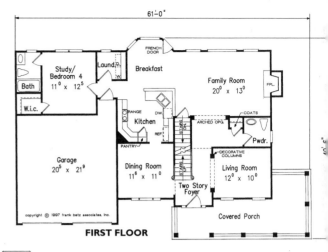

FIRST FLOOR

Units	Single
Price Code	D
Total Finished	2,128 sq. ft.
First Finished	1,257 sq. ft.
Second Finished	871 sq. ft.
Bonus Unfinished	444 sq. ft.
Basement Unfinished	1,275 sq. ft.
Garage Unfinished	462 sq. ft.
Dimensions	61'x40'6"
Foundation	Basement
	Crawlspace
Bedrooms	4
Full Baths	3
Half Baths	1
Primary Roof Pitch	10:12
Max Ridge Height	32'
Roof Framing	Stick
Exterior Walls	2x4

OPTIONAL BONUS SPACE

SECOND FLOOR

Design 97294 BL

See Order Pages and Index for Info

MAIN FLOOR

Units	Single
Price Code	D
Total Finished	2,158 sq. ft.
Main Finished	2,158 sq. ft.
Basement Unfinished	2,190 sq. ft.
Garage Unfinished	485 sq. ft.
Dimensions	63'x63'6"
Foundation	Basement
	Crawlspace
Bedrooms	4
Full Baths	3
Primary Roof Pitch	10:12
Max Ridge Height	25'
Roof Framing	Stick
Exterior Walls	2x4

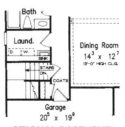

OTIONAL BASEMENT STAIR LOCATION

Design 99875

BL/ML/RRR   See Order Pages and Index for Info

Units	Single
Price Code	F
Total Finished	2,161 sq. ft.
First Finished	1,526 sq. ft.
Second Finished	635 sq. ft.
Bonus Unfinished	355 sq. ft.
Garage Unfinished	610 sq. ft.
Dimensions	76'4"x74'2"
Foundation	Crawl space
Bedrooms	3
Full Baths	2
Half Baths	1
First Ceiling	8'
Second Ceiling	8'
Primary Roof Pitch	12:12
Secondary Roof Pitch	3.5:12
Max Ridge Height	28'6"
Roof Framing	Stick
Exterior Walls	2x4

© Donald A. Gardner Architects, Inc.

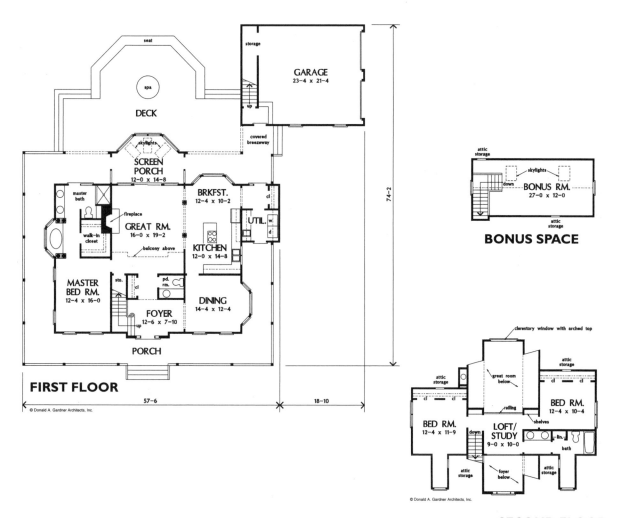

FIRST FLOOR

© Donald A. Gardner Architects, Inc.

BONUS SPACE

SECOND FLOOR

© Donald A. Gardner Architects, Inc.

Design 91343   BL/ML

See Order Pages and Index for Info

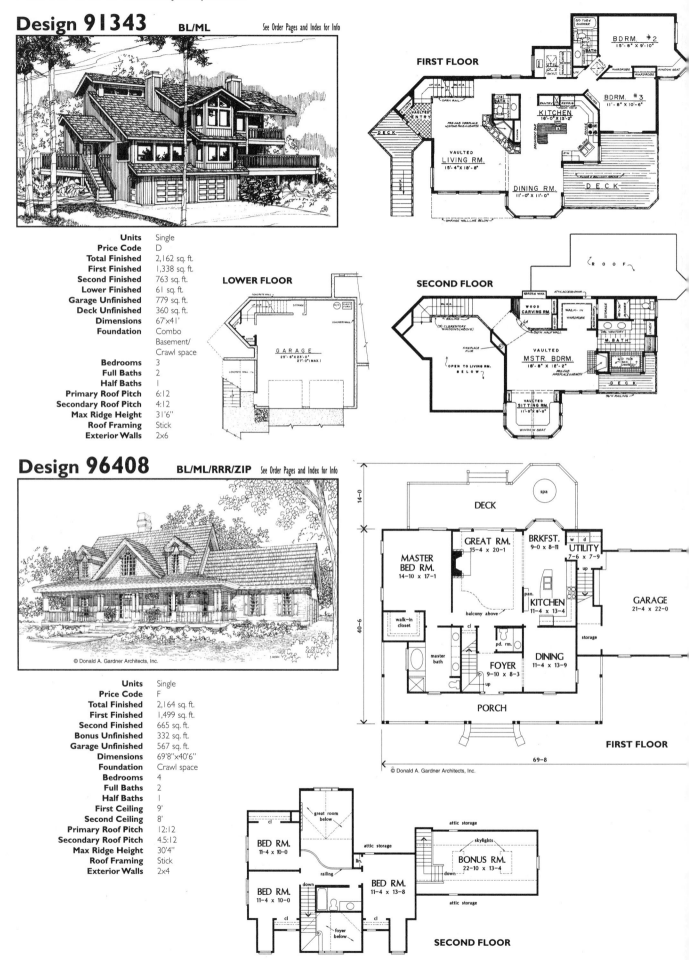

FIRST FLOOR

BDRM. #2
15'-8" X 9'-10"

BDRM. #3
11'-8" X 10'-6"

KITCHEN
16'-0" X 13'-2"

VAULTED
LIVING RM.
15'-4" X 18'-8"

DINING RM.
11'-0" X 11'-0"

DECK

LOWER FLOOR

GARAGE
25'-6" X 23'-0"
27'-0" (MAX.)

SECOND FLOOR

ROOF

WOOD CARVING RM.

WALK-IN WARDROBE

VAULTED
MSTR. BDRM.
18'-8" X 12'-2"

VAULTED
SITTING RM.
11'-0" X 9'-0"

DECK

Units	Single
Price Code	D
Total Finished	2,162 sq. ft.
First Finished	1,338 sq. ft.
Second Finished	763 sq. ft.
Lower Finished	61 sq. ft.
Garage Unfinished	779 sq. ft.
Deck Unfinished	360 sq. ft.
Dimensions	67'x41'
Foundation	Combo Basement/ Crawl space
Bedrooms	3
Full Baths	2
Half Baths	1
Primary Roof Pitch	6:12
Secondary Roof Pitch	4:12
Max Ridge Height	31'6"
Roof Framing	Stick
Exterior Walls	2x6

Design 96408   BL/ML/RRR/ZIP

See Order Pages and Index for Info

© Donald A. Gardner Architects, Inc.

Units	Single
Price Code	F
Total Finished	2,164 sq. ft.
First Finished	1,499 sq. ft.
Second Finished	665 sq. ft.
Bonus Unfinished	332 sq. ft.
Garage Unfinished	567 sq. ft.
Dimensions	69'8"x40'6"
Foundation	Crawl space
Bedrooms	4
Full Baths	2
Half Baths	1
First Ceiling	9'
Second Ceiling	8'
Primary Roof Pitch	12:12
Secondary Roof Pitch	4.5:12
Max Ridge Height	30'4"
Roof Framing	Stick
Exterior Walls	2x4

DECK

spa

GREAT RM.
15-4 x 20-1

BRKFST.
9-0 x 8-11

UTILITY
7-6 x 7-9

MASTER
BED RM.
14-10 x 17-1

KITCHEN
11-4 x 13-4

GARAGE
21-4 x 22-0

walk-in closet

master bath

FOYER
9-10 x 8-3

DINING
11-4 x 13-9

PORCH

FIRST FLOOR

69-8

© Donald A. Gardner Architects, Inc.

BED RM.
11-4 x 10-0

great room below

attic storage

skylights

BONUS RM.
22-10 x 13-4

BED RM.
11-4 x 10-0

BED RM.
11-4 x 13-8

foyer below

attic storage

SECOND FLOOR

Design 96495

BL/ML/RRR   See Order Pages and Index for Info

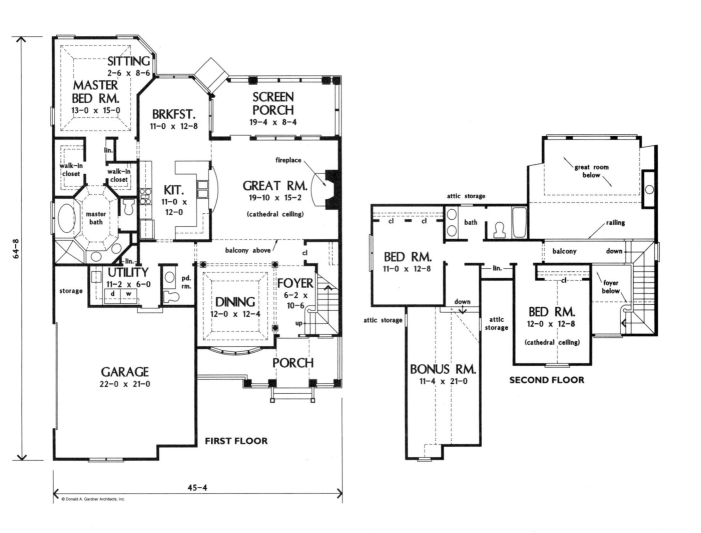

© Donald A. Gardner Architects, Inc.

S. NATHAN

Units	Single
Price Code	F
Total Finished	2,168 sq. ft.
First Finished	1,593 sq. ft.
Second Finished	575 sq. ft.
Bonus Unfinished	303 sq. ft.
Garage Unfinished	550 sq. ft.
Porch Unfinished	330 sq. ft.
Dimensions	45'4"x64'8"
Foundation	Crawl space
Bedrooms	3
Full Baths	2
Half Baths	1
First Ceiling	9'
Second Ceiling	8'
Primary Roof Pitch	10:12
Secondary Roof Pitch	12:12
Max Ridge Height	27'3"
Roof Framing	Stick
Exterior Walls	2x4

FIRST FLOOR

SITTING 2-6 x 8-6

MASTER BED RM. 13-0 x 15-0

BRKFST. 11-0 x 12-8

SCREEN PORCH 19-4 x 8-4

fireplace

walk-in closet

walk-in closet

lin.

KIT. 11-0 x 12-0

GREAT RM. 19-10 x 15-2 (cathedral ceiling)

master bath

balcony above

cl

storage

UTILITY 11-2 x 6-0

d   w

pd. rm.

DINING 12-0 x 12-4

FOYER 6-2 x 10-6

up

GARAGE 22-0 x 21-0

PORCH

64-8

45-4

© Donald A. Gardner Architects, Inc.

SECOND FLOOR

attic storage

great room below

cl   cl

bath

railing

BED RM. 11-0 x 12-8

balcony

down

lin.

cl

down

foyer below

attic storage

down

attic storage

BONUS RM. 11-4 x 21-0

BED RM. 12-0 x 12-8 (cathedral ceiling)

Design 90871 **BL** See Order Pages and Index for Info

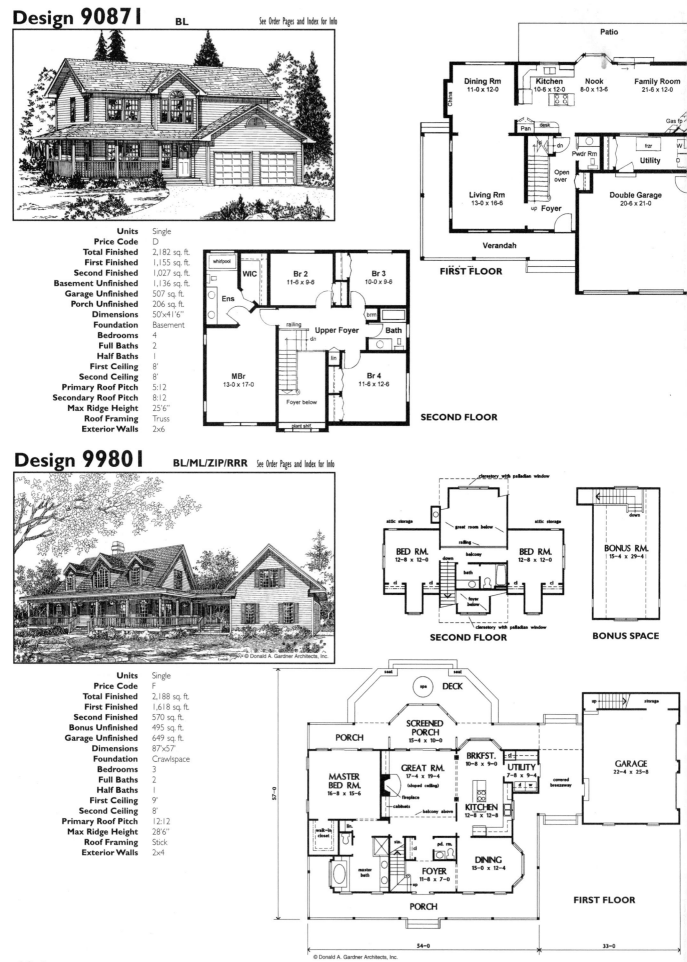

Units	Single
Price Code	D
Total Finished	2,182 sq. ft.
First Finished	1,155 sq. ft.
Second Finished	1,027 sq. ft.
Basement Unfinished	1,136 sq. ft.
Garage Unfinished	507 sq. ft.
Porch Unfinished	206 sq. ft.
Dimensions	50'x41'6"
Foundation	Basement
Bedrooms	4
Full Baths	2
Half Baths	1
First Ceiling	8'
Second Ceiling	8'
Primary Roof Pitch	5:12
Secondary Roof Pitch	8:12
Max Ridge Height	25'6"
Roof Framing	Truss
Exterior Walls	2x6

FIRST FLOOR

SECOND FLOOR

Design 99801 **BL/ML/ZIP/RRR** See Order Pages and Index for Info

© Donald A. Gardner Architects, Inc.

Units	Single
Price Code	F
Total Finished	2,188 sq. ft.
First Finished	1,618 sq. ft.
Second Finished	570 sq. ft.
Bonus Unfinished	495 sq. ft.
Garage Unfinished	649 sq. ft.
Dimensions	87'x57'
Foundation	Crawlspace
Bedrooms	3
Full Baths	2
Half Baths	1
First Ceiling	9'
Second Ceiling	8'
Primary Roof Pitch	12:12
Max Ridge Height	28'6"
Roof Framing	Stick
Exterior Walls	2x4

SECOND FLOOR

BONUS SPACE

FIRST FLOOR

© Donald A. Gardner Architects, Inc.

Design 99838

BL/ML/ZIP/RRR See Order Pages and Index for Info

Units	Single
Price Code	F
Total Finished	2,192 sq. ft.
First Finished	2,192 sq. ft.
Bonus Unfinished	390 sq. ft.
Garage Unfinished	582 sq. ft.
Dimensions	74'10"×55'8"
Foundation	Crawl space
Bedrooms	4
Full Baths	2
Half Baths	1
First Ceiling	9'
Primary Roof Pitch	9.5:12
Secondary Roof Pitch	12:12
Max Ridge Height	26'
Roof Framing	Stick
Exterior Walls	2x4

© Donald A. Gardner Architects, Inc.

S. NATHAN

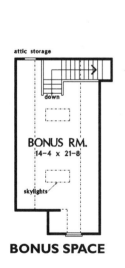

BONUS SPACE

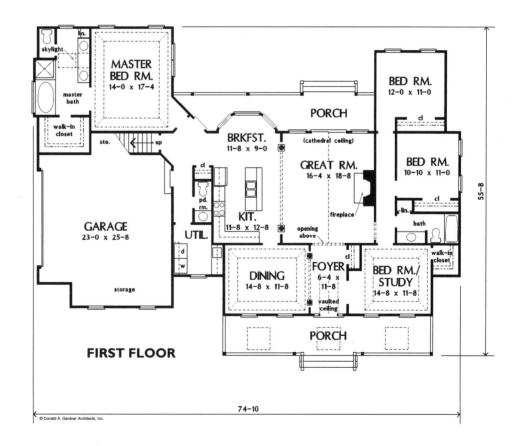

FIRST FLOOR

Design **97228** BL

See Order Pages and Index for Info

Units	Single
Price Code	D
Total Finished	2,201 sq. ft.
Main Finished	2,201 sq. ft.
Basement Unfinished	2,201 sq. ft.
Garage Unfinished	452 sq. ft.
Dimensions	59'6"x62'
Foundation	Basement
	Crawl space
Bedrooms	3
Full Baths	2
Half Baths	1
Primary Roof Pitch	8:12
Max Ridge Height	25'
Roof Framing	Stick
Exterior Walls	2x4

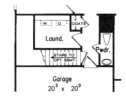

OPTIONAL BASEMENT STAIR LOCATION

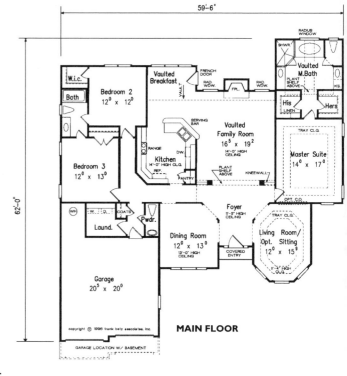

MAIN FLOOR

Design **93710** BL

See Order Pages and Index for Info

Units	Single
Price Code	D
Total Finished	2,201 sq. ft.
Main Finished	2,201 sq. ft.
Garage Unfinished	532 sq. ft.
Porch Unfinished	46 sq. ft.
Dimensions	69'2"x57'2"
Foundation	Crawl space
	Slab
Bedrooms	4
Full Baths	2
Primary Roof Pitch	9:12
Max Ridge Height	22'4"
Roof Framing	Stick
Exterior Walls	2x4

MAIN FLOOR

Design 98120 BL/ML

See Order Pages and Index for Info

© Donald A. Gardner Architects, Inc.

Units	Single
Price Code	F
Total Finished	2,205 sq. ft.
First Finished	1,475 sq. ft.
Second Finished	730 sq. ft.
Bonus Unfinished	430 sq. ft.
Dimensions	71'4"x76'3"
Foundation	Crawlspace
Bedrooms	3
Full Baths	3
Half Baths	1
First Ceiling	9'
Second Ceiling	9'
Primary Roof Pitch	8:12
Secondary Roof Pitch	16:12
Max Ridge Height	28'5"
Exterior Walls	2x4

SECOND FLOOR

FIRST FLOOR

© Donald A. Gardner Architects, Inc.

BONUS SPACE ABOVE GARAGE

Design 93156 BL

See Order Pages and Index for Info

Units	Single
Price Code	D
Total Finished	2,214 sq. ft.
First Finished	1,150 sq. ft.
Second Finished	1,064 sq. ft.
Basement Unfinished	1,150 sq. ft.
Dimensions	66'x44'
Foundation	Basement
Bedrooms	4
Full Baths	2
Half Baths	1
Primary Roof Pitch	10:12
Secondary Roof Pitch	7:12
Max Ridge Height	27'
Roof Framing	Stick
Exterior Walls	2x6

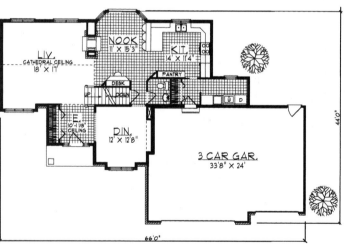

FIRST FLOOR

SECOND FLOOR

Design 97858 BL

See Order Pages and Index for Info

Units	Single
Price Code	D
Total Finished	2,214 sq. ft.
Main Finished	2,214 sq. ft.
Garage Unfinished	599 sq. ft.
Deck Unfinished	136 sq. ft.
Porch Unfinished	42 sq. ft.
Dimensions	55'x77'11"
Foundation	Slab
Bedrooms	3
Full Baths	2
Half Baths	1
First Ceiling	9'-10'
Primary Roof Pitch	10:12
Max Ridge Height	27'
Roof Framing	Stick
Exterior Walls	2x4

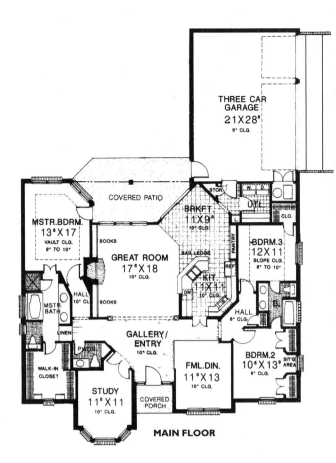

MAIN FLOOR

Design 98819 BL

See Order Pages and Index for Info

Units	Single
Price Code	D
Total Finished	2,216 sq. ft.
First Finished	1,090 sq. ft.
Second Finished	1,126 sq. ft.
Basement Unfinished	1,067 sq. ft.
Garage Unfinished	418 sq. ft.
Dimensions	37'x52'4"
Foundation	Basement
Bedrooms	4
Full Baths	2
Half Baths	1
First Ceiling	8'
Second Ceiling	8'
Primary Roof Pitch	8:12
Max Ridge Height	27'2"
Roof Framing	Truss
Exterior Walls	2x6

SECOND FLOOR

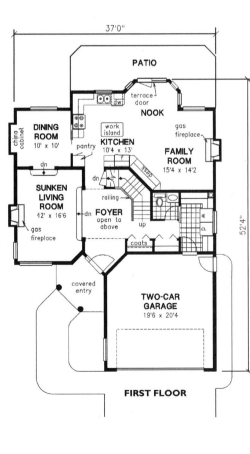

FIRST FLOOR

Design 96423

BL/ML/RRR   See Order Pages and Index for Info

Units	Single
Price Code	F
Total Finished	2,218 sq. ft.
First Finished	1,651 sq. ft.
Second Finished	567 sq. ft.
Dimensions	55'x53'10''
Foundation	Crawl space
Bedrooms	3
Full Baths	2
Half Baths	1
Primary Roof Pitch	12:12
Secondary Roof Pitch	3.5:12
Max Ridge Height	25'
Roof Framing	Stick
Exterior Walls	2x4

Photography by Jon Riley, Riley & Riley Photography

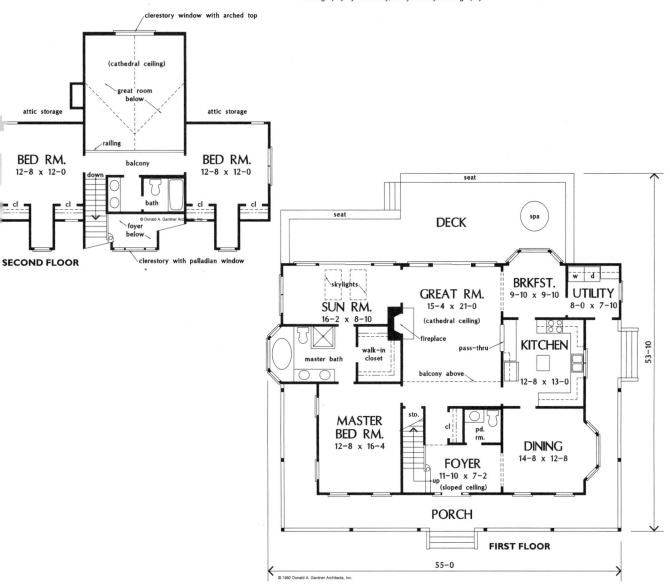

SECOND FLOOR

FIRST FLOOR

Design 34701

BL/ML/RRR/ZIP See Order Pages and Index for Info

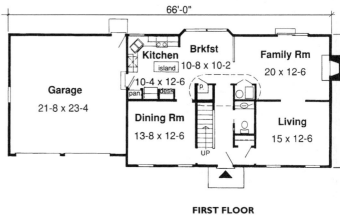

FIRST FLOOR

Units	Single
Price Code	D
Total Finished	2,224 sq. ft.
First Finished	1,090 sq. ft.
Second Finished	1,134 sq. ft.
Basement Unfinished	1,090 sq. ft.
Garage Unfinished	576 sq. ft.
Dimensions	66'x27'
Foundation	Basement
	Crawl space
	Slab
Bedrooms	4
Full Baths	2
Half Baths	1
Primary Roof Pitch	8:12
Max Ridge Height	27'
Roof Framing	Stick
Exterior Walls	2x4,2x6

BASEMENT OPTION

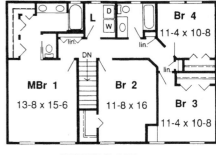

SECOND FLOOR

Design 91591

BL See Order Pages and Index for Info

Units	Single
Price Code	D
Total Finished	2,225 sq. ft.
Main Finished	2,225 sq. ft.
Garage Unfinished	420 sq. ft.
Dimensions	45'x73'
Foundation	Crawl space
Bedrooms	3
Full Baths	2
Primary Roof Pitch	10:12
Max Ridge Height	28'
Roof Framing	Stick
Exterior Walls	2x6

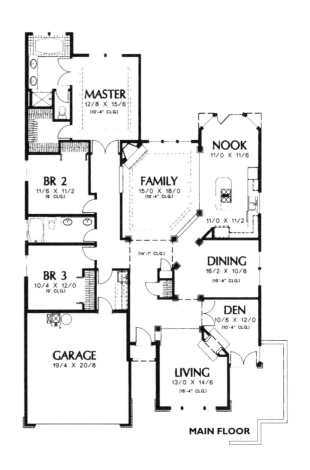

MAIN FLOOR

Design 93302

BL

See Order Pages and Index for Info

Units	Single
Price Code	D
Total Finished	2,226 sq. ft.
First Finished	1,689 sq. ft.
Second Finished	537 sq. ft.
Basement Unfinished	1,689 sq. ft.
Garage Unfinished	524 sq. ft.
Dimensions	68'x64'6''
Foundation	Basement
Bedrooms	3
Full Baths	2
Half Baths	1
Primary Roof Pitch	8:12
Secondary Roof Pitch	12:12
Max Ridge Height	28'
Roof Framing	Stick
Exterior Walls	2x6

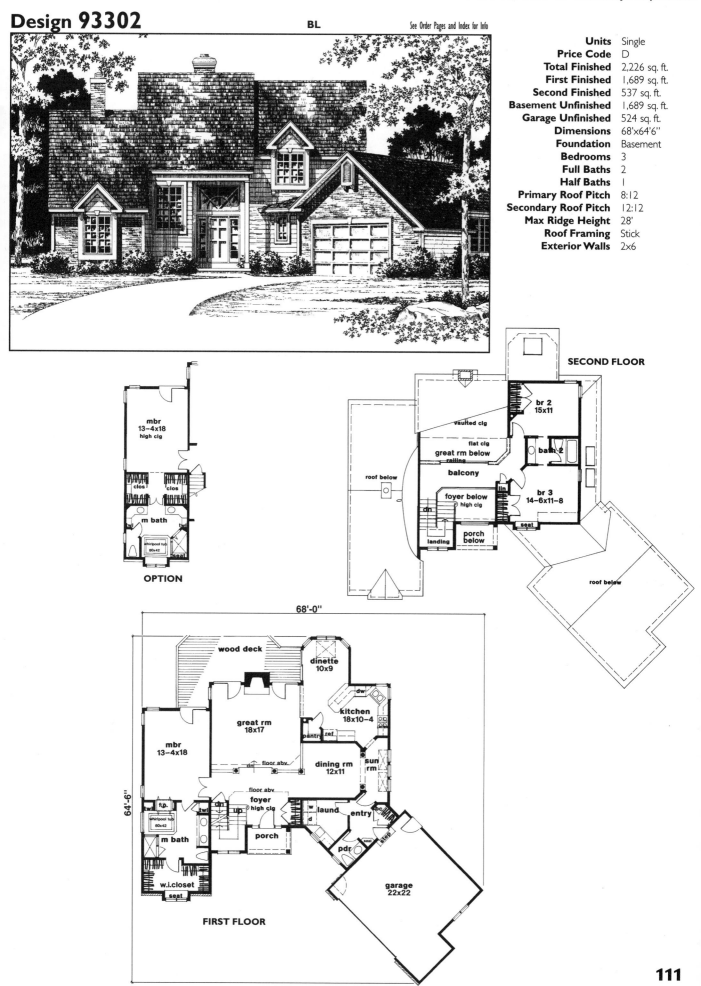

SECOND FLOOR

mbr
13-4x18
high clg

clos clos

m bath

whirlpool tub
60x42

seat

OPTION

vaulted clg

br 2
15x11

flat clg

great rm below
railing

bath 2

balcony

roof below

foyer below
high clg

br 3
14-6x11-8

dn

landing

porch
below

seat

lin

roof below

68'-0"

wood deck

dinette
10x9

dw

kitchen
18x10-4

great rm
18x17

pantry ref

dining rm
12x11

sun
rm

mbr
13-4x18

floor abv.
dn

floor abv

foyer
high clg

w laund
d

entry

bc

whirlpool tub
60x42

up

seat step

m bath

porch

pdr

64'-6"

w.i.closet

seat

garage
22x22

FIRST FLOOR

111

Design 93151 BL

See Order Pages and Index for Info

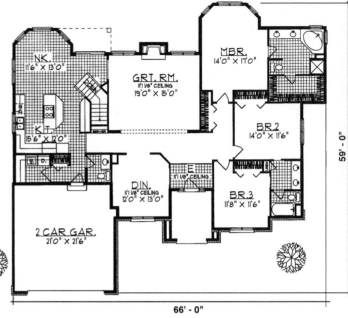

Units	Single
Price Code	D
Total Finished	2,234 sq. ft.
Main Finished	2,234 sq. ft.
Basement Unfinished	2,234 sq. ft.
Dimensions	66'x59'
Foundation	Basement
Bedrooms	3
Full Baths	2
Half Baths	1
Primary Roof Pitch	9:12
Secondary Roof Pitch	7:12
Max Ridge Height	22'6'
Roof Framing	Stick
Exterior Walls	2x6

Design 98031 BL/RRR

See Order Pages and Index for Info

© Donald A. Gardner Architects, Inc.

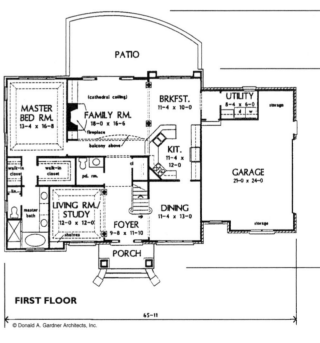

FIRST FLOOR

© Donald A. Gardner Architects, Inc.

Units	Single
Price Code	F
Total Finished	2,235 sq. ft.
First Finished	1,701 sq. ft.
Second Finished	534 sq. ft.
Bonus Unfinished	274 sq. ft.
Garage Unfinished	574 sq. ft.
Porch Unfinished	68 sq. ft.
Dimensions	65'11''x43'5''
Foundation	Crawlspace
Bedrooms	3
Full Baths	2
Half Baths	1
Primary Roof Pitch	10:12
Secondary Roof Pitch	12:12
Max Ridge Height	28'8''
Roof Framing	Stick
Exterior Walls	2x4

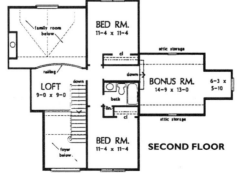

SECOND FLOOR

Design 93445

BL

See Order Pages and Index for Info

Units	Single
Price Code	D
Total Finished	2,235 sq. ft.
First Finished	1,580 sq. ft.
Second Finished	655 sq. ft.
Basement Unfinished	1,580 sq. ft.
Garage Unfinished	436 sq. ft.
Deck Unfinished	63 sq. ft.
Porch Unfinished	57 sq. ft.
Dimensions	59'x38'
Foundation	Basement
Bedrooms	4
Full Baths	2
Half Baths	1
Primary Roof Pitch	12:12
Secondary Roof Pitch	4:12
Max Ridge Height	30'
Roof Framing	Stick
Exterior Walls	2x4

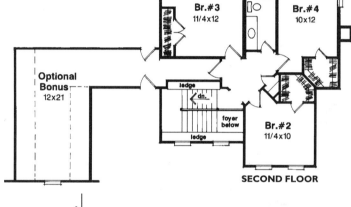

SECOND FLOOR

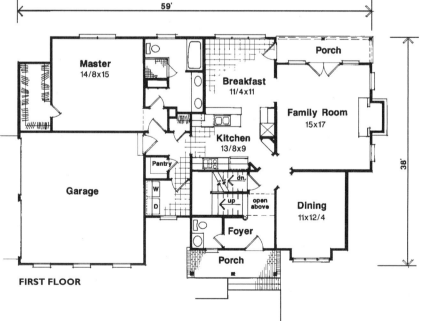

FIRST FLOOR

Design 92570   BL/ML

See Order Pages and Index for Info

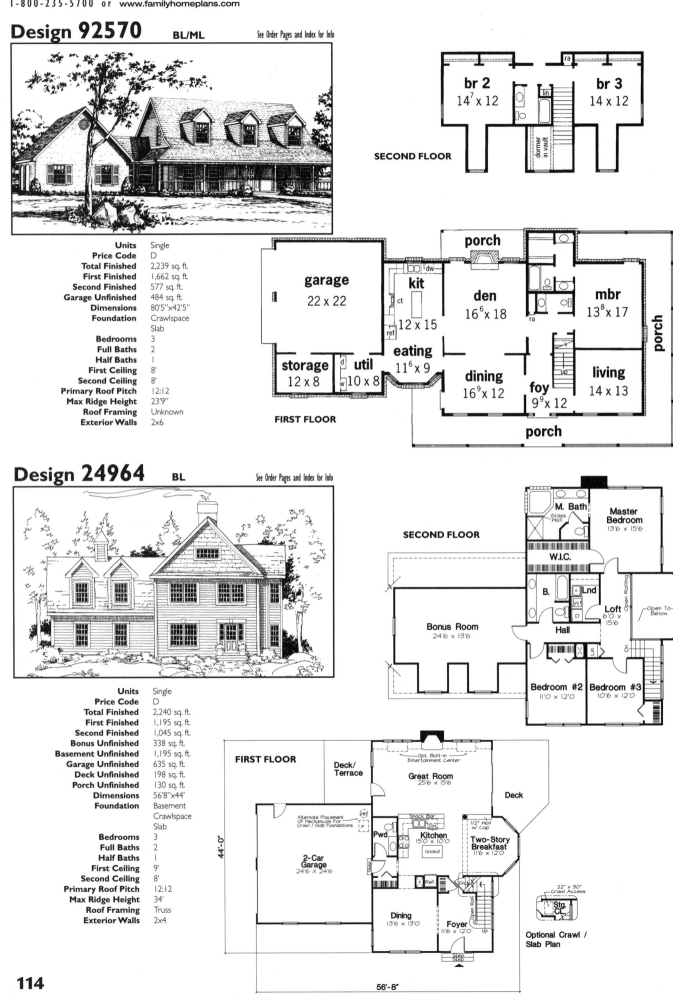

SECOND FLOOR

br 2
14⁷ x 12

br 3
14 x 12

dormer in vault

Units	Single
Price Code	D
Total Finished	2,239 sq. ft.
First Finished	1,662 sq. ft.
Second Finished	577 sq. ft.
Garage Unfinished	484 sq. ft.
Dimensions	80'5"x42'5"
Foundation	Crawlspace
	Slab
Bedrooms	3
Full Baths	2
Half Baths	1
First Ceiling	8'
Second Ceiling	8'
Primary Roof Pitch	12:12
Max Ridge Height	23'9"
Roof Framing	Unknown
Exterior Walls	2x6

FIRST FLOOR

garage
22 x 22

storage
12 x 8

util
10 x 8

kit
12 x 15

eating
11⁶ x 9

porch

den
16⁶ x 18

dining
16⁹ x 12

foy
9⁹ x 12

mbr
13⁸ x 17

living
14 x 13

porch

porch

Design 24964   BL

See Order Pages and Index for Info

SECOND FLOOR

M. Bath

Master Bedroom
13'6 x 15'6

W.I.C.

B.

Lnd

Loft
6'0 x 15'6

Open To Below

Bonus Room
24'6 x 13'6

Hall

Bedroom #2
11'0 x 12'0

Bedroom #3
10'6 x 12'0

Units	Single
Price Code	D
Total Finished	2,240 sq. ft.
First Finished	1,195 sq. ft.
Second Finished	1,045 sq. ft.
Bonus Unfinished	338 sq. ft.
Basement Unfinished	1,195 sq. ft.
Garage Unfinished	635 sq. ft.
Deck Unfinished	198 sq. ft.
Porch Unfinished	130 sq. ft.
Dimensions	56'8"x44'
Foundation	Basement
	Crawlspace
	Slab
Bedrooms	3
Full Baths	2
Half Baths	1
First Ceiling	9'
Second Ceiling	8'
Primary Roof Pitch	12:12
Max Ridge Height	34'
Roof Framing	Truss
Exterior Walls	2x4

FIRST FLOOR

Deck/Terrace

Opt. Built-In Entertainment Center

Great Room
25'6 x 15'6

Deck

Alternate Placement Of Mechanicals For Crawl / Slab Foundations

Snack Bar

Pwd

Kitchen
15'0 x 10'0

Island

1/2" Wall w/ Cap

Two-Story Breakfast
11'6 x 12'0

2-Car Garage
24'6 X 24'6

Ref.

44'-0"

Dining
13'6 x 13'0

Foyer
11'6 x 12'0

Step

22" x 30" Crawl Access

Sta. Cl.

Optional Crawl / Slab Plan

56'-8"

Design 99913

BL/ML   See Order Pages and Index for Info

Units	Single
Price Code	D
Total Finished	2,244 sq. ft.
First Finished	972 sq. ft.
Second Finished	1,272 sq. ft.
Garage Unfinished	270 sq. ft.
Deck Unfinished	80 sq. ft.
Porch Unfinished	80 sq. ft.
Dimensions	32'x45'6''
Foundation	Slab
Bedrooms	3
Full Baths	2
First Ceiling	8'
Second Ceiling	8'
Primary Roof Pitch	6:12
Max Ridge Height	36'
Roof Framing	Truss
Exterior Walls	2x6

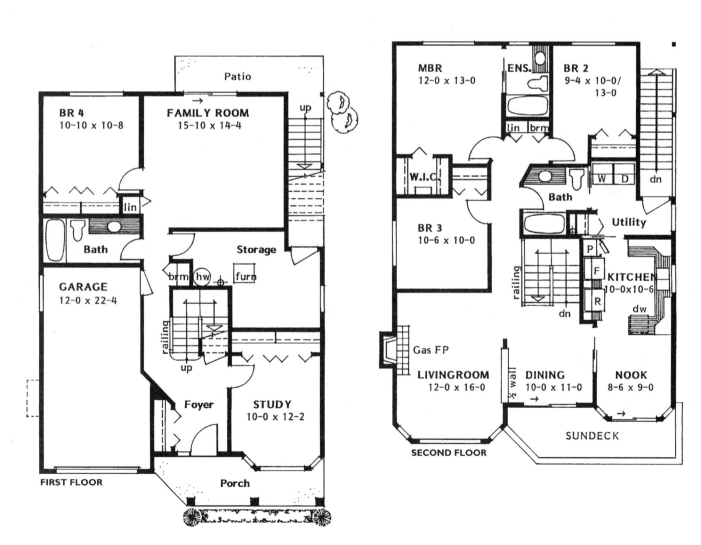

FIRST FLOOR

Patio

BR 4
10-10 x 10-8

FAMILY ROOM
15-10 x 14-4

up

Bath

lin

Storage

GARAGE
12-0 x 22-4

brm hw furm

railing

up

Foyer

STUDY
10-0 x 12-2

Porch

SECOND FLOOR

MBR
12-0 x 13-0

ENS.

BR 2
9-4 x 10-0/
13-0

lin brm

W.I.C

Bath

W D

dn

BR 3
10-6 x 10-0

Utility

railing

P
F
R

dn

KITCHEN
10-0x10-6

dw

Gas FP

LIVINGROOM
12-0 x 16-0

½ wall

DINING
10-0 x 11-0

NOOK
8-6 x 9-0

SUNDECK

Design 98089 BL/ML

See Order Pages and Index for Info

© Donald A. Gardner Architects, Inc.

Units	Single
Price Code	F
Total Finished	2,244 sq. ft.
First Finished	1,644 sq. ft.
Second Finished	600 sq. ft.
Bonus Unfinished	376 sq. ft.
Garage Unfinished	593 sq. ft.
Porch Unfinished	82 sq. ft.
Dimensions	50'8"x55'10"
Foundation	Crawl space
Bedrooms	3
Full Baths	2
Half Baths	1
First Ceiling	9'
Second Ceiling	8'
Primary Roof Pitch	12:12
Secondary Roof Pitch	12:12
Max Ridge Height	28'8"
Roof Framing	Stick
Exterior Walls	2x4

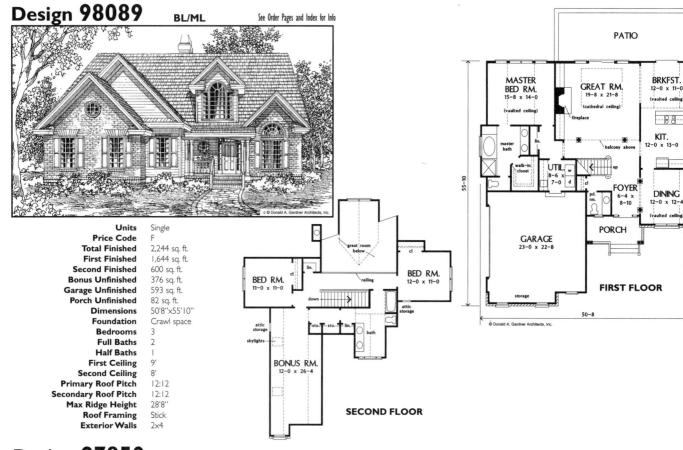

SECOND FLOOR

FIRST FLOOR

© Donald A. Gardner Architects, Inc.

Design 97850 BL

See Order Pages and Index for Info

Units	Single
Price Code	E
Total Finished	2,253 sq. ft.
Main Finished	2,253 sq. ft.
Garage Unfinished	602 sq. ft.
Deck Unfinished	205 sq. ft.
Porch Unfinished	110 sq. ft.
Dimensions	63'x60'3"
Foundation	Slab
Bedrooms	4
Full Baths	3
First Ceiling	8'-10'
Primary Roof Pitch	10:12
Max Ridge Height	26'
Roof Framing	Stick
Exterior Walls	2x4

MAIN FLOOR

Design 99459

BL/ML   See Order Pages and Index for Info

Units	Single
Price Code	E
Total Finished	2,256 sq. ft.
First Finished	1,602 sq. ft.
Second Finished	654 sq. ft.
Dimensions	54'x50'
Foundation	Basement
Bedrooms	4
Full Baths	2
Half Baths	1
Primary Roof Pitch	8:12
Secondary Roof Pitch	12:12
Max Ridge Height	26'
Roof Framing	Stick/Truss
Exterior Walls	2x4

FIRST FLOOR

SECOND FLOOR

Design 98557   BL

See Order Pages and Index for Info

MAIN FLOOR

Units	Single
Price Code	E
Total Finished	2,257 sq. ft.
Main Finished	2,257 sq. ft.
Garage Unfinished	528 sq. ft.
Dimensions	64'7''x77'10''
Foundation	Slab
Bedrooms	3
Full Baths	2
Half Baths	1
First Ceiling	9'-10'
Primary Roof Pitch	10:12
Max Ridge Height	26'6''
Roof Framing	Stick
Exterior Walls	2x4

Design 98548   BL

See Order Pages and Index for Info

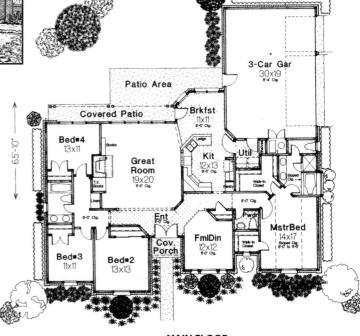

MAIN FLOOR

Units	Single
Price Code	E
Total Finished	2,257 sq. ft.
Main Finished	2,257 sq. ft.
Garage Unfinished	601 sq. ft.
Porch Unfinished	325 sq. ft.
Dimensions	65'x65'10'
Foundation	Crawl space
	Slab
Bedrooms	4
Full Baths	2
Half Baths	1
First Ceiling	9'-11'
Primary Roof Pitch	10:12
Max Ridge Height	25'
Roof Framing	Stick
Exterior Walls	2x4

Design 98044

BL/ML

See Order Pages and Index for Info

Units	Single
Price Code	G
Total Finished	2,261 sq. ft.
First Finished	1,699 sq. ft.
Second Finished	562 sq. ft.
Bonus Unfinished	235 sq. ft.
Garage Unfinished	510 sq. ft.
Dimensions	69'3"x45'10"
Foundation	Crawl space
Bedrooms	3
Full Baths	2
Half Baths	1
Primary Roof Pitch	12:12
Max Ridge Height	33'
Roof Framing	Stick
Exterior Walls	2x4

© Donald A. Gardner Architects, Inc.

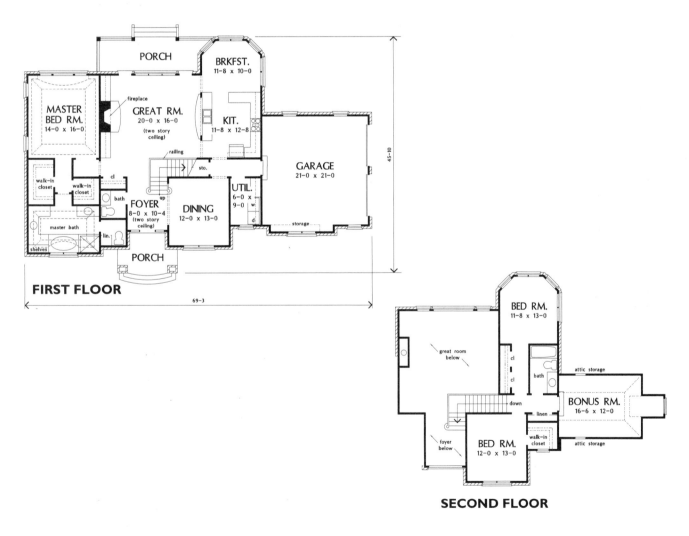

FIRST FLOOR

SECOND FLOOR

Design 90458

BL/ML/ZIP   See Order Pages and Index for Info

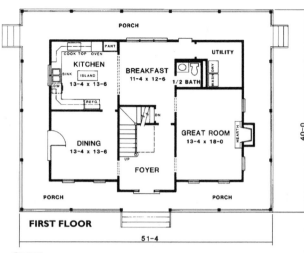

FIRST FLOOR

Units	Single
Price Code	E
Total Finished	2,263 sq. ft.
First Finished	1,125 sq. ft.
Second Finished	1,138 sq. ft.
Basement Unfinished	1,125 sq. ft.
Porch Unfinished	936 sq. ft.
Dimensions	51'4"x40'
Foundation	Basement
	Crawl space
Bedrooms	3
Full Baths	2
Half Baths	1
First Ceiling	8'
Second Ceiling	8'
Primary Roof Pitch	7:12
Secondary Roof Pitch	5:12
Max Ridge Height	26'4"
Roof Framing	Stick
Exterior Walls	2x4

SECOND FLOOR

Design 96815

BL/ML   See Order Pages and Index for Info

FIRST FLOOR

Units	Single
Price Code	E
Total Finished	2,266 sq. ft.
First Finished	1,216 sq. ft.
Second Finished	1,050 sq. ft.
Basement Unfinished	1,216 sq. ft.
Garage Unfinished	729 sq. ft.
Porch Unfinished	823 sq. ft.
Dimensions	64'6"x47'7"
Foundation	Basement
	Crawl space
	Slab
Bedrooms	4
Full Baths	3
Half Baths	1
First Ceiling	9'
Second Ceiling	8'
Tray Ceiling	10'
Primary Roof Pitch	8:12
Secondary Roof Pitch	12:12
Max Ridge Height	29'6"
Roof Framing	Truss
Exterior Walls	2x4

ALTERNATE MEDIA ROOM BATH

SECOND FLOOR

ALTERNATE SECOND FLOOR BATH/LAUNDRY

Design 98595

BL   See Order Pages and Index for Info

Units	Single
Price Code	E
Total Finished	2,272 sq. ft.
First Finished	1,572 sq. ft.
Second Finished	700 sq. ft.
Bonus Unfinished	202 sq. ft.
Dimensions	70'x38'5''
Foundation	Basement
	Crawl space
	Slab
Bedrooms	3
Full Baths	2
Half Baths	1
First Ceiling	9'
Second Ceiling	8'
Primary Roof Pitch	9:12
Max Ridge Height	26'
Roof Framing	Stick
Exterior Walls	2x4

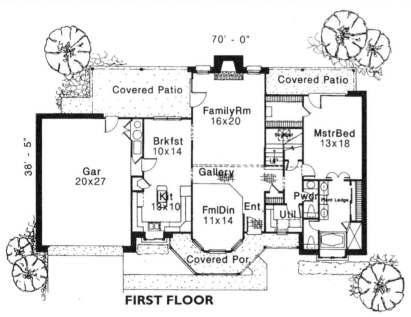

FIRST FLOOR

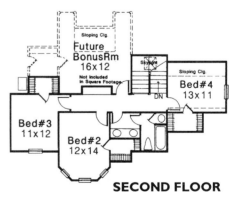

SECOND FLOOR

Design 98347 BL/ML

See Order Pages and Index for Info

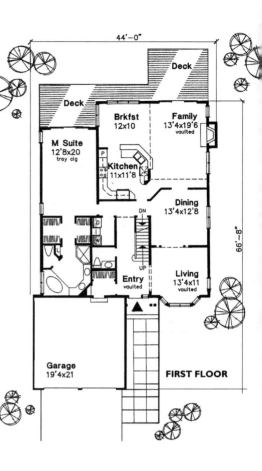

FIRST FLOOR

Units	Single
Price Code	E
Total Finished	2,272 sq. ft.
First Finished	1,750 sq. ft.
Second Finished	522 sq. ft.
Bonus Unfinished	216 sq. ft.
Basement Unfinished	1,750 sq. ft.
Garage Unfinished	420 sq. ft.
Deck Unfinished	280 sq. ft.
Dimensions	44'x66'8''
Foundation	Basement
Bedrooms	2
Full Baths	2
Half Baths	1
First Ceiling	8'
Second Ceiling	8'
Vaulted Ceiling	17'
Primary Roof Pitch	6:12
Secondary Roof Pitch	10:12
Max Ridge Height	26'4''
Roof Framing	Truss
Exterior Walls	2x6

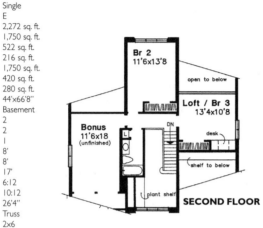

SECOND FLOOR

Design 93172 BL

See Order Pages and Index for Info

Units	Single
Price Code	E
Total Finished	2,274 sq. ft.
Main Finished	2,274 sq. ft.
Basement Unfinished	2,274 sq. ft.
Porch Unfinished	232 sq. ft.
Dimensions	77'8''x56'
Foundation	Basement
Bedrooms	3
Full Baths	2
Primary Roof Pitch	8:12
Secondary Roof Pitch	8:12
Max Ridge Height	24'6''
Roof Framing	Stick
Exterior Walls	2x6

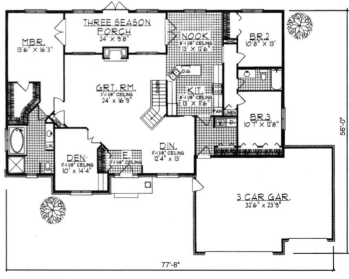

MAIN FLOOR

Design 98593

BL

See Order Pages and Index for Info

Units	Single
Price Code	E
Total Finished	2,285 sq. ft.
First Finished	2,285 sq. ft.
Garage Unfinished	653 sq. ft.
Dimensions	74'10''x56'10''
Foundation	Slab
Bedrooms	4
Full Baths	3
Primary Roof Pitch	9:12
Max Ridge Height	22'
Roof Framing	Stick
Exterior Walls	2x4

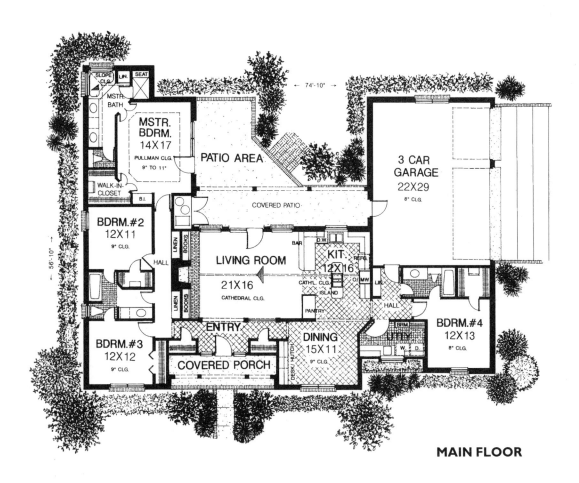

MAIN FLOOR

Design 91095 BL

See Order Pages and Index for Info

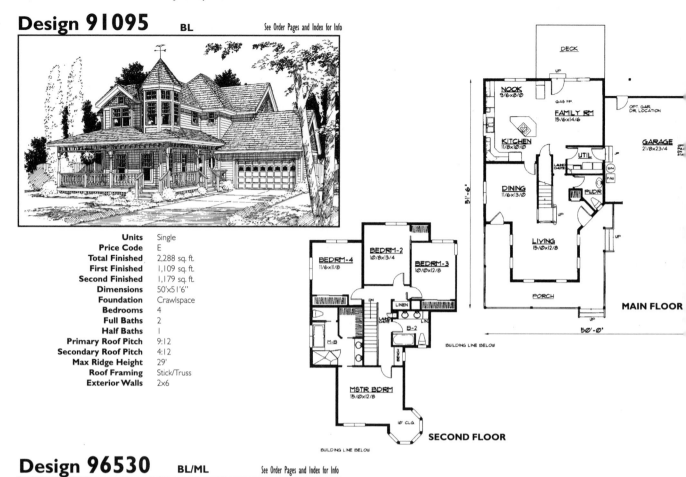

Units	Single
Price Code	E
Total Finished	2,288 sq. ft.
First Finished	1,109 sq. ft.
Second Finished	1,179 sq. ft.
Dimensions	50'x51'6"
Foundation	Crawlspace
Bedrooms	4
Full Baths	2
Half Baths	1
Primary Roof Pitch	9:12
Secondary Roof Pitch	4:12
Max Ridge Height	29'
Roof Framing	Stick/Truss
Exterior Walls	2x6

Design 96530 BL/ML

See Order Pages and Index for Info

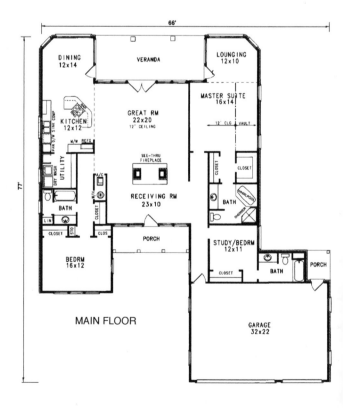

Units	Single
Price Code	E
Total Finished	2,289 sq. ft.
Main Finished	2,289 sq. ft.
Garage Unfinished	758 sq. ft.
Dimensions	66'x77'
Foundation	Crawlspace
	Slab
Bedrooms	3
Full Baths	3
First Ceiling	8'
Primary Roof Pitch	6:12
Max Ridge Height	22'
Roof Framing	Stick
Exterior Walls	2x4

Design 90474

BL/ML

See Order Pages and Index for Info

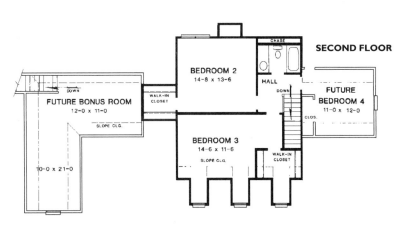

Units	Single
Price Code	E
Total Finished	2,297 sq. ft.
First Finished	1,580 sq. ft.
Second Finished	717 sq. ft.
Bonus Unfinished	410 sq. ft.
Basement Unfinished	1,342 sq. ft.
Garage Unfinished	484 sq. ft.
Deck Unfinished	288 sq. ft.
Porch Unfinished	144 sq. ft.
Dimensions	72'x40'
Foundation	Basement
	Crawl space
Bedrooms	3
Half Baths	1
First Ceiling	8'
Second Ceiling	8'
Vaulted Ceiling	11'4"
Primary Roof Pitch	12:12
Secondary Roof Pitch	5:12
Max Ridge Height	25'6"
Roof Framing	Stick
Exterior Walls	2x4

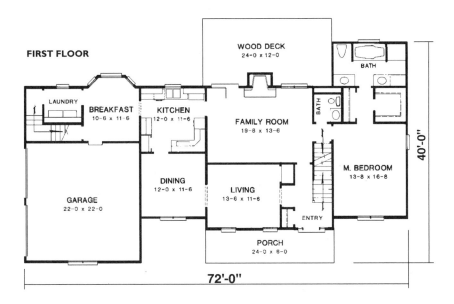

FIRST FLOOR

WOOD DECK
24-0 x 12-0

BATH

LAUNDRY

BREAKFAST
10-6 x 11-6

KITCHEN
12-0 x 11-6

FAMILY ROOM
19-8 x 13-6

BATH

GARAGE
22-0 x 22-0

DINING
12-0 x 11-6

LIVING
13-6 x 11-6

M. BEDROOM
13-8 x 16-8

ENTRY

PORCH
24-0 x 6-0

40'-0"

72'-0"

SECOND FLOOR

CHASE

FUTURE BONUS ROOM
12-0 x 11-0

DOWN

WALK-IN CLOSET

BEDROOM 2
14-8 x 13-6

HALL

DOWN

FUTURE BEDROOM 4
11-0 x 12-0

SLOPE CLG.

10-0 x 21-0

BEDROOM 3
14-6 x 11-6

SLOPE CLG.

CLOS.

WALK-IN CLOSET

Design 98057 BL

See Order Pages and Index for Info

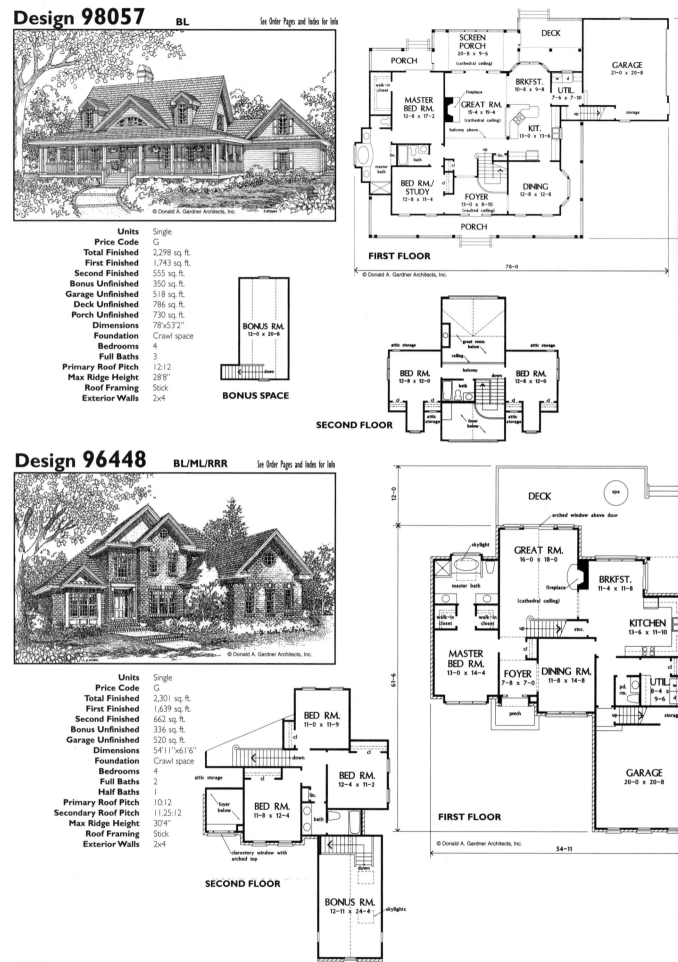

Units	Single
Price Code	G
Total Finished	2,298 sq. ft.
First Finished	1,743 sq. ft.
Second Finished	555 sq. ft.
Bonus Unfinished	350 sq. ft.
Garage Unfinished	518 sq. ft.
Deck Unfinished	786 sq. ft.
Porch Unfinished	730 sq. ft.
Dimensions	78'x53'2"
Foundation	Crawl space
Bedrooms	4
Full Baths	3
Primary Roof Pitch	12:12
Max Ridge Height	28'8"
Roof Framing	Stick
Exterior Walls	2x4

Design 96448 BL/ML/RRR

See Order Pages and Index for Info

Units	Single
Price Code	G
Total Finished	2,301 sq. ft.
First Finished	1,639 sq. ft.
Second Finished	662 sq. ft.
Bonus Unfinished	336 sq. ft.
Garage Unfinished	520 sq. ft.
Dimensions	54'11"x61'6"
Foundation	Crawl space
Bedrooms	4
Full Baths	2
Half Baths	1
Primary Roof Pitch	10:12
Secondary Roof Pitch	11.25:12
Max Ridge Height	30'4"
Roof Framing	Stick
Exterior Walls	2x4

126

Design 97869

BL

See Order Pages and Index for Info

Units	Single
Price Code	E
Total Finished	2,307 sq. ft.
First Finished	2,307 sq. ft.
Garage Unfinished	572 sq. ft.
Deck Unfinished	189 sq. ft.
Porch Unfinished	35 sq. ft.
Dimensions	60'10''x70'11''
Foundation	Slab
Bedrooms	3
Full Baths	3
First Ceiling	10'
Primary Roof Pitch	10:12
Max Ridge Height	26'
Roof Framing	Stick
Exterior Walls	2x4

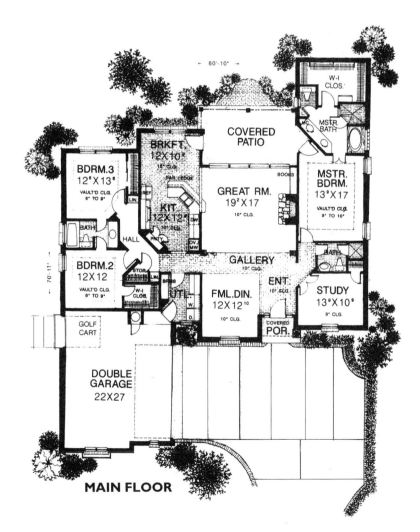

MAIN FLOOR

Design 93089

BL/ML

See Order Pages and Index for Info

Units	Single
Price Code	I
Total Finished	3,494 sq. ft.
First Finished	2,469 sq. ft.
Second Finished	1,025 sq. ft.
Bonus Unfinished	320 sq. ft.
Garage Unfinished	795 sq. ft.
Porch Unfinished	249 sq. ft.
Dimensions	67'8"×74'2"
Foundation	Basement
	Crawl space
	Slab
Bedrooms	4
Full Baths	3
Half Baths	1
Primary Roof Pitch	9:12
Secondary Roof Pitch	12:12
Max Ridge Height	31'
Roof Framing	Stick
Exterior Walls	2x4

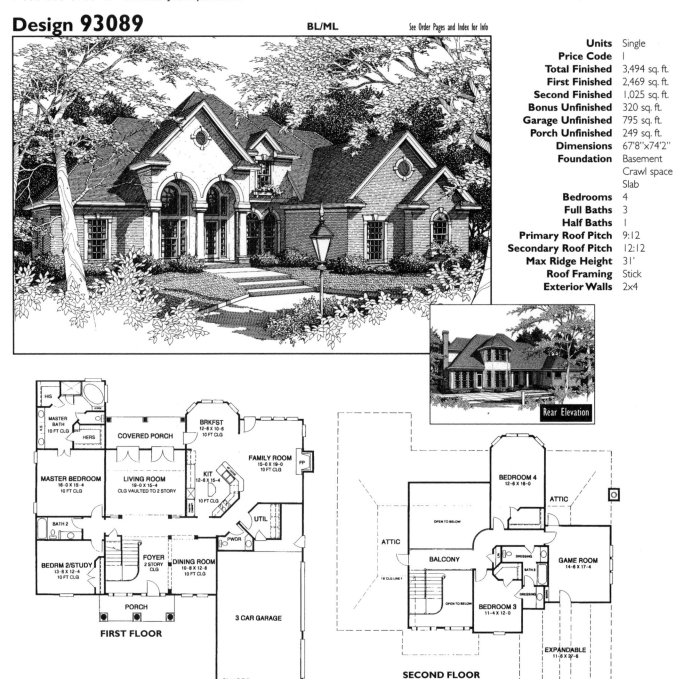

Rear Elevation

FIRST FLOOR

SECOND FLOOR

© Larry E. Belk

Inside, the two-story foyer opens the view directly through the living room to the rear grounds. The use of square columns to define the dining room adds an air of elegance to the home. The kitchen breakfast area and family room are conveniently grouped for family gatherings and informal entertaining. The master bedroom and elegantly appointed master bath are located on the first floor. A large game room completes this wonderful family home. Additional expandable area is available over the three-car garage.

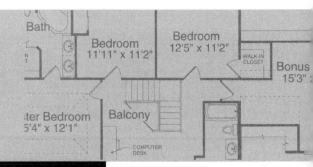

ARCHITECTURAL IMPACT

Design 92630

BL/ZIP   See Order Pages and Index for Info

Units	Single
Price Code	C
Total Finished	1,782 sq. ft.
Main Finished	1,782 sq. ft.
Basement Unfinished	1,735 sq. ft.
Garage Unfinished	407 sq. ft.
Dimensions	67'2"×47'
Foundation	Basement
Bedrooms	3
Full Baths	2
Primary Roof Pitch	7:12
Secondary Roof Pitch	9:12
Max Ridge Height	20'
Roof Framing	Truss
Exterior Walls	2x4

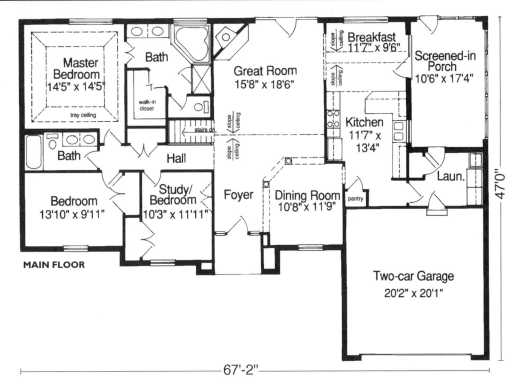

MAIN FLOOR

67'-2"

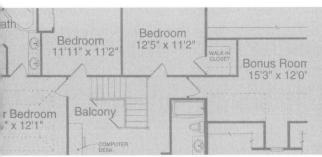

The appeal of this Ranch-style home is not only in its charm and exterior style. The Great room and the dining room are accented by a sloped ceiling, columns and custom moldings. The breakfast area also has sloped ceiling and the light permeates through the rear windows and the French doors, which leads to the spacious screened porch. Convenience was the order of the day when this kitchen was designed. Relaxing in the master bedroom suite is enhanced by the ultra bath with a whirlpool tub.

HOME PLAN OF THE YEAR

Design 97246 BL

See Order Pages and Index for Info

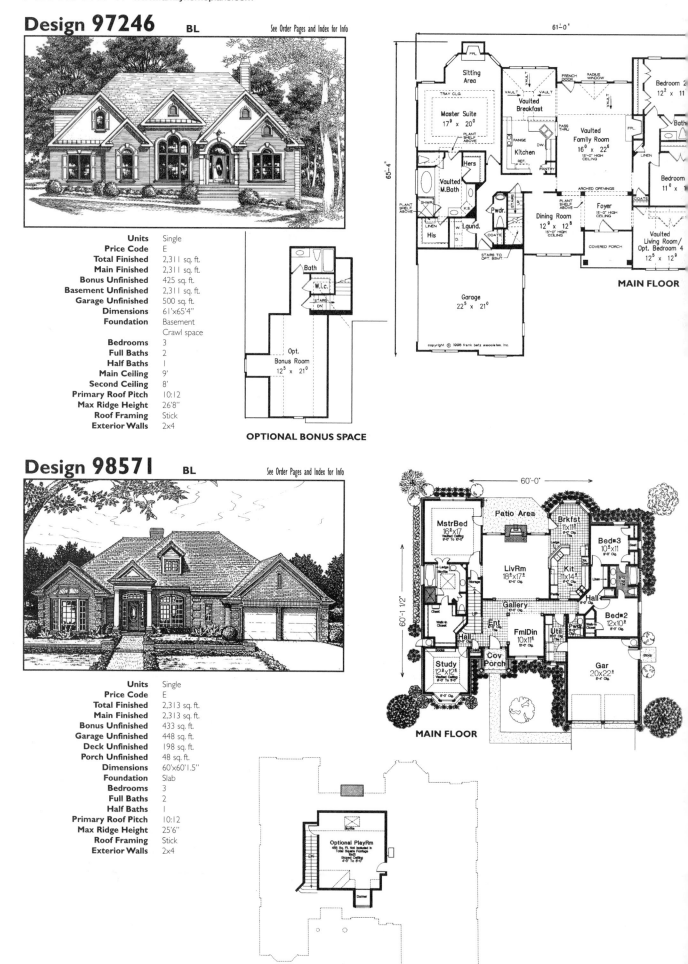

Units	Single
Price Code	E
Total Finished	2,311 sq. ft.
Main Finished	2,311 sq. ft.
Bonus Unfinished	425 sq. ft.
Basement Unfinished	2,311 sq. ft.
Garage Unfinished	500 sq. ft.
Dimensions	61'x65'4"
Foundation	Basement
	Crawl space
Bedrooms	3
Full Baths	2
Half Baths	1
Main Ceiling	9'
Second Ceiling	8'
Primary Roof Pitch	10:12
Max Ridge Height	26'8"
Roof Framing	Stick
Exterior Walls	2x4

OPTIONAL BONUS SPACE

Opt. Bonus Room 12⁵ x 21⁰

Bath
W.i.c.
STAIRS DN

MAIN FLOOR

61'-0"
65'-4"

Sitting Area
FPL
TRAY CLG
Master Suite 17⁹ x 20⁰
Vaulted Breakfast
RADIUS WINDOW
FRENCH DOORS
Bedroom 2 12² x 11
VAULT VAULT VAULT
Kitchen
RANGE DW
Vaulted Family Room 16⁰ x 22⁶ 15'-0" HIGH CEILING
FPL
Hers
PASS THRU
REF
PANTRY
LINEN
Bath
Vaulted M.Bath
PLANT SHELF ABOVE
Pwdr.
PLANT SHELF ABOVE
Bedroom 11⁰ x
SHWR
Dining Room 12⁸ x 12⁸ 15'-0" HIGH CEILING
Foyer 15'-0" HIGH CEILING
ARCHED OPENINGS
COATS
LINEN
His
Lqund.
COATS
STAIRS TO OPT. BSMT.
Covered Porch
Vaulted Living Room/ Opt. Bedroom 4 12⁵ x 12⁹
Garage 22⁵ x 21⁰

copyright 1996 frank betz associates, inc.

Design 98571 BL

See Order Pages and Index for Info

Units	Single
Price Code	E
Total Finished	2,313 sq. ft.
Main Finished	2,313 sq. ft.
Bonus Unfinished	433 sq. ft.
Garage Unfinished	448 sq. ft.
Deck Unfinished	198 sq. ft.
Porch Unfinished	48 sq. ft.
Dimensions	60'x60'1.5"
Foundation	Slab
Bedrooms	3
Full Baths	2
Half Baths	1
Primary Roof Pitch	10:12
Max Ridge Height	25'6"
Roof Framing	Stick
Exterior Walls	2x4

MAIN FLOOR

60'-0"
60'-1 1/2'

MstrBed 16⁸x17
Patio Area
Brkfst 11x11⁵
Bed#3 10⁵x11
LivRm 18⁸x17⁵
Kit 11x14⁵
Storage
Gallery
Hall
Bed#2 12x10
Walk-in Closet
Ent
FmlDin 10x11⁸
Util
Pwdr
Study 12⁸x12⁸
Cov Porch
Gar 20x22⁸

OPTIONAL PLAY ROOM

Optional PlayRm 433 Sq. Ft. Not Included in Total Square Footage 13x23 Sloped Ceiling 4'-0" To 8'-0"
Skylite
DN
Dormer

Design 98578

BL

See Order Pages and Index for Info

Units	Single
Price Code	E
Total Finished	2,314 sq. ft.
First Finished	1,595 sq. ft.
Second Finished	719 sq. ft.
Garage Unfinished	440 sq. ft.
Deck Unfinished	96 sq. ft.
Porch Unfinished	32 sq. ft.
Dimensions	52'4"x63'4"
Foundation	Slab
Bedrooms	4
Full Baths	3
Half Baths	1
Primary Roof Pitch	12:12
Max Ridge Height	27'
Roof Framing	Stick
Exterior Walls	2x4

LOWER LEVEL

UPPER LEVEL

Design 94633 BL

See Order Pages and Index for Info

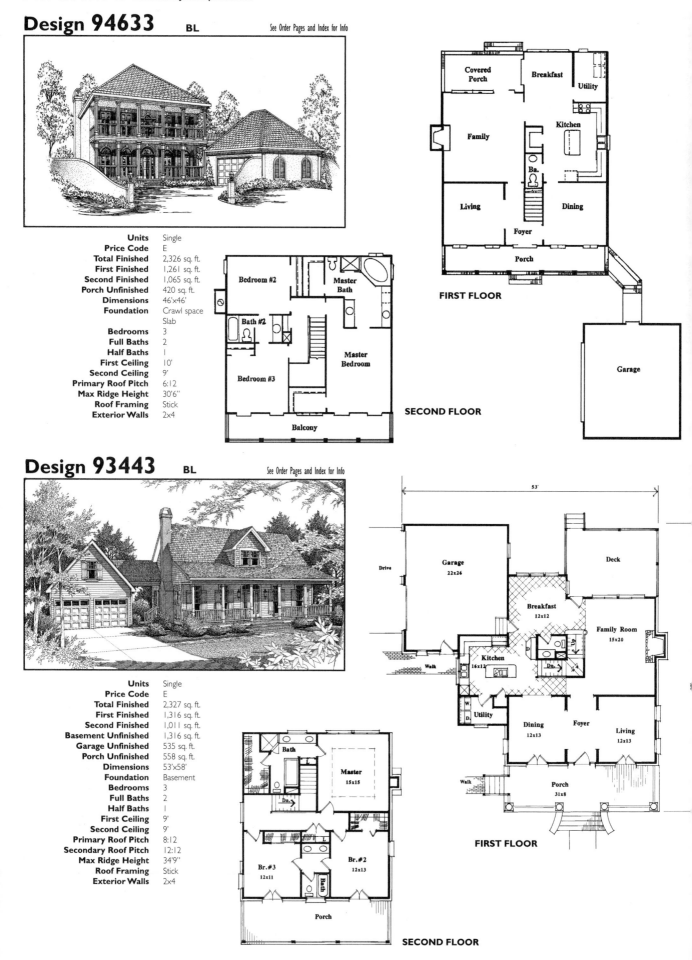

Units	Single
Price Code	E
Total Finished	2,326 sq. ft.
First Finished	1,261 sq. ft.
Second Finished	1,065 sq. ft.
Porch Unfinished	420 sq. ft.
Dimensions	46'x46'
Foundation	Crawl space
	Slab
Bedrooms	3
Full Baths	2
Half Baths	1
First Ceiling	10'
Second Ceiling	9'
Primary Roof Pitch	6:12
Max Ridge Height	30'6"
Roof Framing	Stick
Exterior Walls	2x4

FIRST FLOOR

SECOND FLOOR

Design 93443 BL

See Order Pages and Index for Info

Units	Single
Price Code	E
Total Finished	2,327 sq. ft.
First Finished	1,316 sq. ft.
Second Finished	1,011 sq. ft.
Basement Unfinished	1,316 sq. ft.
Garage Unfinished	535 sq. ft.
Porch Unfinished	558 sq. ft.
Dimensions	53'x58'
Foundation	Basement
Bedrooms	3
Full Baths	2
Half Baths	1
First Ceiling	9'
Second Ceiling	9'
Primary Roof Pitch	8:12
Secondary Roof Pitch	12:12
Max Ridge Height	34'9"
Roof Framing	Stick
Exterior Walls	2x4

FIRST FLOOR

SECOND FLOOR

Design 98336

BL

See Order Pages and Index for Info

Units	Single
Price Code	E
Total Finished	2,328 sq. ft.
First Finished	1,487 sq. ft.
Second Finished	841 sq. ft.
Garage Unfinished	542 sq. ft.
Deck Unfinished	400 sq. ft.
Dimensions	56'4''x51'
Foundation	Slab
Bedrooms	3
Full Baths	2
Half Baths	1
First Ceiling	8'
Second Ceiling	8'
Primary Roof Pitch	6:12
Secondary Roof Pitch	12:12
Max Ridge Height	25'
Roof Framing	Truss
Exterior Walls	2x4

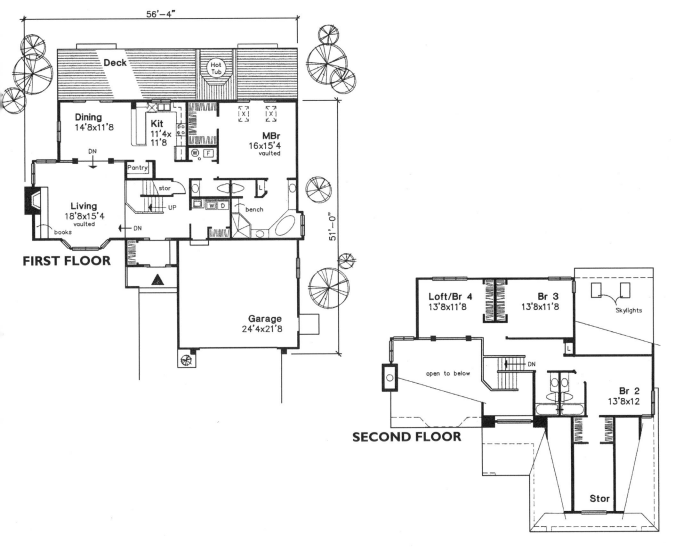

133

Design 97427 BL/ML/RRR

See Order Pages and Index for Info

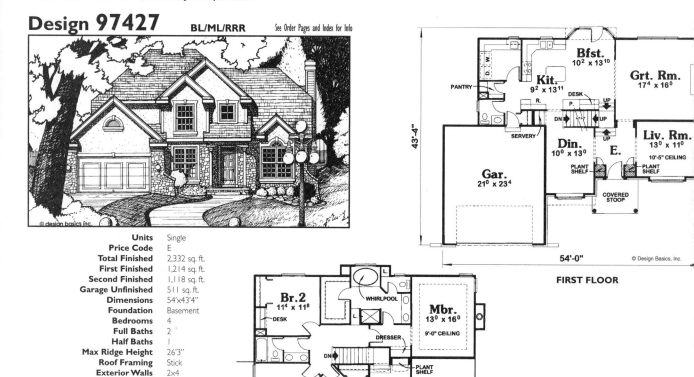

© design basics inc.

Units	Single
Price Code	E
Total Finished	2,332 sq. ft.
First Finished	1,214 sq. ft.
Second Finished	1,118 sq. ft.
Garage Unfinished	511 sq. ft.
Dimensions	54'x43'4''
Foundation	Basement
Bedrooms	4
Full Baths	2
Half Baths	1
Max Ridge Height	26'3''
Roof Framing	Stick
Exterior Walls	2x4

© Design Basics, Inc.

FIRST FLOOR

SECOND FLOOR

Design 97857 BL

See Order Pages and Index for Info

Units	Single
Price Code	E
Total Finished	2,332 sq. ft.
Main Finished	2,332 sq. ft.
Garage Unfinished	620 sq. ft.
Deck Unfinished	80 sq. ft.
Porch Unfinished	48 sq. ft.
Dimensions	82'3''x86'6''
Foundation	Slab
Bedrooms	3
Full Baths	2
Half Baths	1
Main Ceiling	9'-10'
Primary Roof Pitch	12:12
Max Ridge Height	29'
Roof Framing	Stick
Exterior Walls	2x4

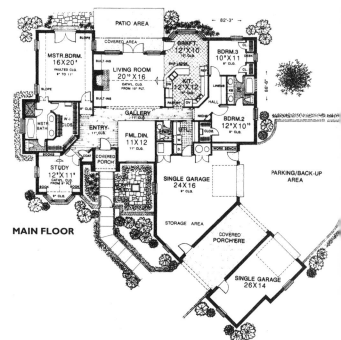

MAIN FLOOR

Design 92613

BL

See Order Pages and Index for Info

Units	Single
Price Code	G
Total Finished	2,846 sq. ft.
First Finished	2,192 sq. ft.
Second Finished	654 sq. ft.
Bonus Unfinished	325 sq. ft.
Basement Unfinished	1,922 sq. ft.
Garage Unfinished	706 sq. ft.
Dimensions	74'4"x69'11"
Foundation	Basement
Bedrooms	3
Full Baths	2
Half Baths	2
First Ceiling	9'
Primary Roof Pitch	8:12
Secondary Roof Pitch	12:12
Max Ridge Height	29'
Roof Framing	Truss
Exterior Walls	2x4

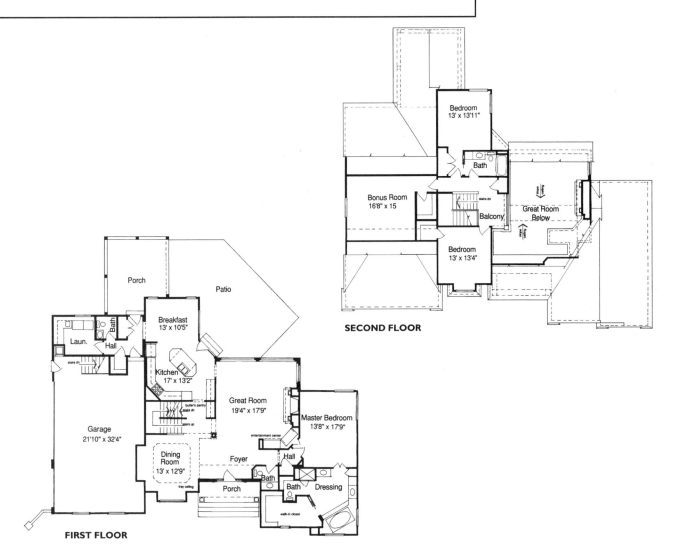

SECOND FLOOR

FIRST FLOOR

Design 97209   BL

See Order Pages and Index for Info

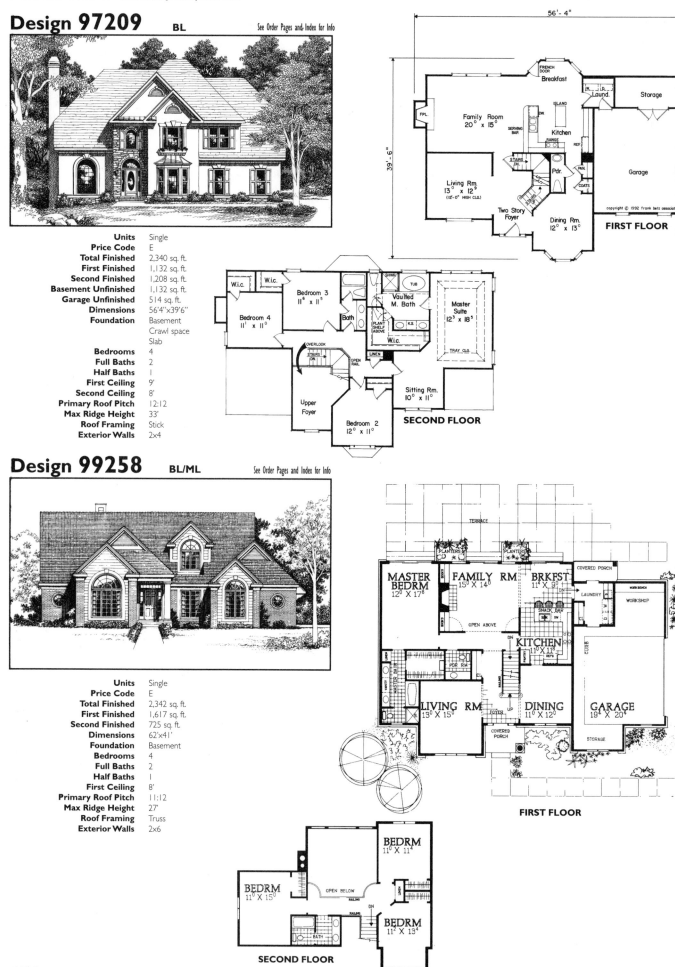

Units	Single
Price Code	E
Total Finished	2,340 sq. ft.
First Finished	1,132 sq. ft.
Second Finished	1,208 sq. ft.
Basement Unfinished	1,132 sq. ft.
Garage Unfinished	514 sq. ft.
Dimensions	56'4"x39'6"
Foundation	Basement
	Crawl space
	Slab
Bedrooms	4
Full Baths	2
Half Baths	1
First Ceiling	9'
Second Ceiling	8'
Primary Roof Pitch	12:12
Max Ridge Height	33'
Roof Framing	Stick
Exterior Walls	2x4

FIRST FLOOR

SECOND FLOOR

Design 99258   BL/ML

See Order Pages and Index for Info

Units	Single
Price Code	E
Total Finished	2,342 sq. ft.
First Finished	1,617 sq. ft.
Second Finished	725 sq. ft.
Dimensions	62'x41'
Foundation	Basement
Bedrooms	4
Full Baths	2
Half Baths	1
First Ceiling	8'
Primary Roof Pitch	11:12
Max Ridge Height	27'
Roof Framing	Truss
Exterior Walls	2x6

FIRST FLOOR

SECOND FLOOR

Design 81003

BL

See Order Pages and Index for Info

Units	Single
Price Code	E
Total Finished	2,342 sq. ft.
First Finished	1,234 sq. ft.
Second Finished	1,108 sq. ft.
Dimensions	56'x74'6''
Foundation	Crawl space
Bedrooms	3
Full Baths	2
Half Baths	1
First Ceiling	9'
Second Ceiling	8'
Primary Roof Pitch	10:12
Max Ridge Height	34'6''
Roof Framing	Truss
Exterior Walls	2x6

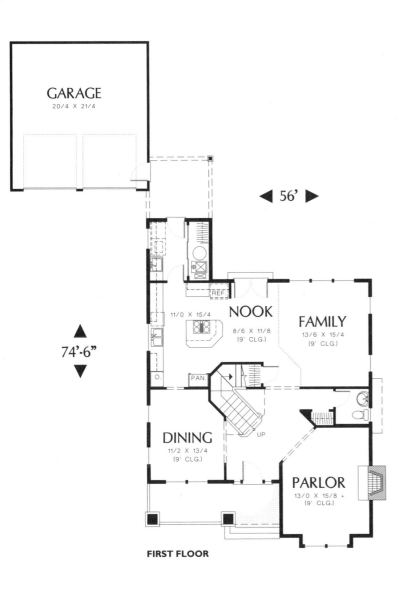

GARAGE
20/4 X 21/4

◄ **56'** ►

▲
74'-6"
▼

NOOK
8/6 X 11/8
(9' CLG.)

FAMILY
13/6 X 15/4
(9' CLG.)

REF.

PAN.

UP

DINING
11/2 X 13/4
(9' CLG.)

PARLOR
13/0 X 15/8 +
(9' CLG.)

FIRST FLOOR

BR. 3
12/6X 11/8

LIN

DEN/BR.4
12/10 X 10/0 +/-

DN.

BR. 2
11/2 X 12/4

LIN

VAULTED
MASTER
13/0 X 15/0

SECOND FLOOR

137

Design 94639   BL

See Order Pages and Index for Info

Units	Single
Price Code	E
Total Finished	2,345 sq. ft.
Main Finished	2,345 sq. ft.
Garage Unfinished	510 sq. ft.
Porch Unfinished	62 sq. ft.
Dimensions	59'10"x66'3"
Foundation	Slab
Bedrooms	3
Full Baths	3
Primary Roof Pitch	8:12
Max Ridge Height	23'
Roof Framing	Stick
Exterior Walls	2x4

MAIN FLOOR

Garage 23'-4" X 20'-7"

Ma. Bath

Patio

Brk'fst 9' X 13'

Util.

Ma. Bedroom 14'-3" X 17'

Living 20'-1" X 18'

Kitchen 12'-7" X 12'-6"

Bath

Bath

Bedroom #2 10'-9" X 13'

Foyer

Dining 11'-4" X 13'

Bedroom #3 11'-6" X 11"

Porch

Study 10'-8" X 12'

Design 20228   BL/ZIP

See Order Pages and Index for Info

Units	Single
Price Code	E
Total Finished	2,345 sq. ft.
First Finished	1,395 sq. ft.
Second Finished	950 sq. ft.
Basement Unfinished	1,395 sq. ft.
Garage Unfinished	396 sq. ft.
Dimensions	48'6"x47'
Foundation	Basement Crawlspace Slab
Bedrooms	3
Full Baths	2
Half Baths	1
First Ceiling	9'
Second Ceiling	9'
Primary Roof Pitch	10:12
Secondary Roof Pitch	12:12
Max Ridge Height	30'9"
Roof Framing	Truss
Exterior Walls	2x4

FIRST FLOOR

Nook 10-2 x 10-2

Kitchen 14'5 x 14'0

Great Room 20-2 x 19-9

Sunroom 10-1 x 10-5

Pantry

Hall

Two Car Garage 20-0 x 20-0

Dining Room 11-9 x 14-9

Foyer

Porch

SECOND FLOOR

Master Bedroom 12-0 x 17-0

Open To Below

Bedroom #3 12-0 x 12-0

Bedroom #2 11-8 x 14-9

CRAWLSPACE/SLAB OPTION

Design 98455

BL/ML/ZIP   See Order Pages and Index for Info

Units	Single
Price Code	E
Total Finished	2,349 sq. ft.
First Finished	1,761 sq. ft.
Second Finished	588 sq. ft.
Bonus Unfinished	267 sq. ft.
Basement Unfinished	1,761 sq. ft.
Garage Unfinished	435 sq. ft.
Dimensions	56'x47'6''
Foundation	Basement
	Crawl space
Bedrooms	4
Full Baths	3
First Ceiling	9'
Second Ceiling	8'
Primary Roof Pitch	12:12
Max Ridge Height	31'6''
Roof Framing	Stick
Exterior Walls	2x4

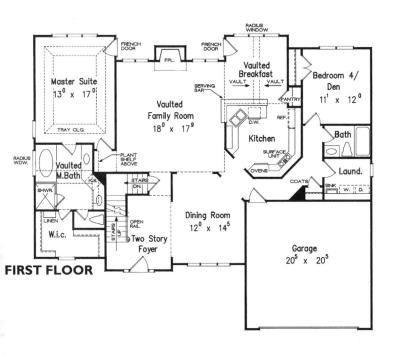

FIRST FLOOR

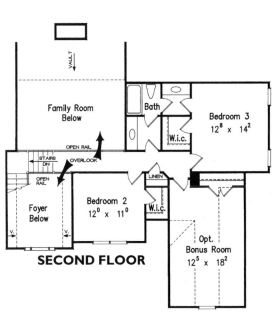

SECOND FLOOR

Design 96413

BL/ML/ZIP/RRR See Order Pages and Index for Info

© 1997 Donald A. Gardner Architects, Inc.

Units	Single
Price Code	G
Total Finished	2,349 sq. ft.
Main Finished	2,349 sq. ft.
Bonus Unfinished	435 sq. ft.
Garage Unfinished	615 sq. ft.
Dimensions	83'2"x60'6"
Foundation	Crawl space
Bedrooms	4
Full Baths	3
Main Ceiling	9'
Primary Roof Pitch	10:12
Secondary Roof Pitch	12:12
Roof Framing	Stick
Exterior Walls	2x4

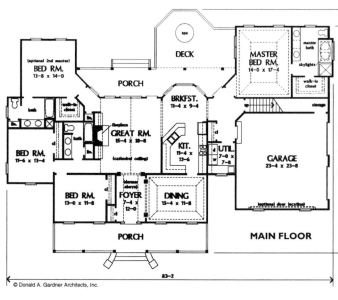

MAIN FLOOR

© Donald A. Gardner Architects, Inc.

**OPTIONAL HANDICAP
ACCESS BATH**

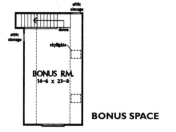

BONUS RM.
14-6 x 23-8

BONUS SPACE

Design 98084

BL/ML See Order Pages and Index for Info

© Donald A. Gardner Architects, Inc.

Units	Single
Price Code	G
Total Finished	2,356 sq. ft.
First Finished	1,718 sq. ft.
Second Finished	638 sq. ft.
Dimensions	71'x42'8"
Foundation	Crawl space
Bedrooms	4
Full Baths	3
First Ceiling	9'
Second Ceiling	9'
Primary Roof Pitch	10:12
Secondary Roof Pitch	12:12
Max Ridge Height	29'4"
Roof Framing	Stick
Exterior Walls	2x4

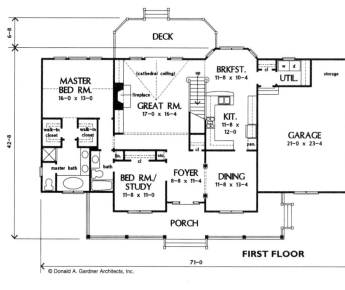

FIRST FLOOR

© Donald A. Gardner Architects, Inc.

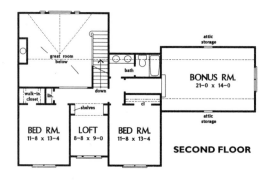

SECOND FLOOR

Design 94632

BL

See Order Pages and Index for Info

Units	Single
Price Code	E
Total Finished	2,365 sq. ft.
Main Finished	2,365 sq. ft.
Dimensions	67'6"x73'
Foundation	Crawl space
	Slab
Bedrooms	4
Full Baths	2
Main Ceiling	9'
Primary Roof Pitch	10:12
Secondary Roof Pitch	14:12
Max Ridge Height	31'6"
Roof Framing	Stick
Exterior Walls	2x4

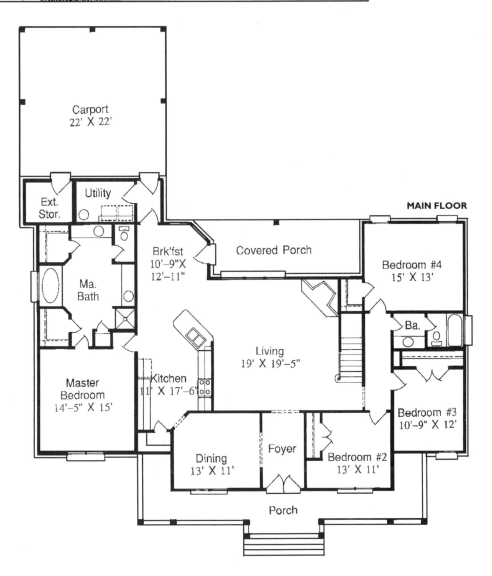

MAIN FLOOR

Carport
22' X 22'

Ext. Stor.

Utility

Ma. Bath

Brk'fst
10'-9"X 12'-11"

Covered Porch

Bedroom #4
15' X 13'

Master Bedroom
14'-5" X 15'

Kitchen
11' X 17'-6"

Living
19' X 19'-5"

Ba.

Bedroom #3
10'-9" X 12'

Dining
13' X 11'

Foyer

Bedroom #2
13' X 11'

Porch

Design 98409 BL/ML

See Order Pages and Index for Info

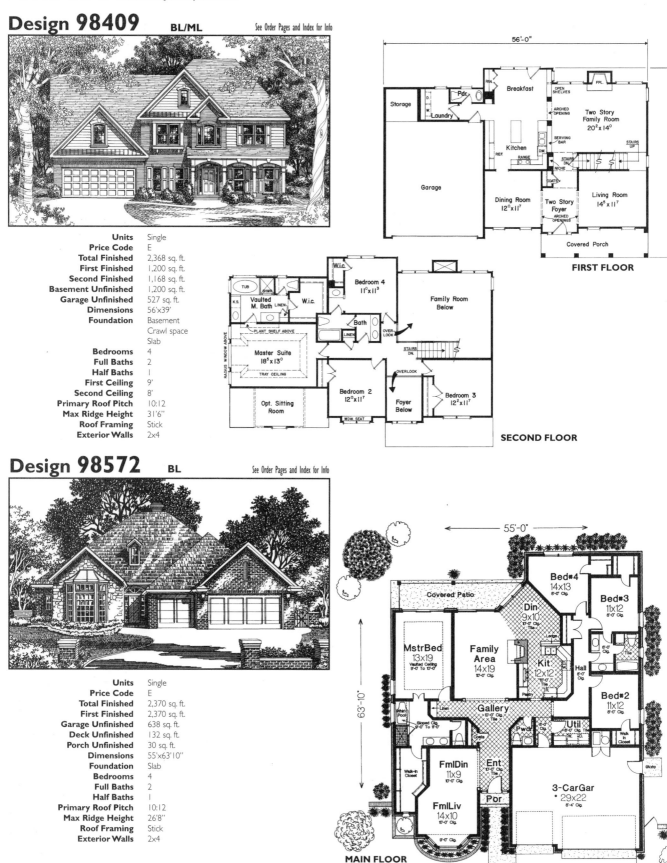

Units	Single
Price Code	E
Total Finished	2,368 sq. ft.
First Finished	1,200 sq. ft.
Second Finished	1,168 sq. ft.
Basement Unfinished	1,200 sq. ft.
Garage Unfinished	527 sq. ft.
Dimensions	56'x39'
Foundation	Basement
	Crawl space
	Slab
Bedrooms	4
Full Baths	2
Half Baths	1
First Ceiling	9'
Second Ceiling	8'
Primary Roof Pitch	10:12
Max Ridge Height	31'6"
Roof Framing	Stick
Exterior Walls	2x4

FIRST FLOOR

SECOND FLOOR

Design 98572 BL

See Order Pages and Index for Info

Units	Single
Price Code	E
Total Finished	2,370 sq. ft.
First Finished	2,370 sq. ft.
Garage Unfinished	638 sq. ft.
Deck Unfinished	132 sq. ft.
Porch Unfinished	30 sq. ft.
Dimensions	55'x63'10"
Foundation	Slab
Bedrooms	4
Full Baths	2
Half Baths	1
Primary Roof Pitch	10:12
Max Ridge Height	26'8"
Roof Framing	Stick
Exterior Walls	2x4

MAIN FLOOR

Design 24255

BL/ML

See Order Pages and Index for Info

Units	Single
Price Code	E
Total Finished	2,370 sq. ft.
First Finished	1,370 sq. ft.
Second Finished	1,000 sq. ft.
Bonus Unfinished	194 sq. ft.
Basement Unfinished	1,370 sq. ft.
Garage Unfinished	667 sq. ft.
Dimensions	60'9"x49'4"
Foundation	Basement
Bedrooms	4
Full Baths	2
Half Baths	1
Primary Roof Pitch	8:12
Max Ridge Height	30'
Roof Framing	Truss
Exterior Walls	2x4

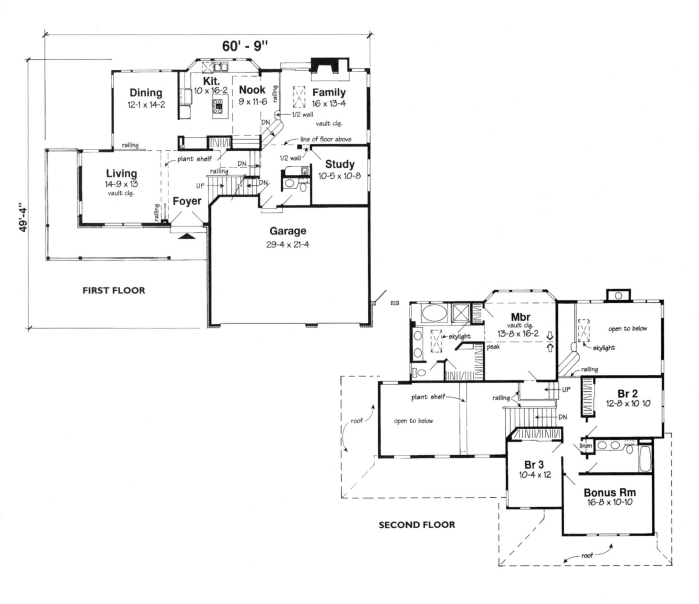

FIRST FLOOR

60' - 9"

49' - 4"

Dining 12-1 x 14-2

Kit. 10 x 16-2

Nook 9 x 11-6

Family 16 x 13-4
vault clg.

1/2 wall

Living 14-9 x 13
vault clg.

plant shelf

line of floor above

1/2 wall

Study 10-5 x 10-8

Foyer

railing

Garage 29-4 x 21-4

SECOND FLOOR

Mbr vault clg. 13-8 x 16-2

skylight

peak

open to below

skylight

railing

plant shelf

railing

Br 2 12-8 x 10 10

open to below

UP

DN

linen

Br 3 10-4 x 12

Bonus Rm 16-8 x 10-10

roof

roof

143

Design 20368

BL/ML/RRR/ZIP See Order Pages and Index for Info

FIRST FLOOR

64'-0"

52'-0"

Deck

Family Rm 15-6 x 19-2 vaulted

MBr 1 15 x 13-2 pan vault

Dinette/Kitchen 22 x 13-8 bench

Balcony above

UP DN

desk ov

spa

pantry

Living Rm 13 x 13-8

Foyer vaulted

Dining Rm 11 x 13-8

Garage 21-4 x 31-4

vaulted

Br 2 13-2 x 13-10

shelves

Loft

linen

DN

lin

Br 3 12-6 x 10-8

SECOND FLOOR

Units	Single
Price Code	E
Total Finished	2,372 sq. ft.
First Finished	1,752 sq. ft.
Second Finished	620 sq. ft.
Basement Unfinished	1,726 sq. ft.
Garage Unfinished	714 sq. ft.
Dimensions	64'x52'
Foundation	Basement
	Crawl space, Slab
Bedrooms	3
Full Baths	2
Half Baths	1
First Ceiling	8'
Second Ceiling	8'
Primary Roof Pitch	12:12
Secondary Roof Pitch	7:12
Max Ridge Height	29'6''
Roof Framing	Stick
Exterior Walls	2x4, 2x6

REAR ELEVATION

Design 99068

BL See Order Pages and Index for Info

Units	Single
Price Code	E
Total Finished	2,375 sq. ft.
First Finished	1,770 sq. ft.
Second Finished	605 sq. ft.
Basement Unfinished	1,770 sq. ft.
Garage Unfinished	460 sq. ft.
Dimensions	78'x37'
Foundation	Basement
Bedrooms	3
Full Baths	2
Half Baths	1
Primary Roof Pitch	12:12
Secondary Roof Pitch	9:12
Max Ridge Height	25'
Roof Framing	Stick
Exterior Walls	2x4

BEDROOM 13'-4" x 12'-2"

BATH

CL.

CL.

CL.

BEDROOM 13'-0" x 12'-0"

DN

BALCONY

OPEN TO BELOW

OPEN TO BELOW

SECOND FLOOR

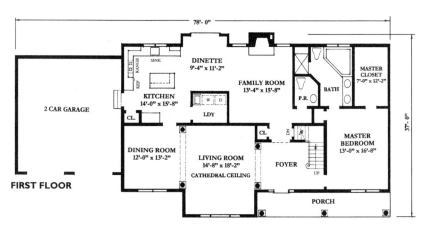

78'-0"

37'-0"

2 CAR GARAGE

REF RANGE SINK

KITCHEN 14'-0" x 15'-8"

DINETTE 9'-4" x 11'-2"

W D

LDY

FAMILY ROOM 13'-4" x 15'-8"

P.R.

BATH

MASTER CLOSET 7'-0" x 12'-2"

CL.

DINING ROOM 12'-0" x 13'-2"

LIVING ROOM 14'-8" x 18'-2" CATHEDRAL CEILING

CL.

DN

FOYER

UP

MASTER BEDROOM 13'-0" x 16'-8"

FIRST FLOOR

PORCH

Design 92546

BL/ML

See Order Pages and Index for Info

Units	Single
Price Code	E
Total Finished	2,387 sq. ft.
Main Finished	2,387 sq. ft.
Garage Unfinished	505 sq. ft.
Porch Unfinished	194 sq. ft.
Dimensions	64'10''×54'10''
Foundation	Crawl space
	Slab
Bedrooms	4
Full Baths	2
Half Baths	1
Main Ceiling	9'
Primary Roof Pitch	8:12
Secondary Roof Pitch	12:12
Max Ridge Height	28'
Roof Framing	Truss
Exterior Wall	2x4

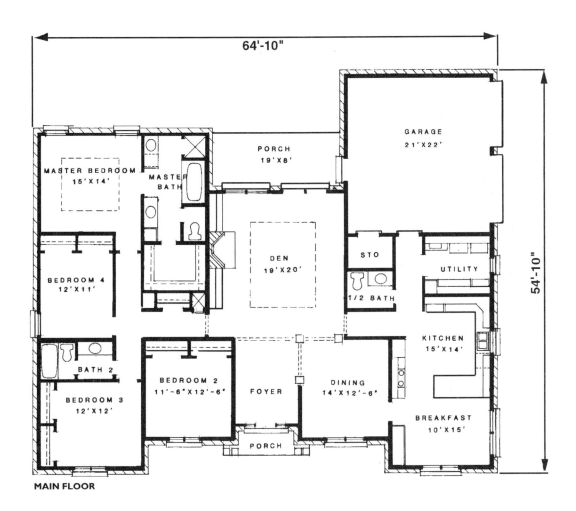

MAIN FLOOR

Design 97879 BL

See Order Pages and Index for Info

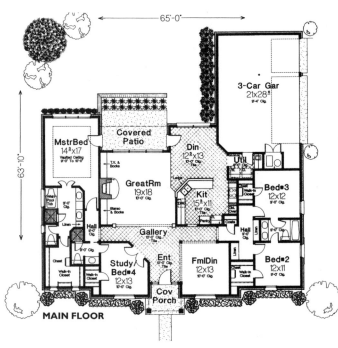

MAIN FLOOR

Units	Single
Price Code	E
Total Finished	2,389 sq. ft.
Main Finished	2,389 sq. ft.
Garage Unfinished	609 sq. ft.
Deck Unfinished	193 sq. ft.
Porch Unfinished	62 sq. ft.
Dimensions	65'x63'10''
Foundation	Slab
Bedrooms	4
Full Baths	3
First Ceiling	9'-10'
Primary Roof Pitch	12:12
Max Ridge Height	28'
Roof Framing	Stick
Exterior Walls	2x4

Design 93033 BL

See Order Pages and Index for Info

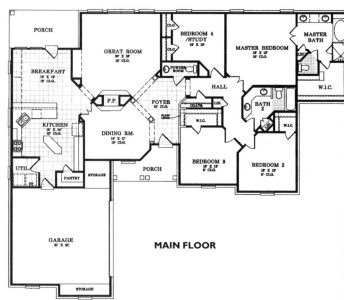

MAIN FLOOR

Units	Single
Price Code	E
Total Finished	2,389 sq. ft.
Main Finished	2,389 sq. ft.
Garage Unfinished	543 sq. ft.
Porch Unfinished	208 sq. ft.
Dimensions	75'2''x61'4''
Foundation	Crawl space
	Slab
Bedrooms	4
Full Baths	2
Half Baths	1
Primary Roof Pitch	8:12
Secondary Roof Pitch	12:12
Max Ridge Height	22'
Roof Framing	Stick
Exterior Walls	2x4

Design 98574

BL

See Order Pages and Index for Info

Units	Single
Price Code	E
Total Finished	2,389 sq. ft.
First Finished	2,389 sq. ft.
Dimensions	65'x63'10''
Foundation	Slab
Bedrooms	4
Full Baths	3
Primary Roof Pitch	12:12
Max Ridge Height	28'
Roof Framing	Stick
Exterior Walls	2x4

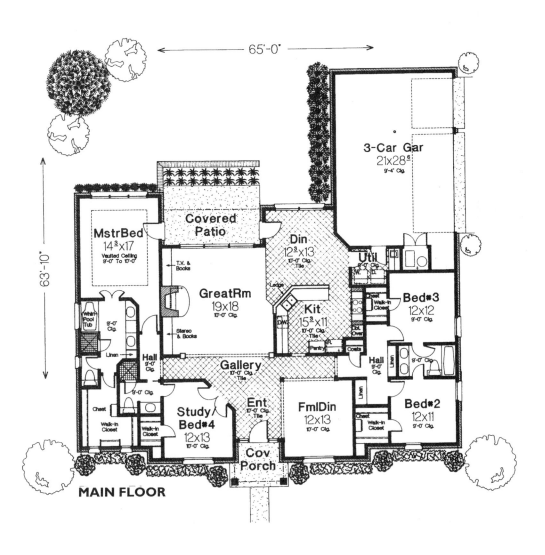

MAIN FLOOR

65'-0"

63'-10"

3-Car Gar
21x28⁶
9'-4" Clg.

MstrBed
14³x17
Vaulted Ceiling
9'-0" To 10'-0"

Covered Patio

Din
12³x13
10'-0" Clg. Tile

Util

Bed#3
12x12
9'-0" Clg.

GreatRm
19x18
10'-0" Clg.

T.V. & Books

Whirl Pool Tub

9'-0" Clg.

Stereo & Books

Kit
15³x11
10'-0" Clg. Tile

Walk-in Closet

Linen

Hall
9'-0" Clg.

Pantry

Hall
10'-0" Clg. Tile

Linen

Gallery
10'-0" Clg. Tile

Chest

Walk-in Closet

Walk-in Closet

Study
Bed#4
12x13
10'-0" Clg.

Ent
10'-0" Clg. Tile

FmlDin
12x13
10'-0" Clg.

Chest

Walk-in Closet

Bed#2
12x11
9'-0" Clg.

Cov Porch

147

Increase the beauty and efficiency of your home ...

Heat-N-Glo Fireplaces

Beauty

If you thought you couldn't enjoy the beauty and warmth of a glowing fireplace in your home, think again. Because Heat-N-Glo's direct vent gas fireplaces don't require a chimney, they can be installed virtually anywhere in your home, under a window, in an entertainment center or even in a bedroom or master bath. Create a dramatic look by using a multi-sided direct vent between rooms or as a bar.

There's something about a warm glowing campfire that draws everyone together. And now, thanks to Heat-N-Glo's gas fireplace technology, a realistic campfire can come to life at a moment's notice right in the comfort of your home.

Value

Installing a fireplace increases the value of your home and offers you one of the best returns on investment for a home upgrade. National studies show that homeowners prefer homes with fireplaces and because Heat-N-Glo's patented direct vent technology vents out the back to the outside, installation of a beautiful and realistic fireplace is made simple. In addition to having the reputation

as the innovation and technology leader, Heat-N-Glo is known throughout the industry as a company that listens to its customers and is responsive to changes in the market. They became ISO9001 certified in 1996, ensuring their goal of providing customers with assurance that products and services delivered will meet and exceed expectations.

Efficiency & Warmth

Nothing brings the family together like the roar of a fire. Now you can have that beautiful ambiance in your home along with true energy efficiency and comfortable warmth.

Heat-N-Glo the innovator in gas fireplaces, invented and patented the first direct vent fireplace in 1987. Direct vents use a sealed combustion chamber that draws air from outside your home through an 8" pipe. The exhaust is then vented through a 5" pipe back outside. These fireplaces never steal the warm air from inside, and deliver the most effective heating design on the market. This effective design also maintains the clean air in your home and does not contribute to the negative pressure concerns so common in today's tightly sealed homes. Because no room air is used for combustion, Heat-N-Glo's direct vents are especially efficient (up to 70%+).

Introduction of this proprietary technology combined with many other industry firsts illustrates Heat-N-Glo's commitment to innovation in fireplaces today and into the future.

Many of Heat-N-Glo's direct vent fireplaces have been A.F.U.E. rated.

This means they have been tested to the same standards as today's energy efficient furnaces. These heater rated furnaces can even be operated by a remote control thermostat. Set the temperature for your room, then sit back and relax in the beautiful glow of the fire while it keeps you toasty warm.

Commitment

At Heat-N-Glo, their goal is to continually develop new products, enhance performance, and maintain a high level of customer satisfaction by developing efficient, clean-burning, convenient, and aesthetically appealing fireplaces, inserts and related products.

Heat-N-Glo, a division of Hearth Technologies, Inc., manufactures a complete line of gas, wood-burning and electric fireplace, insert and stove products. Heat-N-Glo also recently introduced a line of Outdoor Comfort products that includes fireplaces, firepits and grills. ■

No one builds a better fire

HEAT-N-GLO, a division of Hearth Technologies Inc.
20802 Kensington Blvd., Lakeville, MN 55044
(612) 985-6000 • FAX (612) 985-6001 • Email: info@heatnglo.com • www.heatnglo.com

Design 97413

BL

See Order Pages and Index for Info

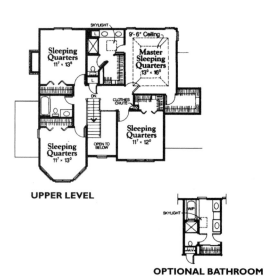

© Design Basics, Inc.

G. MACDONALD

Units	Single
Price Code	E
Total Finished	2,392 sq. ft.
First Finished	1,183 sq. ft.
Second Finished	1,209 sq. ft.
Garage Unfinished	483 sq. ft.
Dimensions	60'x38'
Foundation	Basement
Bedrooms	4
Full Baths	2
Half Baths	1
Primary Roof Pitch	8:12
Secondary Roof Pitch	12:12
Max Ridge Height	28'

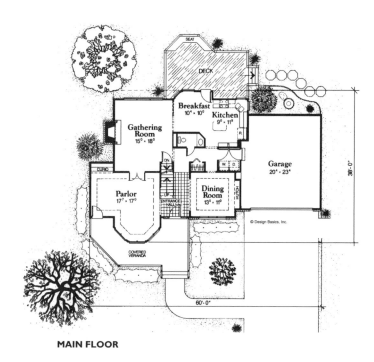

MAIN FLOOR

SEAT

DECK

Breakfast
10⁴ × 10⁰

Kitchen
9⁰ × 11⁹

Gathering Room
15⁰ × 18⁰

Garage
20⁴ × 23⁴

CURIO

Parlor
17⁷ × 17⁰

Dining Room
13⁰ × 11⁰

ENTRANCE HALL

COVERED VERANDA

© Design Basics, Inc.

38'-0"

60'-0"

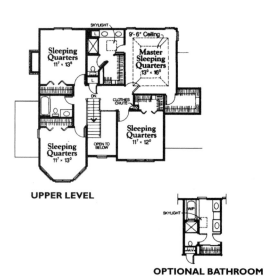

SKYLIGHT

9'-6" Ceiling

Sleeping Quarters
11⁷ × 13⁴

Master Sleeping Quarters
13⁰ × 16⁰

CLOTHES CHUTE

Sleeping Quarters
11⁷ × 13⁰

OPEN TO BELOW

Sleeping Quarters
11⁷ × 12⁰

UPPER LEVEL

SKYLIGHT

OPTIONAL BATHROOM

Design 97143

BL

See Order Pages and Index for Info

Units	Single
Price Code	E
Total Finished	2,396 sq. ft.
First Finished	1,930 sq. ft.
Second Finished	466 sq. ft.
Basement Unfinished	1,930 sq. ft.
Porch Unfinished	217 sq. ft.
Dimensions	62'8"x66'8"
Foundation	Basement
Bedrooms	3
Full Baths	2
Half Baths	1
First Ceiling	9'
Primary Roof Pitch	12:12
Max Ridge Height	33'
Roof Framing	Truss
Exterior Walls	2x6

MAIN FLOOR

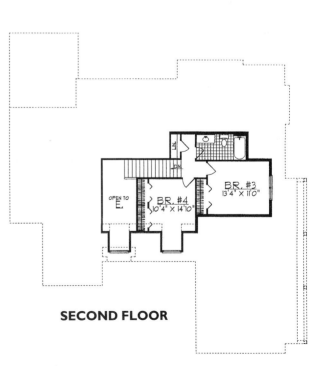

SECOND FLOOR

Design 98144

BL/ML

See Order Pages and Index for Info

© Donald A. Gardner Architects, Inc.

Units	Single
Price Code	G
Total Finished	2,398 sq. ft.
First Finished	1,856 sq. ft.
Second Finished	542 sq. ft.
Bonus Unfinished	366 sq. ft.
Garage Unfinished	570 sq. ft.
Deck Unfinished	161 sq. ft.
Porch Unfinished	50 sq. ft.
Dimensions	45'8"x64'8"
Foundation	Crawl space
Bedrooms	4
Full Baths	3
First Ceiling	9'
Second Ceiling	8'
Primary Roof Pitch	10:12
Secondary Roof Pitch	12:12
Max Ridge Height	28'
Exterior Walls	2x4

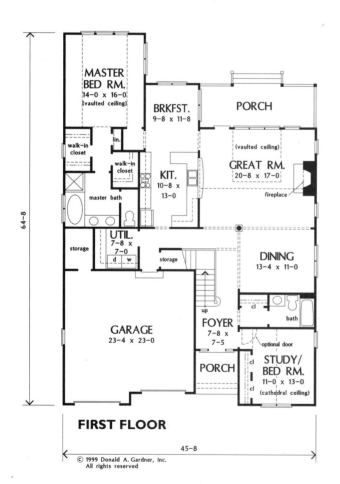

FIRST FLOOR

MASTER BED RM.
14-0 x 16-0
(vaulted ceiling)

walk-in closet

walk-in closet

master bath

lin.

storage

UTIL.
7-8 x 7-0
d w

storage

BRKFST.
9-8 x 11-8

KIT.
10-8 x 13-0

PORCH

GREAT RM.
20-8 x 17-0
(vaulted ceiling)

fireplace

DINING
13-4 x 11-0

GARAGE
23-4 x 23-0

up

FOYER
7-8 x 7-5

cl

bath

optional door

PORCH

STUDY/
BED RM.
11-0 x 13-0
(cathedral ceiling)

cl

cl

64-8

45-8

© 1999 Donald A. Gardner, Inc.
All rights reserved

SECOND FLOOR

great room below

BED RM.
13-0 x 11-0

bath

cl   cl

lin.

down

BED RM.
13-4 x 11-0

BONUS RM.
16-6 x 21-0

foyer below

cl

© 1999 Donald A. Gardner, Inc.
All rights reserved

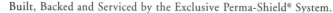

Design 92651

BL/ZIP

See Order Pages and Index for Info

Units	Single
Price Code	E
Total Finished	2,403 sq. ft.
First Finished	1,710 sq. ft.
Second Finished	693 sq. ft.
Basement Unfinished	1,620 sq. ft.
Garage Unfinished	467 sq. ft.
Porch Unfinished	43 sq. ft.
Dimensions	63'4"x48'
Foundation	Basement
	Slab
Bedrooms	4
Full Baths	3
Half Baths	1
First Ceiling	8'
Second Ceiling	8'
Vaulted Ceiling	11'
Tray Ceiling	17'
Primary Roof Pitch	12:8
Secondary Roof Pitch	12:12
Max Ridge Height	20'
Roof Framing	Truss
Exterior Walls	2x4

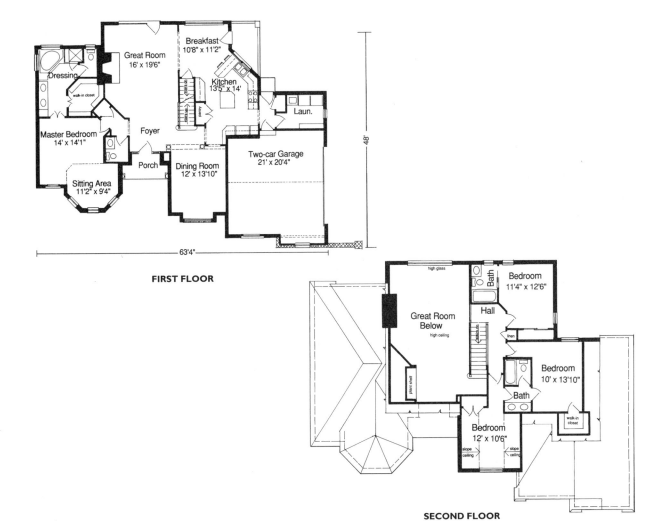

FIRST FLOOR

SECOND FLOOR

Design 98511

BL/ZIP

See Order Pages and Index for Info

Units	Single
Price Code	E
Total Finished	2,445 sq. ft.
First Finished	2,445 sq. ft.
Garage Unfinished	630 sq. ft.
Deck Unfinished	234 sq. ft.
Porch Unfinished	32 sq. ft.
Dimensions	65'x68'8''
Foundation	Crawl space
	Slab
Bedrooms	4
Full Baths	3
Half Baths	1
First Ceiling	9'-12'
Primary Roof Pitch	12:12
Max Ridge Height	32'
Roof Framing	Stick
Exterior Walls	2x4

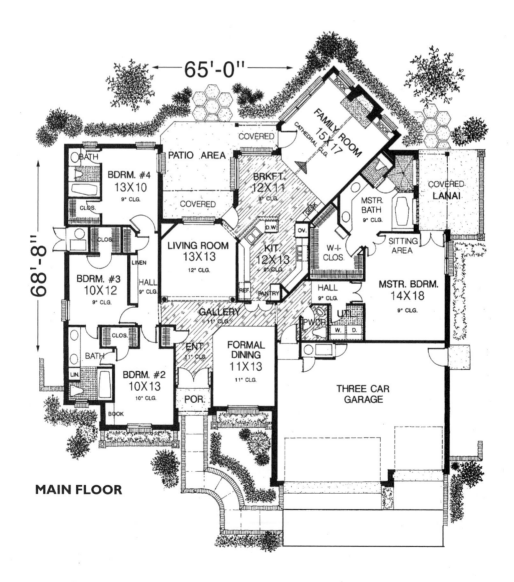

MAIN FLOOR

Design 93147

BL

See Order Pages and Index for Info

Units	Single
Price Code	E
Total Finished	2,451 sq. ft.
First Finished	1,296 sq. ft.
Second Finished	1,155 sq. ft.
Basement Unfinished	1,296 sq. ft.
Dimensions	56'x43'
Foundation	Basement
Bedrooms	4
Full Baths	2
Half Baths	1
Primary Roof Pitch	10:12
Secondary Roof Pitch	8:12
Max Ridge Height	27'
Roof Framing	Stick
Exterior Walls	2x6

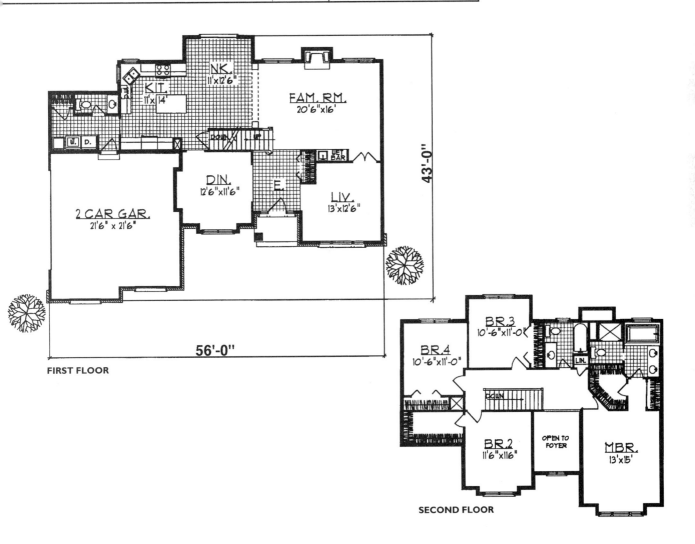

FIRST FLOOR

NK. 11'x12'6"

KIT. 11'x14'

FAM. RM. 20'6"x16'

W. D.

DIN. 12'6"x11'6"

LIV. 13'x12'6"

2 CAR GAR. 21'6" x 21'6"

56'-0"

43'-0"

SECOND FLOOR

BR.4 10'-6"x11'-0"

BR.3 10'-6"x11'-0"

BR.2 11'6"x11'6"

MBR. 13'x15'

OPEN TO FOYER

LIN.

155

Design 94634

BL

See Order Pages and Index for Info

Units	Single
Price Code	E
Total Finished	2,453 sq. ft.
First Finished	1,804 sq. ft.
Second Finished	649 sq. ft.
Porch Unfinished	346 sq. ft.
Dimensions	36'6"x65'6"
Foundation	Crawl space
	Slab
Bedrooms	4
Full Baths	3
First Ceiling	10'
Primary Roof Pitch	10:12
Max Ridge Height	33'6"
Roof Framing	Stick
Exterior Walls	2x4

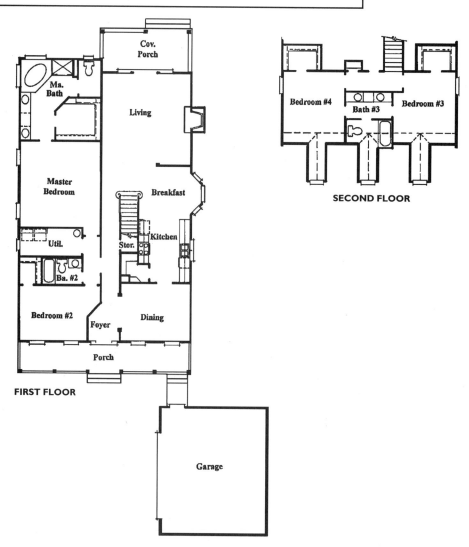

SECOND FLOOR

FIRST FLOOR

Design 98518

BL/ZIP

See Order Pages and Index for Info

Units	Single
Price Code	E
Total Finished	2,455 sq. ft.
First Finished	1,447 sq. ft.
Second Finished	1,008 sq. ft.
Garage Unfinished	756 sq. ft.
Deck Unfinished	220 sq. ft.
Porch Unfinished	210 sq. ft.
Dimensions	65'x37'11"
Foundation	Basement
	Slab
Bedrooms	3
Full Baths	2
Half Baths	1
First Ceiling	9'
Second Ceiling	8'
Primary Roof Pitch	10:12
Max Ridge Height	30'
Roof Framing	Stick
Exterior Walls	2x4

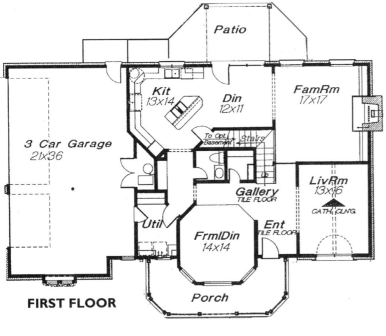

FIRST FLOOR

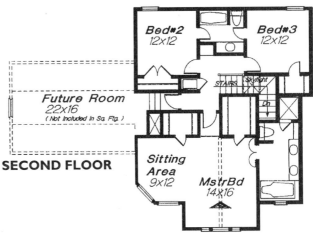

SECOND FLOOR

Design 94638

BL

See Order Pages and Index for Info

Units	Single
Price Code	E
Total Finished	2,461 sq. ft.
First Finished	1,449 sq. ft.
Second Finished	1,012 sq. ft.
Porch Unfinished	109 sq. ft.
Dimensions	44'x52'6"
Foundation	Crawl space
	Slab
Bedrooms	4
Full Baths	2
Half Baths	1
First Ceiling	8'
Second Ceiling	8'
Primary Roof Pitch	12:12
Secondary Roof Pitch	5:12
Roof Framing	Stick
Exterior Walls	2x4

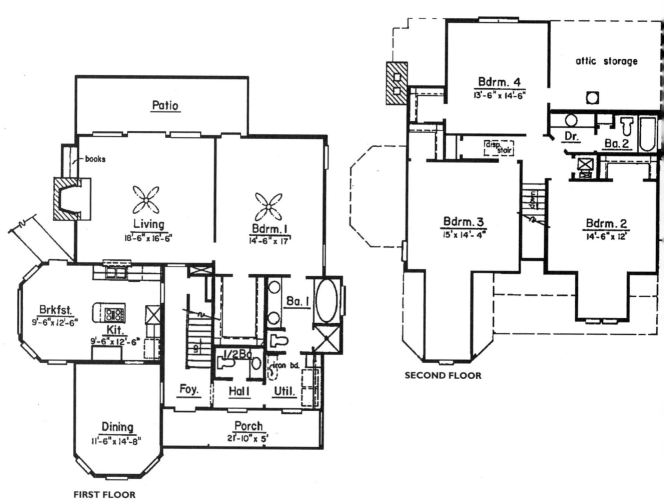

FIRST FLOOR

Patio

books

Living
18'-6" x 16'-6"

Bdrm. 1
14'-6" x 17'

Brkfst.
9'-6" x 12'-6"

Kit.
9'-6" x 12'-6"

Ba. 1

1/2 Ba

iron bd.

Foy.   Hall   Util.

Dining
11'-6" x 14'-8"

Porch
21'-10" x 5'

SECOND FLOOR

attic storage

Bdrm. 4
13'-6" x 14'-6"

disp.
stair

Dr.

Ba. 2

Bdrm. 3
15' x 14'-4"

Bdrm. 2
14'-6" x 12'

Design 93013

BL

See Order Pages and Index for Info

Units	Single
Price Code	E
Total Finished	2,463 sq. ft.
First Finished	1,831 sq. ft.
Second Finished	632 sq. ft.
Garage Unfinished	525 sq. ft.
Dimensions	50'7"x66'2"
Foundation	Slab
Bedrooms	3
Full Baths	2
Half Baths	1
Primary Roof Pitch	8:12
Secondary Roof Pitch	12:12
Max Ridge Height	30
Roof Framing	Stick
Exterior Walls	2x4

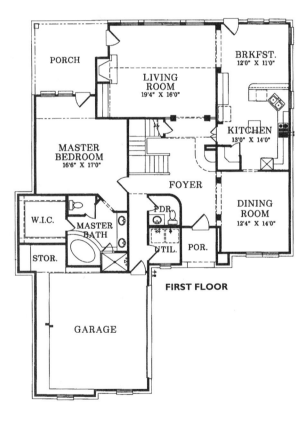

FIRST FLOOR

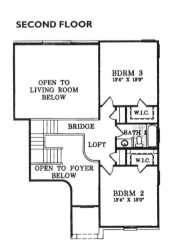

SECOND FLOOR

Design 98335

BL/ML

See Order Pages and Index for Info

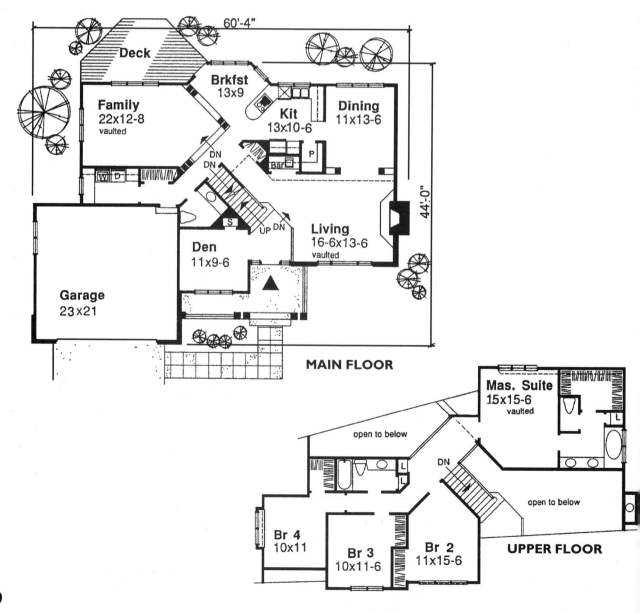

Units	Single
Price Code	E
Total Finished	2,463 sq. ft.
Main Finished	1,380 sq. ft.
Upper Finished	1,083 sq. ft.
Basement Unfinished	1,380 sq. ft.
Garage Unfinished	523 sq. ft.
Porch Unfinished	72 sq. ft.
Dimensions	60'4"×44'
Foundation	Basement
Bedrooms	4
Full Baths	2
Half Baths	1
Primary Roof Pitch	7:12
Secondary Roof Pitch	9:12
Max Ridge Height	26'
Roof Framing	Truss
Exterior Walls	2x4

MAIN FLOOR

Deck

Brkfst 13x9

Family 22x12-8 vaulted

Kit 13x10-6

Dining 11x13-6

DN DN

Bar P

W D

S

UP DN

Den 11x9-6

Living 16-6x13-6 vaulted

Garage 23x21

60'-4"

44'-0"

UPPER FLOOR

Mas. Suite 15x15-6 vaulted

open to below

DN

open to below

Br 4 10x11

Br 3 10x11-6

Br 2 11x15-6

Design 94635

BL

See Order Pages and Index for Info

Units	Single
Price Code	E
Total Finished	2,473 sq. ft.
First Finished	1,504 sq. ft.
Second Finished	969 sq. ft.
Porch Unfinished	212 sq. ft.
Dimensions	36'x53'
Foundation	Crawl space
	Slab
Bedrooms	4
Full Baths	2
Half Baths	1
First Ceiling	10'
Second Ceiling	9'
Primary Roof Pitch	10:12
Max Ridge Height	32'6"
Roof Framing	Stick
Exterior Walls	2x4

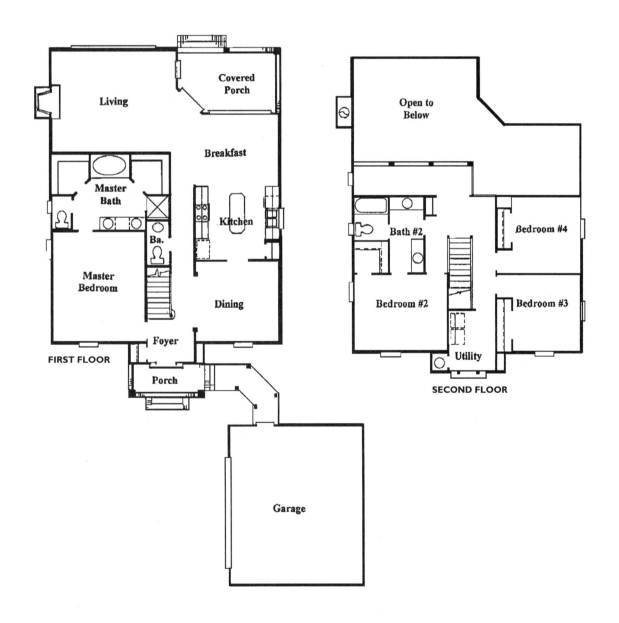

FIRST FLOOR

SECOND FLOOR

Design 91526

BL/ML

See Order Pages and Index for Info

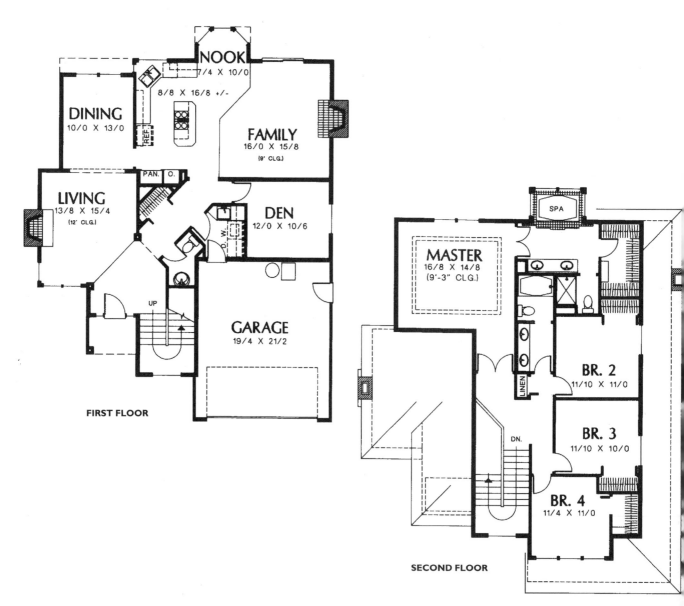

Units	Single
Price Code	E
Total Finished	2,476 sq. ft.
First Finished	1,321 sq. ft.
Second Finished	1,155 sq. ft.
Garage Unfinished	420 sq. ft.
Dimensions	42'x53'4"
Foundation	Crawl space
Bedrooms	4
Full Baths	2
Half Baths	1
Primary Roof Pitch	7:12
Max Ridge Height	27'
Roof Framing	Stick
Exterior Walls	2x6

NOOK
7/4 X 10/0

8/8 X 16/8 +/-

DINING
10/0 X 13/0

FAMILY
16/0 X 15/8
(9' CLG.)

PAN.   O.

LIVING
13/8 X 15/4
(12' CLG.)

DEN
12/0 X 10/6

D. W.

UP

GARAGE
19/4 X 21/2

FIRST FLOOR

SPA

MASTER
16/8 X 14/8
(9'-3" CLG.)

LINEN

BR. 2
11/10 X 11/0

BR. 3
11/10 X 10/0

DN.

BR. 4
11/4 X 11/0

SECOND FLOOR

Design 93163

BL

See Order Pages and Index for Info

Units	Single
Price Code	E
Total Finished	2,477 sq. ft.
First Finished	1,764 sq. ft.
Second Finished	713 sq. ft.
Basement Unfinished	1,764 sq. ft.
Dimensions	61'x52'8''
Foundation	Basement
Bedrooms	4
Full Baths	2
Half Baths	1
Primary Roof Pitch	12:12
Secondary Roof Pitch	8:12
Max Ridge Height	29'6''
Roof Framing	Stick
Exterior Walls	2x6

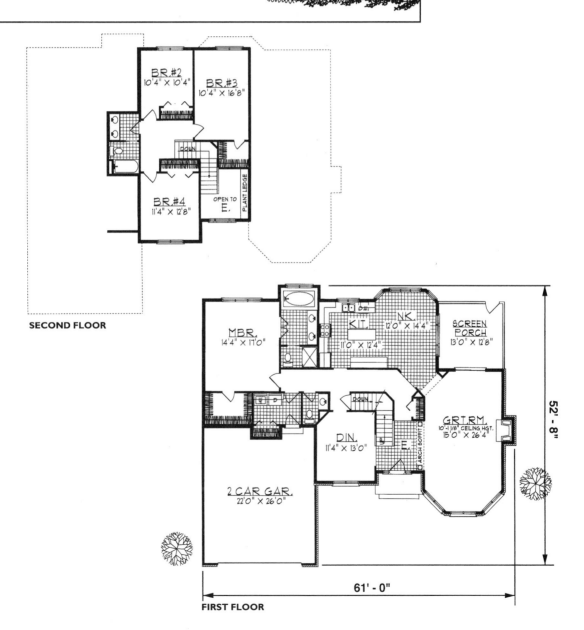

SECOND FLOOR

BR.#2
10'4'' X 10'4''

BR.#3
10'4'' X 16'8''

DOWN

BR.#4
11'4'' X 12'8''

OPEN TO E.

PLANT LEDGE

MBR.
14'4'' X 17'0''

KIT.
11'0'' X 12'4''

NK.
12'0'' X 14'4''

SCREEN PORCH
13'0'' X 12'8''

DOWN

DIN.
11'4'' X 13'0''

ARCH BOFFIT

GRT. RM.
10'-1 1/8'' CEILING HGT.
15'0'' X 26'4''

2 CAR GAR.
22'0'' X 26'0''

52' - 8''

61' - 0''

FIRST FLOOR

Design 93159

BL

See Order Pages and Index for Info

Units	Single
Price Code	E
Total Finished	2,493 sq. ft.
First Finished	1,298 sq. ft.
Second Finished	1,195 sq. ft.
Basement Unfinished	1,298 sq. ft.
Dimensions	66'4"x46'4"
Foundation	Basement
Bedrooms	4
Full Baths	2
Half Baths	1
Primary Roof Pitch	9:12
Secondary Roof Pitch	9:12
Max Ridge Height	29'8"
Roof Framing	Stick
Exterior Walls	2x6

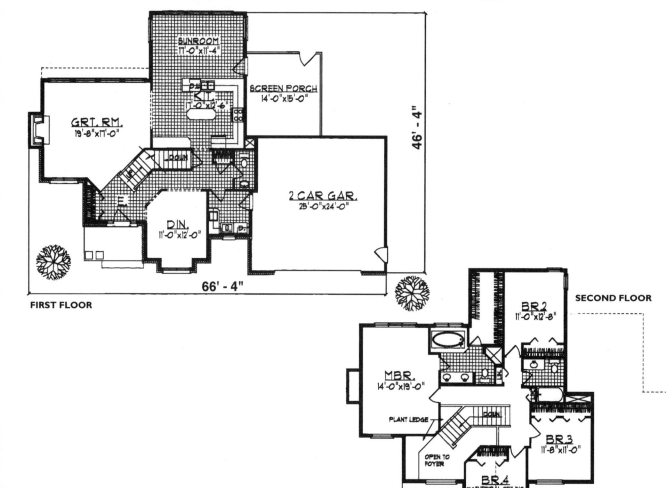

FIRST FLOOR

SUNROOM 11'-0"x11'-4"

SCREEN PORCH 14'-0"x15'-0"

KIT. 11'-0"x12'-6"

GRT. RM. 19'-8"x17'-0"

DOWN

2 CAR GAR. 25'-0"x24'-0"

DIN. 11'-0"x12'-0"

66'-4"

46'-4"

SECOND FLOOR

BR.2 11'-0"x12'-8"

MBR. 14'-0"x19'-0"

PLANT LEDGE

DOWN

BR.3 11'-8"x11'-0"

OPEN TO FOYER

BR.4 CATHEDRAL CEILING 11'-0"x11'-0"

Design 93173

BL

See Order Pages and Index for Info

Units	Single
Price Code	F
Total Finished	2,510 sq. ft.
First Finished	1,982 sq. ft.
Second Finished	528 sq. ft.
Basement Unfinished	1,982 sq. ft.
Porch Unfinished	168 sq. ft.
Dimensions	64'x68'8"
Foundation	Basement
Bedrooms	3
Full Baths	2
Half Baths	1
Primary Roof Pitch	8:12
Secondary Roof Pitch	8:12
Max Ridge Height	24'6"
Roof Framing	Stick
Exterior Walls	2x6

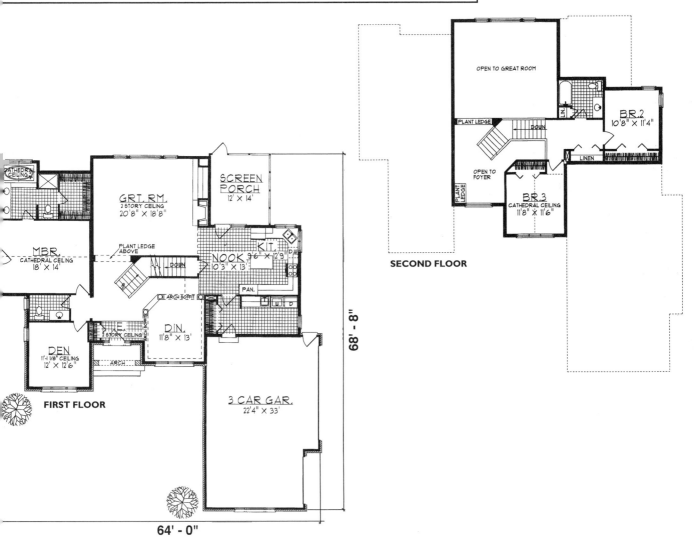

SECOND FLOOR

OPEN TO GREAT ROOM

BR.2
10'8" X 11'4"

BR.3
CATHEDRAL CEILING
11'8" X 11'6"

PLANT LEDGE

OPEN TO FOYER

LIN

LINEN

DOWN

FIRST FLOOR

GRT. RM.
2 STORY CEILING
20'8" X 18'8"

SCREEN PORCH
12' X 14'

KIT.
9'6" X 12'9"

NOOK
10'3" X 13'

MBR
CATHEDRAL CEILING
18' X 14'

PLANT LEDGE ABOVE

DOWN

DIN.
11'8" X 13'

DEN
11'-1 1/8" CEILING
12' X 12'6"

3 CAR GAR.
22'4" X 33'

PAN.

ARCH SOFFIT

68' - 8"

64' - 0"

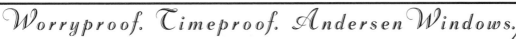

Design 93050

BL   See Order Pages and Index for Info

Units	Single
Price Code	F
Total Finished	2,511 sq. ft.
Main Finished	2,511 sq. ft.
Garage Unfinished	469 sq. ft.
Dimensions	69'x63'6"
Foundation	Crawl space
	Slab
Bedrooms	4
Full Baths	2
Half Baths	1
Primary Roof Pitch	9:12
Secondary Roof Pitch	12:12
Max Ridge Height	21'4"
Roof Framing	Stick
Exterior Walls	2x4

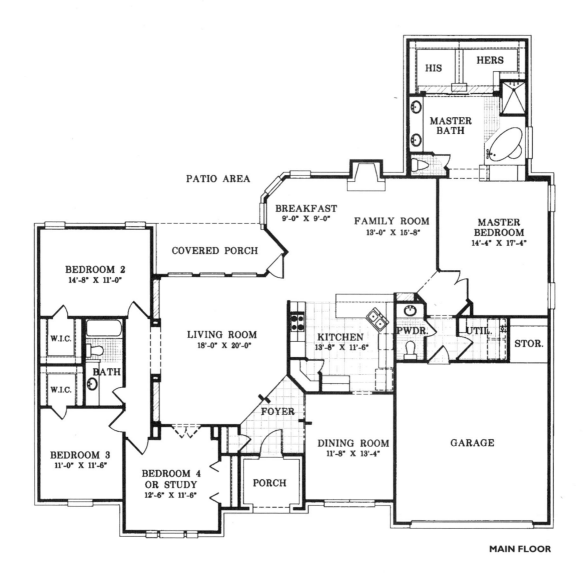

MAIN FLOOR

Design 99161

BL   See Order Pages and Index for Info

Units	Single
Price Code	F
Total Finished	2,513 sq. ft.
First Finished	1,887 sq. ft.
Second Finished	626 sq. ft.
Dimensions	69'4''x53'
Foundation	Basement
Bedrooms	3
Full Baths	2
Half Baths	1
Primary Roof Pitch	10:12
Secondary Roof Pitch	12:12
Max Ridge Height	30'
Roof Framing	Truss
Exterior Walls	2x6

MAIN FLOOR

SECOND FLOOR

Visit us at www.merillat.com

Merillat.

167

Design 86021

BL

See Order Pages and Index for Info

Units	Single
Price Code	F
Total Finished	2,529 sq. ft.
Main Finished	2,529 sq. ft.
Basement Unfinished	2,495 sq. ft.
Garage Unfinished	675 sq. ft.
Deck Unfinished	126 sq. ft.
Porch Unfinished	280 sq. ft.
Dimensions	77'4"x49'4"
Foundation	Basement
Bedrooms	3
Full Baths	2
Primary Roof Pitch	10'8:12
Secondary Roof Pitch	12:12
Max Ridge Height	26'11.2"
Roof Framing	Stick/Truss
Exterior Walls	2x6

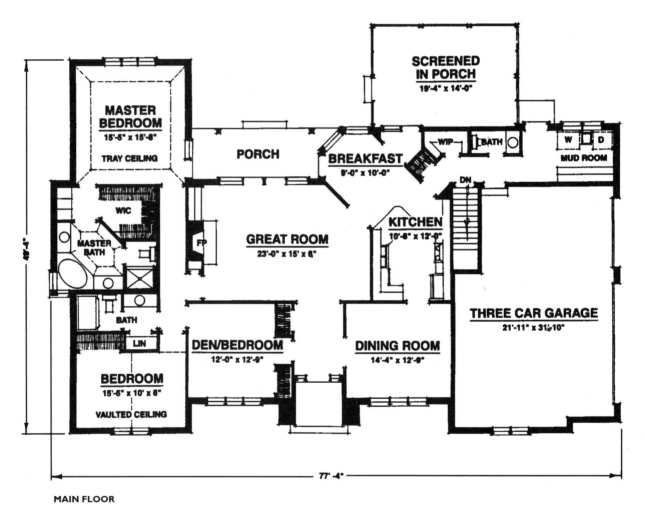

MAIN FLOOR

Design 94643

BL   See Order Pages and Index for Info

Units	Single
Price Code	F
Total Finished	2,533 sq. ft.
First Finished	1,916 sq. ft.
Second Finished	617 sq. ft.
Garage Unfinished	516 sq. ft.
Deck Unfinished	264 sq. ft.
Porch Unfinished	390 sq. ft.
Dimensions	66'x66'
Foundation	Crawl space
	Slab
Bedrooms	4
Full Baths	3
Half Baths	1
Primary Roof Pitch	10:12
Secondary Roof Pitch	12:12
Max Ridge Height	32'
Roof Framing	Stick
Exterior Walls	2x4

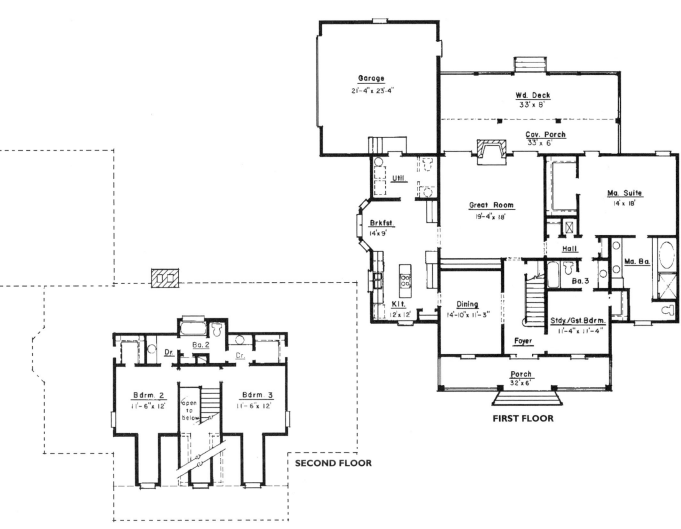

FIRST FLOOR

SECOND FLOOR

Design 91813

BL/ML

See Order Pages and Index for Info

Units	Single
Price Code	F
Total Finished	2,541 sq. ft.
First Finished	1,507 sq. ft.
Second Finished	1,034 sq. ft.
Garage Unfinished	832 sq. ft.
Dimensions	58'x54'7''
Foundation	Basement
	Crawl space
	Slab
Bedrooms	4
Full Baths	3
Primary Roof Pitch	7:12
Exterior Walls	2x6

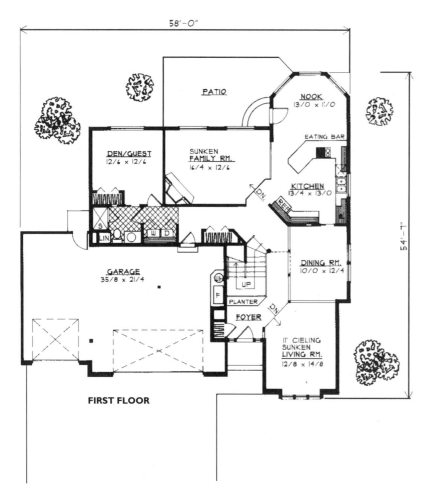

FIRST FLOOR

58'-0"

54'-7"

PATIO

NOOK
13/0 x 11/0

EATING BAR

DEN/GUEST
12/6 x 12/6

SUNKEN
FAMILY RM.
16/4 x 12/6

KITCHEN
13/4 x 13/0

GARAGE
35/8 x 21/4

DINING RM.
10/0 x 12/4

UP

PLANTER

FOYER

11' CIELING
SUNKEN
LIVING RM.
12/8 x 14/8

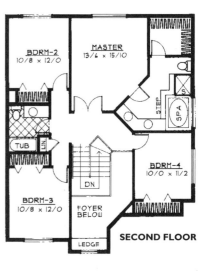

SECOND FLOOR

BDRM-2
10/8 x 12/0

MASTER
13/6 x 15/10

SPA

STEP

TUB

LIN

BDRM-4
10/0 x 11/2

BDRM-3
10/8 x 12/0

DN

FOYER
BELOW

LEDGE

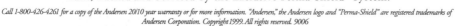

Design 93035

BL

See Order Pages and Index for Info

Units	Single
Price Code	F
Total Finished	2,545 sq. ft.
Main Finished	2,545 sq. ft.
Garage Unfinished	436 sq. ft.
Dimensions	69'x63'6''
Foundation	Crawl space
	Slab
Bedrooms	4
Full Baths	2
Half Baths	1
Primary Roof Pitch	9:12
Secondary Roof Pitch	12:12
Max Ridge Height	23'
Roof Framing	Stick
Exterior Walls	2x4

MAIN FLOOR

HERS HIS

SLOPE CLG   SLOPE CLG

KS

MSTR BATH

ARCH   SEAT

SLOPE CLG →   ← SLOPE CLG

FP

PATIO

BRKFST
9-6x9-6
10 FT CLG

FAMILY RM
13-4x14-8
10 FT CLG

MSTR BEDRM
14-4x17-4
CATHEDRAL CLG

BEDRM 2
14-8x11-0

42" LEDGE   B/C

LIVING RM
17-0x18-8
12 FT CLG

KITCHEN
13-8x12-6
10 FT CLG

PWDR

UTILITY

PAN

BATH
2

OPTIONAL
FR DOORS

SLOPE
CLG

FOYER
DN

DINING RM
11-8x13-4
12 FT CLG

GARAGE

BEDRM 3
11-0x11-6

DN

DN

STUDY/
BEDRM 4
11-6x13-0
COFFERED CLG

PORCH

SLOPE
CLG

© Larry E. Belk

Design 96520

BL/ML   See Order Pages and Index for Info

Units	Single
Price Code	F
Total Finished	2,558 sq. ft.
First Finished	1,577 sq. ft.
Second Finished	981 sq. ft.
Garage Unfinished	484 sq. ft.
Porch Unfinished	977 sq. ft.
Dimensions	84'x54'
Foundation	Crawl space
	Slab
Bedrooms	4
Full Baths	2
Half Baths	1
Primary Roof Pitch	10:12
Secondary Roof Pitch	5:12
Max Ridge Height	26'
Roof Framing	Stick
Exterior Walls	2x4

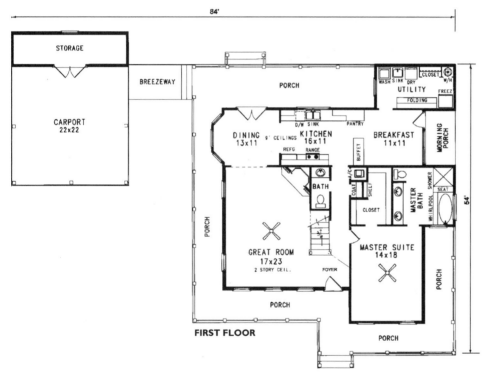

FIRST FLOOR

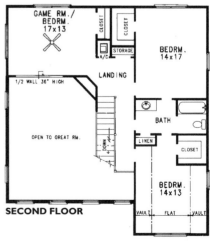

SECOND FLOOR

Design 98112

BL/ML

See Order Pages and Index for Info

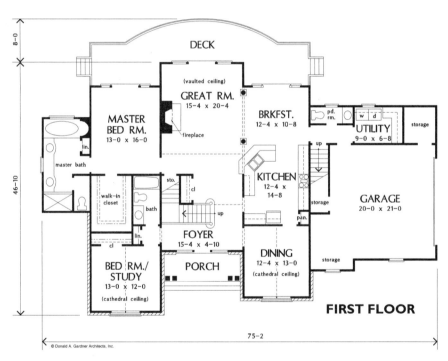

© Donald A. Gardner Architects, Inc.

B. NATHAN

Units	Single
Price Code	H
Total Finished	2,578 sq. ft.
First Finished	1,957 sq. ft.
Second Finished	621 sq. ft.
Bonus Unfinished	396 sq. ft.
Garage Unfinished	569 sq. ft.
Deck Unfinished	351 sq. ft.
Porch Unfinished	72 sq. ft.
Dimensions	75'2"x46'10"
Foundation	Crawl space
Bedrooms	4
Full Baths	3
Half Baths	1
Primary Roof Pitch	10:12
Secondary Roof Pitch	12:12
Max Ridge Height	26'5"
Exterior Walls	2x4

FIRST FLOOR

DECK

GREAT RM.
15-4 x 20-4
(vaulted ceiling)

fireplace

BRKFST.
12-4 x 10-8

pd. rm.

w d

UTILITY
9-0 x 6-8

storage

MASTER BED RM.
13-0 x 16-0

master bath

lin.

walk-in closet

sto.

cl

bath

up

KITCHEN
12-4 x 14-8

up

storage

pan.

GARAGE
20-0 x 21-0

lin.

cl

FOYER
15-4 x 4-10

DINING
12-4 x 13-0
(cathedral ceiling)

storage

BED RM./ STUDY
13-0 x 12-0
(cathedral ceiling)

PORCH

8-0

46-10

75-2

© Donald A. Gardner Architects, Inc.

great room below

railing

BED RM.
13-0 x 12-4

down

bath

BED RM.
12-4 x 12-4

down

BONUS RM.
23-8 x 15-10

cl   cl

cl   cl

foyer below

SECOND FLOOR

Design 10678

BL/ML

See Order Pages and Index for Info

Units	Single
Price Code	F
Total Finished	2,581 sq. ft.
First Finished	1,375 sq. ft.
Second Finished	1,206 sq. ft.
Basement Unfinished	1,375 sq. ft.
Dimensions	52'x49'4''
Foundation	Basement
Bedrooms	3
Full Baths	2
Half Baths	1
Primary Roof Pitch	8:12
Max Ridge Height	35'
Roof Framing	Truss
Exterior Walls	2x6

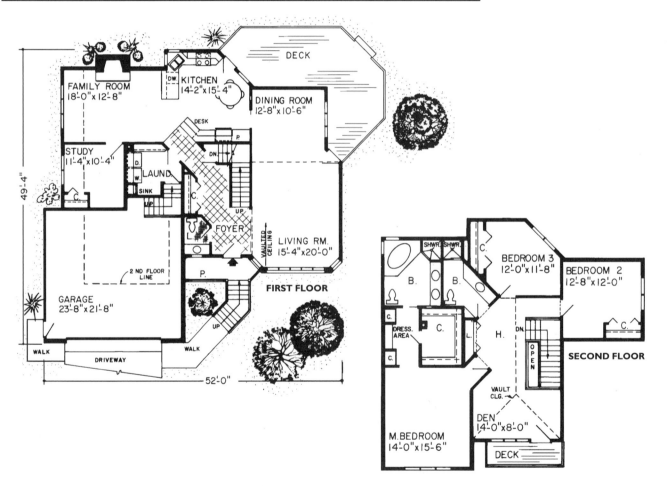

Design 98040

BL/ML

See Order Pages and Index for Info

© Donald A. Gardner Architects, Inc.

B. NATHAN.

Units	Single
Price Code	H
Total Finished	2,587 sq. ft.
First Finished	1,572 sq. ft.
Second Finished	1,015 sq. ft.
Bonus Unfinished	380 sq. ft.
Garage Unfinished	603 sq. ft.
Dimensions	63'10"x58'10"
Foundation	Crawl space
Bedrooms	4
Full Baths	3
First Ceiling	9
Second Ceiling	9
Primary Roof Pitch	12:12
Secondary Roof Pitch	5:12
Max Ridge Height	34'6"
Roof Framing	Stick
Exterior Walls	2x4

FIRST FLOOR

SCREEN PORCH
16-2 x 12-1
(cathedral ceiling)

PORCH

DINING
12-0 x 14-4

KIT.
12-4 x 16-10

BRKFST.
11-0 x 10-6

GREAT RM.
15-6 x 24-8
(cathedral ceiling)

fireplace

sto.

pan.

cl

UTIL.
7-0 x 11-4

bath

w d

up
(two story)

FOYER
8-4 x 9-6

BED RM./
STUDY
11-4 x 11-8

cl

cl

PORCH

GARAGE
21-0 x 23-4

storage

58-10

63-10

© Donald A. Gardner Architects, Inc.

SECOND FLOOR

BED RM.
14-4 x 12-0

cl cl

MASTER
BED RM.
14-4 x 12-10

master
bath

walk-in
closet

lin.

lin.

down

down

foyer
below

cl

BED RM.
11-4 x 11-8

bath

cl

sto.

skylights

BONUS RM.
15-6 x 17-8

Design 99144

BL

See Order Pages and Index for Info

Units	Single
Price Code	F
Total Finished	2,588 sq. ft.
First Finished	1,423 sq. ft.
Second Finished	1,165 sq. ft.
Bonus Unfinished	250 sq. ft.
Basement Unfinished	1,423 sq. ft.
Dimensions	60'4"x46'
Foundation	Basement
Bedrooms	3
Full Baths	2
Half Baths	1
Primary Roof Pitch	7:12
Secondary Roof Pitch	9:12
Max Ridge Height	30'5"
Roof Framing	Truss
Exterior Walls	2x6

FIRST FLOOR

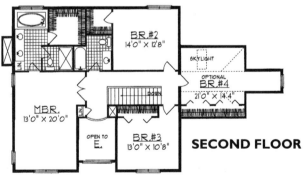

SECOND FLOOR

Design 96411

BL/ML/RRR See Order Pages and Index for Info

Units	Single
Price Code	H
Total Finished	2,596 sq. ft.
First Finished	1,939 sq. ft.
Second Finished	657 sq. ft.
Bonus Unfinished	386 sq. ft.
Garage Unfinished	526 sq. ft.
Porch Unfinished	897 sq. ft.
Dimensions	80'10''x55'8''
Foundation	Crawl space
Bedrooms	4
Full Baths	3
First Ceiling	9'
Second Ceiling	9'
Primary Roof Pitch	12:12
Max Ridge Height	30'2''
Roof Framing	Stick
Exterior Walls	2x4

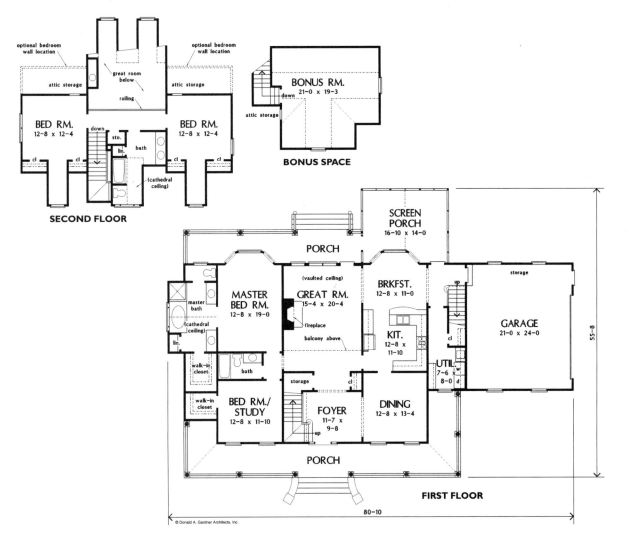

© Donald A. Gardner Architects, Inc.

Design 99894

BL/ML/RRR See Order Pages and Index for Info

© Donald A. Gardner Architects, Inc.

B. NATHAN

Units	Single
Price Code	H
Total Finished	2,602 sq. ft.
First Finished	1,871 sq. ft.
Second Finished	731 sq. ft.
Bonus Unfinished	402 sq. ft.
Garage Unfinished	600 sq. ft.
Dimensions	77'6"x70'0"
Foundation	Crawl space
Bedrooms	4
Full Baths	3
First Ceiling	9'
Second Ceiling	8'
Primary Roof Pitch	11:12
Secondary Roof Pitch	12:12
Max Ridge Height	28
Roof Framing	Stick
Exterior Walls	2x4

MAIN FLOOR

© Donald A. Gardner Architects, Inc.

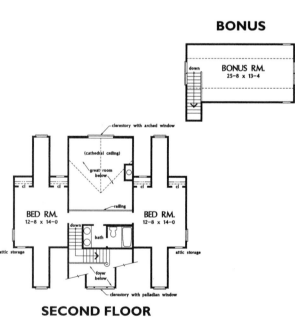

BONUS

BONUS RM.
25-8 x 13-4

SECOND FLOOR

Design 97715

BL

See Order Pages and Index for Info

Units	Single
Price Code	F
Total Finished	2,603 sq. ft.
First Finished	1,836 sq. ft.
Second Finished	767 sq. ft.
Basement Unfinished	1,836 sq. ft.
Dimensions	58'6''x61'
Foundation	Basement
Bedrooms	4
Full Baths	3
Half Baths	1
Primary Roof Pitch	8:12
Secondary Roof Pitch	10:12
Max Ridge Height	29'
Roof Framing	Truss
Exterior Walls	2x4

FIRST FLOOR

SECOND FLOOR

179

Design 93709

BL

See Order Pages and Index for Info

Units	Single
Price Code	F
Total Finished	2,607 sq. ft.
First Finished	1,910 sq. ft.
Second Finished	697 sq. ft.
Garage Unfinished	536 sq. ft.
Deck Unfinished	192 sq. ft.
Porch Unfinished	26 sq. ft.
Dimensions	58'4"x58'4"
Foundation	Crawl space
Bedrooms	4
Full Baths	2
Half Baths	1
Primary Roof Pitch	10:12
Max Ridge Height	29'8"
Roof Framing	Stick
Exterior Walls	2x4

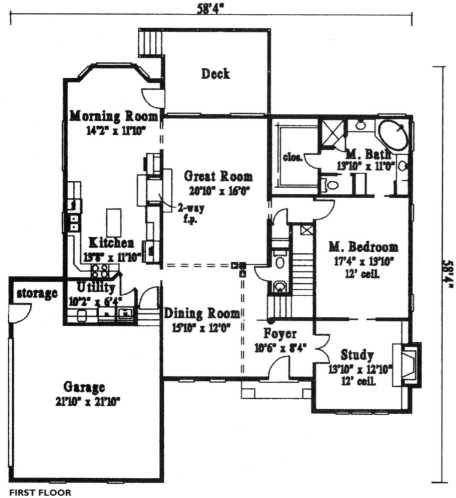

58'4"

Deck

Morning Room
14'2" x 11'10"

Great Room
20'10" x 16'0"

2-way f.p.

clos.

M. Bath
13'10" x 11'0"

Kitchen
15'8" x 11'10"

M. Bedroom
17'4" x 13'10"
12' ceil.

Utility
10'2" x 6'4"

storage

Dining Room
15'10" x 12'0"

Foyer
10'6" x 8'4"

Study
13'10" x 12'10"
12' ceil.

Garage
21'10" x 21'10"

58'4"

FIRST FLOOR

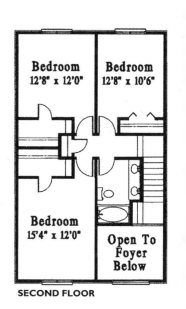

Bedroom
12'8" x 12'0"

Bedroom
12'8" x 10'6"

Bedroom
15'4" x 12'0"

Open To Foyer Below

SECOND FLOOR

Design 93407

BL/RRR

See Order Pages and Index for Info

Units	Single
Price Code	F
Total Finished	2,613 sq. ft.
First Finished	1,625 sq. ft.
Second Finished	988 sq. ft.
Basement Unfinished	1,625 sq. ft.
Garage Unfinished	491 sq. ft.
Dimensions	59'x50'
Foundation	Basement
Bedrooms	4
Full Baths	2
Half Baths	1
Primary Roof Pitch	10:12
Secondary Roof Pitch	6:12
Max Ridge Height	32'
Roof Framing	Stick
Exterior Walls	2x4

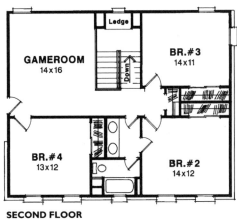

SECOND FLOOR

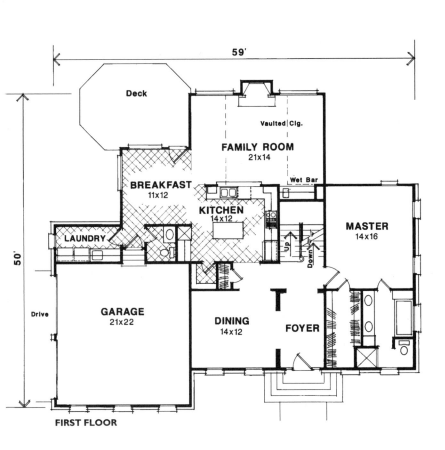

FIRST FLOOR

Design 99146

BL

See Order Pages and Index for Info

Units	Single
Price Code	G
Total Finished	2,629 sq. ft.
First Finished	2,629 sq. ft.
Basement Unfinished	2,629 sq. ft.
Dimensions	65'x72'
Foundation	Basement
Bedrooms	3
Full Baths	2
Half Baths	1
Primary Roof Pitch	8:12
Secondary Roof Pitch	12:12
Max Ridge Height	27'5"
Roof Framing	Truss
Exterior Walls	2x6

MAIN FLOOR

DESIGN 94637

BL

See Order Pages and Index for Info

Units	Single
Price Code	F
Total Finished	2,664 sq. ft.
First Finished	1,977 sq. ft.
Second Finished	687 sq. ft.
Bonus Unfinished	346 sq. ft.
Garage Unfinished	487 sq. ft.
Porch Unfinished	668 sq. ft.
Dimensions	69'6''x69'8.5''
Foundation	Crawl space
Bedrooms	4
Full Baths	3
Primary Roof Pitch	14:12
Secondary Roof Pitch	12:12
Roof Framing	Stick
Exterior Walls	2x4

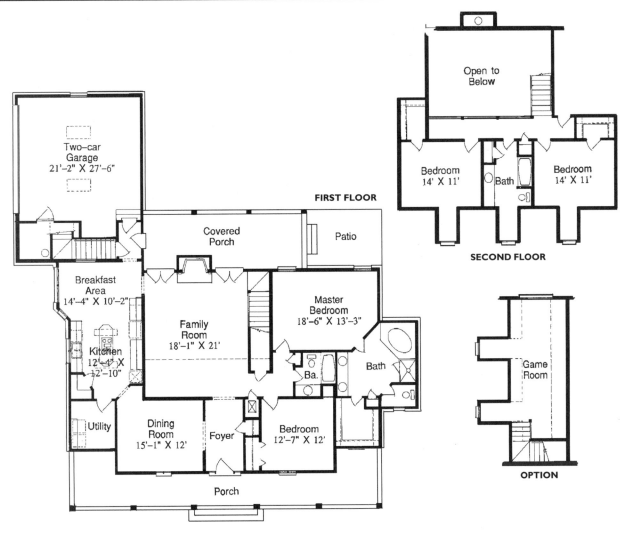

FIRST FLOOR

Two-car Garage
21'-2" X 27'-6"

Breakfast Area
14'-4" X 10'-2"

Kitchen
12'-4" X 12'-10"

Family Room
18'-1" X 21'

Covered Porch

Patio

Master Bedroom
18'-6" X 13'-3"

Ba.

Bath

Dining Room
15'-1" X 12'

Foyer

Bedroom
12'-7" X 12'

Utility

Porch

SECOND FLOOR

Open to Below

Bedroom
14' X 11'

Bath

Bedroom
14' X 11'

OPTION

Game Room

Design 97192

BL

See Order Pages and Index for Info

Units	Single
Price Code	F
Total Finished	2,673 sq. ft.
First Finished	2,018 sq. ft.
Second Finished	655 sq. ft.
Basement Unfinished	2,018 sq. ft.
Porch Unfinished	224 sq. ft.
Dimensions	81'x53'
Foundation	Basement
Bedrooms	3
Full Baths	2
Half Baths	1
Primary Roof Pitch	8:12
Secondary Roof Pitch	10:12
Max Ridge Height	30'
Roof Framing	Truss
Exterior Walls	2x6

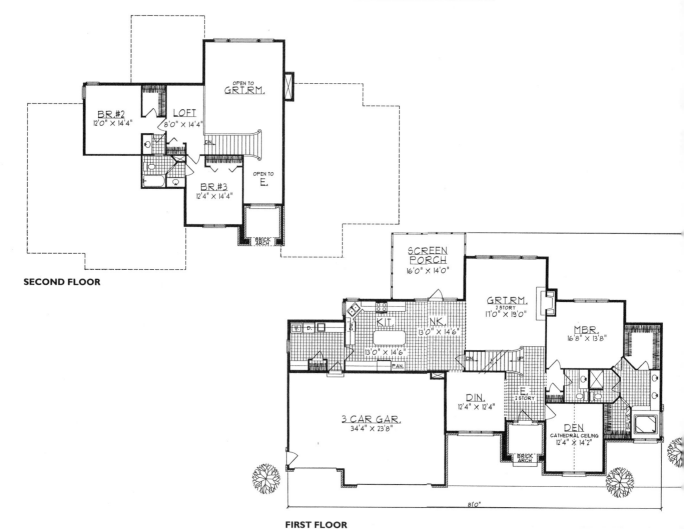

SECOND FLOOR

FIRST FLOOR

Design 99853

BL/ML/ZIP/RRR See Order Pages and Index for Info

© Donald A. Gardner Architects, Inc.

Units	Single
Price Code	H
Total Finished	2,692 sq. ft.
First Finished	1,734 sq. ft.
Second Finished	958 sq. ft.
Dimensions	55'x59'10''
Foundation	Crawl space
Bedrooms	4
Full Baths	3
Half Baths	1
First Ceiling	8'
Second Ceiling	8'
Primary Roof Pitch	6:12
Secondary Roof Pitch	12:12
Max Ridge Height	27'
Roof Framing	Stick
Exterior Walls	2x4

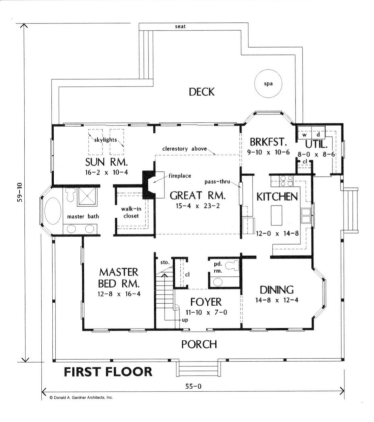

FIRST FLOOR

© Donald A. Gardner Architects, Inc.

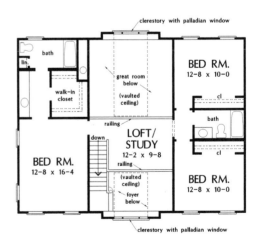

SECOND FLOOR

Design 93332

BL   See Order Pages and Index for Info

Units	Single
Price Code	F
Total Finished	2,707 sq. ft.
First Finished	1,484 sq. ft.
Second Finished	1,223 sq. ft.
Basement Unfinished	1,484 sq. ft.
Dimensions	82'x48'8''
Foundation	Basement
Bedrooms	3
Full Baths	2
Half Baths	1
First Ceiling	9'
Second Ceiling	8'
Primary Roof Pitch	12:12
Secondary Roof Pitch	5:12
Max Ridge Height	32'
Roof Framing	Stick
Exterior Walls	2x4

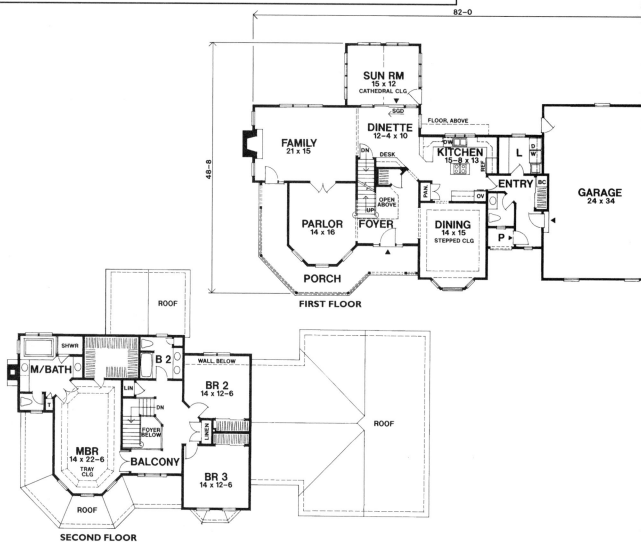

FIRST FLOOR

82-0

48-8

SUN RM 15 x 12 CATHEDRAL CLG
DINETTE 12-4 x 10
FAMILY 21 x 15
KITCHEN 15-8 x 13
FLOOR, ABOVE
DESK
DN
PAN.
OPEN ABOVE
UP
ENTRY
GARAGE 24 x 34
PARLOR 14 x 16
FOYER
DINING 14 x 15 STEPPED CLG
PORCH

SECOND FLOOR

ROOF
M/BATH
SHWR
B 2
WALL BELOW
LIN
BR 2 14 x 12-6
ROOF
DN
FOYER BELOW
LINEN
MBR 14 x 22-6 TRAY CLG
BALCONY
BR 3 14 x 12-6
ROOF

Visit us at www.merillat.com

186   Merillat.

Design 99160

BL

See Order Pages and Index for Info

Units	Single
Price Code	F
Total Finished	2,731 sq. ft.
First Finished	1,692 sq. ft.
Lower Finished	1,039 sq. ft.
Basement Unfinished	653 sq. ft.
Garage Unfinished	751 sq. ft.
Deck Unfinished	205 sq. ft.
Dimensions	67'x58'
Foundation	Basement
Bedrooms	3
Full Baths	3
Primary Roof Pitch	8:12
Max Ridge Height	24'
Roof Framing	Truss
Exterior Walls	2x6

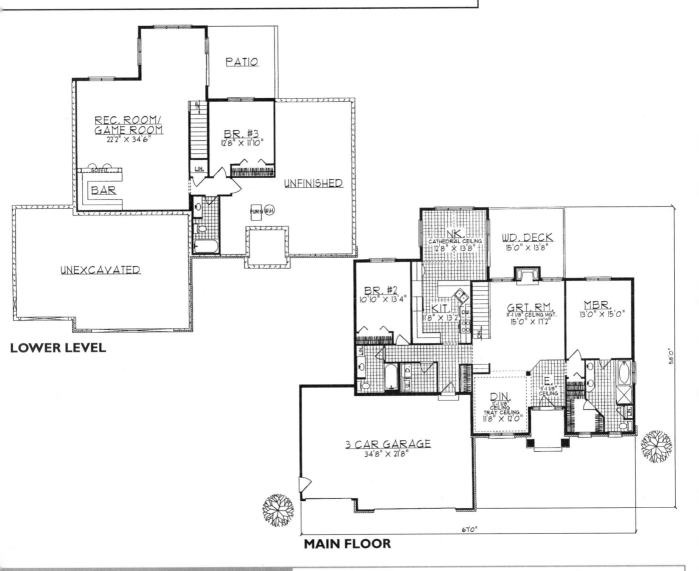

LOWER LEVEL

PATIO

REC. ROOM/ GAME ROOM
22'2" X 34'6"

BAR

SOFFIT

BR. #3
12'8" X 11'10"

LIN.

UNFINISHED

FURN. W.H.

UNEXCAVATED

NK.
CATHEDRAL CEILING
12'8" X 13'8"

WD. DECK
15'0" X 13'8"

BR. #2
10'10" X 13'4"

KIT.
11'8" X 13'2"

GRT. RM.
11'-1 1/8" CEILING HGT.
15'0" X 17'2"

MBR.
13'0" X 15'0"

DIN.
11'-1 1/8" CEILING
TRAY CEILING
11'8" X 12'0"

11'-1 1/8" CEILING

3 CAR GARAGE
34'8" X 21'8"

58'-0"

67'-0"

MAIN FLOOR

Design 94631

BL

See Order Pages and Index for Info

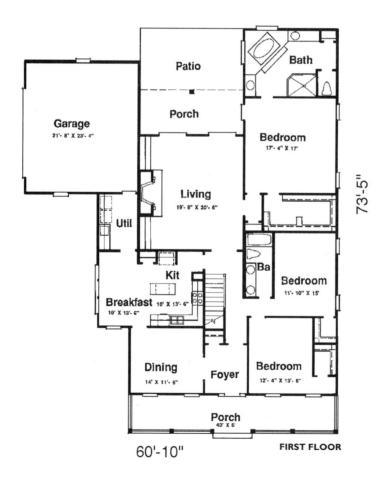

Units	Single
Price Code	F
Total Finished	2,732 sq. ft.
First Finished	2,346 sq. ft.
Second Finished	386 sq. ft.
Garage Unfinished	530 sq. ft.
Porch Unfinished	436 sq. ft.
Dimensions	60'10"x73'5"
Foundation	Crawl space
	Slab
Bedrooms	4
Full Baths	3
First Ceiling	9'
Second Ceiling	8'
Primary Roof Pitch	10:12
Secondary Roof Pitch	6:12
Max Ridge Height	26'
Roof Framing	Stick
Exterior Walls	2x4

Bath
13'- 2" X 13'- 9"

Bedroom

SECOND FLOOR

Garage
21'- 8" X 23'- 4"

Patio

Porch

Bath

Bedroom
17'- 4" X 17'

Living
19'- 8" X 20'- 6"

Util

73'-5"

Kit

Ba

Bedroom
11'- 10" X 15'

Breakfast 10' X 13'- 6"
10' X 13'- 6"

Dining
14' X 11'- 8"

Foyer

Bedroom
12'- 4" X 13'- 6"

Porch
40' X 6'

60'-10"

FIRST FLOOR

Design 91560

BL/ML/RRR   See Order Pages and Index for Info

Units	Single
Price Code	F
Total Finished	2,739 sq. ft.
First Finished	1,470 sq. ft.
Second Finished	1,269 sq. ft.
Dimensions	70'x47'
Foundation	Crawl space
Bedrooms	4
Full Baths	2
Half Baths	1
Primary Roof Pitch	10:12
Max Ridge Height	33'
Roof Framing	Truss
Exterior Walls	2x6

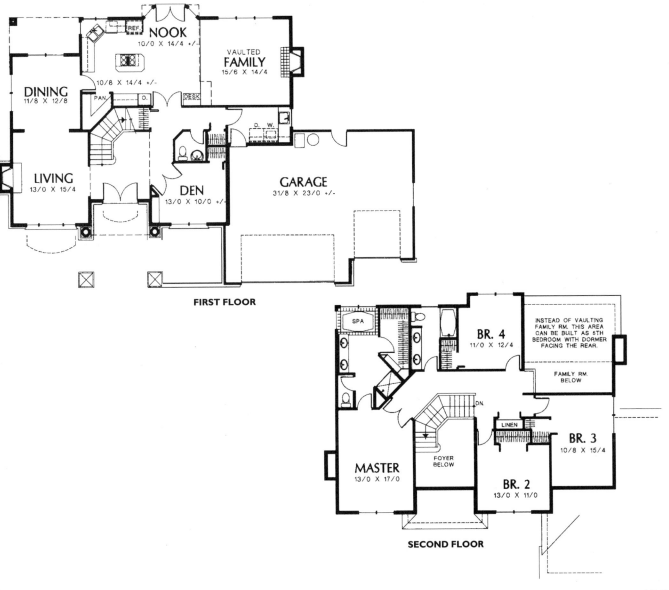

FIRST FLOOR

NOOK 10/0 X 14/4

VAULTED FAMILY 15/6 X 14/4

10/8 X 14/4 +/-

DINING 11/8 X 12/8

LIVING 13/0 X 15/4

DEN 13/0 X 10/0 +/-

GARAGE 31/8 X 23/0 +/-

SECOND FLOOR

SPA

BR. 4 11/0 X 12/4

INSTEAD OF VAULTING FAMILY RM. THIS AREA CAN BE BUILT AS 5TH BEDROOM WITH DORMER FACING THE REAR.

FAMILY RM. BELOW

MASTER 13/0 X 17/0

FOYER BELOW

LINEN

BR. 3 10/8 X 15/4

BR. 2 13/0 X 11/0

189

Design 99128

BL

See Order Pages and Index for Info

Units	Single
Price Code	G
Total Finished	2,751 sq. ft.
First Finished	1,888 sq. ft.
Second Finished	863 sq. ft.
Basement Unfinished	1,888 sq. ft.
Dimensions	86'x39'
Foundation	Basement
Bedrooms	4
Full Baths	2
Half Baths	1
First Ceiling	9'
Second Ceiling	8'
Primary Roof Pitch	12:12
Secondary Roof Pitch	9:12
Max Ridge Height	32'6"
Roof Framing	Truss
Exterior Walls	2x6

SECOND FLOOR

OPEN TO FAM. RM.

BR. #2
15'4" × 12'4"

LIN.

BR. #4
12'0" × 12'0"

OPEN TO E.

BR. #3
12'0" × 16'0"

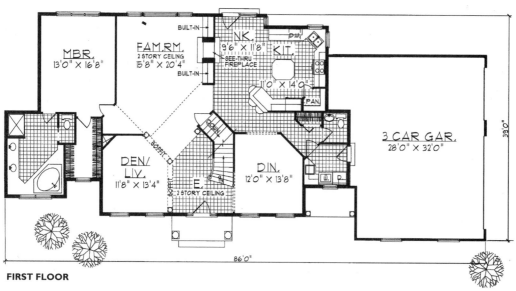

FIRST FLOOR

MBR.
13'0" × 16'8"

FAM. RM.
2 STORY CEILING
15'8" × 20'4"

BUILT-IN

BUILT-IN

NK.
9'6" × 11'8"

KIT.
11'0" × 14'0"

SEE-THRU FIREPLACE

PAN.

DEN/LIV.
11'8" × 13'4"

E.
2 STORY CEILING

DIN.
12'0" × 13'8"

3 CAR GAR.
28'0" × 32'0"

39'0"

86'0"

Merillat

Visit us at www.merillat.com

Design 90483

BL/ML

See Order Pages and Index for Info

Units	Single
Price Code	G
Total Finished	2,754 sq. ft.
First Finished	1,822 sq. ft.
Second Finished	932 sq. ft.
Basement Unfinished	1,822 sq. ft.
Garage Unfinished	484 sq. ft.
Deck Unfinished	312 sq. ft.
Dimensions	53'10"x50'5"
Foundation	Basement
	Crawl space
Bedrooms	3
Full Baths	2
Half Baths	1
Primary Roof Pitch	12:12
Max Ridge Height	27'8"
Roof Framing	Stick
Exterior Walls	2x4

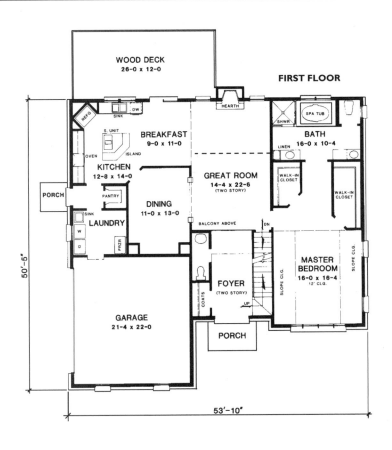

FIRST FLOOR

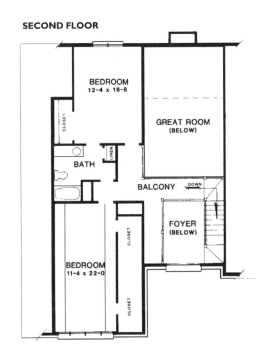

SECOND FLOOR

Design 97868

BL   See Order Pages and Index for Info

Units	Single
Price Code	G
Total Finished	2,757 sq. ft.
Main Finished	2,757 sq. ft.
Garage Unfinished	682 sq. ft.
Deck Unfinished	220 sq. ft.
Porch Unfinished	40 sq. ft.
Dimensions	64'x76'4''
Foundation	Slab
Bedrooms	4
Full Baths	3
First Ceiling	9'-11'
Primary Roof Pitch	12:12
Max Ridge Height	32'6''
Roof Framing	Stick
Exterior Walls	2x4

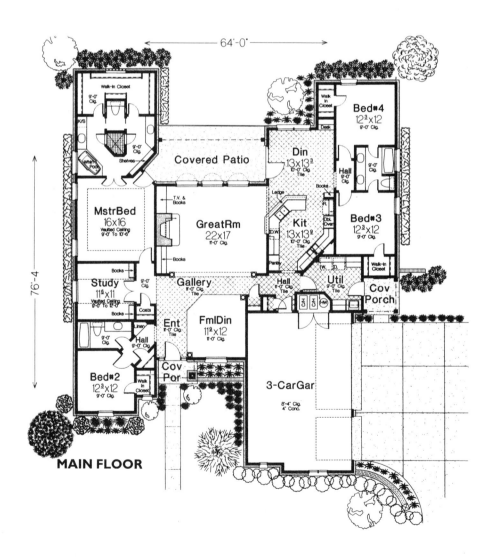

MAIN FLOOR

Design 32101

BL/ML/ZIP

See Order Pages and Index for Info

Photography supplied by the Meredith Corporation

Units	Single
Price Code	G
Total Finished	2,764 sq. ft.
First Finished	1,546 sq. ft.
Second Finished	1,218 sq. ft.
Bonus Unfinished	403 sq. ft.
Garage Unfinished	624 sq. ft.
Deck Unfinished	90 sq. ft.
Porch Unfinished	410 sq. ft.
Dimensions	89'x63'8''
Foundation	Crawl space
Bedrooms	3
Full Baths	2
Half Baths	1
First Ceiling	10'
Second Ceiling	8'
Primary Roof Pitch	12:12
Max Ridge Height	35'6''
Roof Framing	Stick
Exterior Walls	2x4

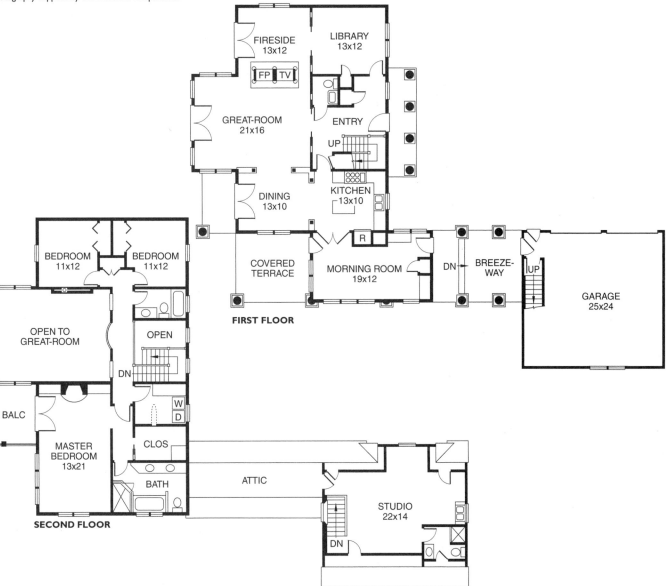

FIRST FLOOR

SECOND FLOOR

193

Design 93609

BL

See Order Pages and Index for Info

Units	Single
Price Code	G
Total Finished	2,771 sq. ft.
First Finished	1,535 sq. ft.
Second Finished	1,236 sq. ft.
Garage Unfinished	418 sq. ft.
Deck Unfinished	100 sq. ft.
Dimensions	54'x45'4"
Foundation	Basement
	Slab
Bedrooms	4
Full Baths	2
Half Baths	1
Primary Roof Pitch	8:12
Secondary Roof Pitch	12:12
Max Ridge Height	29'
Roof Framing	Stick
Exterior Walls	2x4

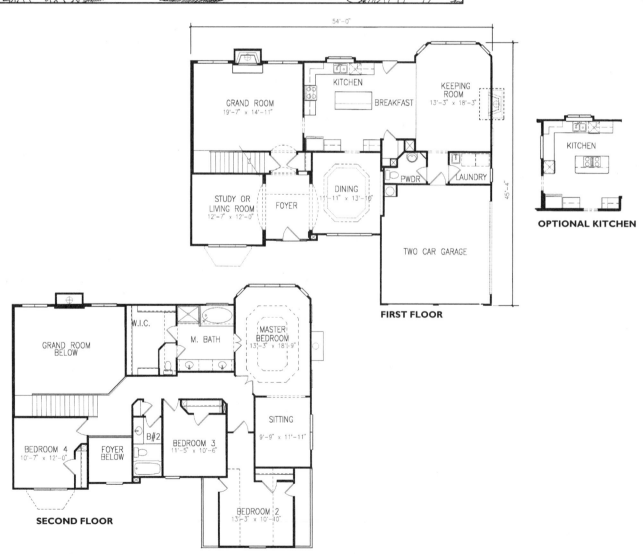

OPTIONAL KITCHEN

FIRST FLOOR

SECOND FLOOR

Visit us at www.merillat.com

Merillat.

DESIGN 93068

BL

See Order Pages and Index for Info

Units	Single
Price Code	G
Total Finished	2,777 sq. ft.
Main Finished	2,777 sq. ft.
Garage Unfinished	501 sq. ft.
Porch Unfinished	88 sq. ft.
Dimensions	88'4''x54'9''
Foundation	Slab
Bedrooms	4
Full Baths	2
Half Baths	1
Main Ceiling	10'8''
Primary Roof Pitch	9:12
Secondary Roof Pitch	12:12
Max Ridge Height	21'8''
Roof Framing	Stick
Exterior Walls	2x4

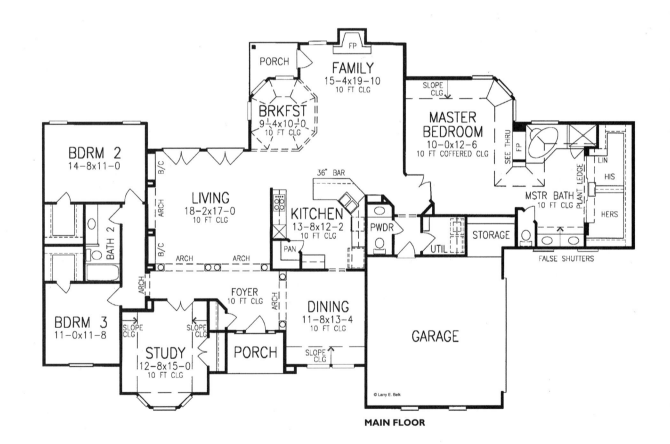

MAIN FLOOR

© Larry E. Belk

Design 93274

BL

See Order Pages and Index for Info

Units	Single
Price Code	G
Total Finished	2,796 sq. ft.
First Finished	1,358 sq. ft.
Second Finished	1,369 sq. ft.
Lower Finished	69 sq. ft.
Basement Unfinished	1,358 sq. ft.
Garage Unfinished	482 sq. ft.
Deck Unfinished	315 sq. ft.
Porch Unfinished	60 sq. ft.
Dimensions	52'×65'10''
Foundation	Slab
Bedrooms	5
Full Baths	4
Primary Roof Pitch	12:12
Secondary Roof Pitch	6.5:12
Max Ridge Height	32'
Roof Framing	Stick
Exterior Walls	2×4

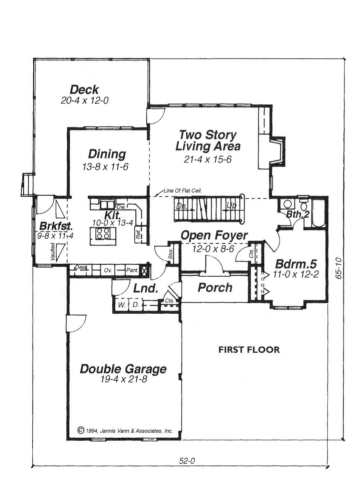

Deck
20-4 x 12-0

Dining
13-8 x 11-6

Two Story Living Area
21-4 x 15-6

Line Of Flat Ceil.

Brkfst.
9-8 x 11-4
Vaulted

Kit.
10-0 x 13-4

Dw.

Ref.

Dn   Up

Bth.2

Open Foyer
12-0 x 8-6

Stor.

Desk   Ov.   Pant.

Lnd.

W. D.   Cts.

Porch

Cts.

Bdrm.5
11-0 x 12-2

FIRST FLOOR

Double Garage
19-4 x 21-8

© 1994, Jannis Vann & Associates, Inc.

52-0

65-10

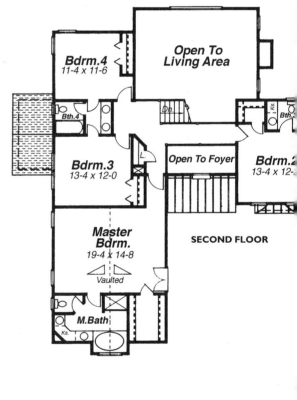

Bdrm.4
11-4 x 11-6

Bth.4

Open To Living Area

Dn.

Ks.
Bth.

Bdrm.3
13-4 x 12-0

L.

Open To Foyer

Bdrm.2
13-4 x 12-

SECOND FLOOR

Master Bdrm.
19-4 x 14-8
Vaulted

M.Bath

Ks.

Design 94636

BL   See Order Pages and Index for Info

Units	Single
Price Code	G
Total Finished	2,801 sq. ft.
First Finished	1,651 sq. ft.
Second Finished	1,150 sq. ft.
Dimensions	46'4"x79'1"
Foundation	Crawl space
	Slab
Bedrooms	5
Full Baths	3
First Ceiling	9'
Second Ceiling	8'
Primary Roof Pitch	9:12
Secondary Roof Pitch	3:12
Roof Framing	Stick
Exterior Walls	2x4

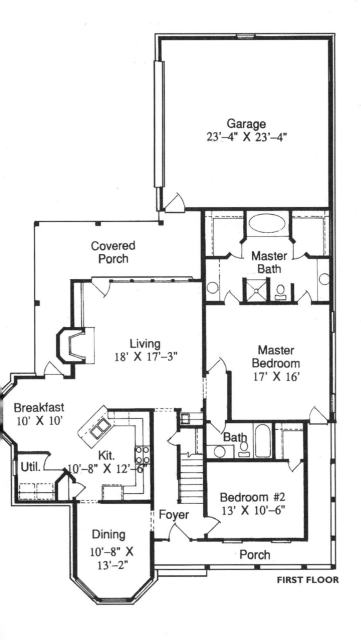

FIRST FLOOR

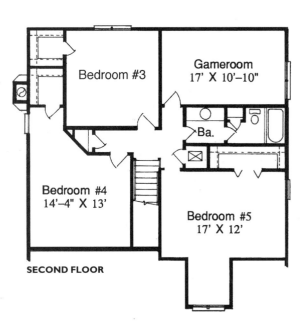

SECOND FLOOR

Design 99145

BL   See Order Pages and Index for Info

Units	Single
Price Code	G
Total Finished	2,830 sq. ft.
First Finished	2,082 sq. ft.
Second Finished	748 sq. ft.
Basement Unfinished	2,082 sq. ft.
Dimensions	66'x61'
Foundation	Basement
Bedrooms	4
Full Baths	2
Half Baths	1
Primary Roof Pitch	8:12
Secondary Roof Pitch	10:12
Max Ridge Height	32'8"
Roof Framing	Truss
Exterior Walls	2x6

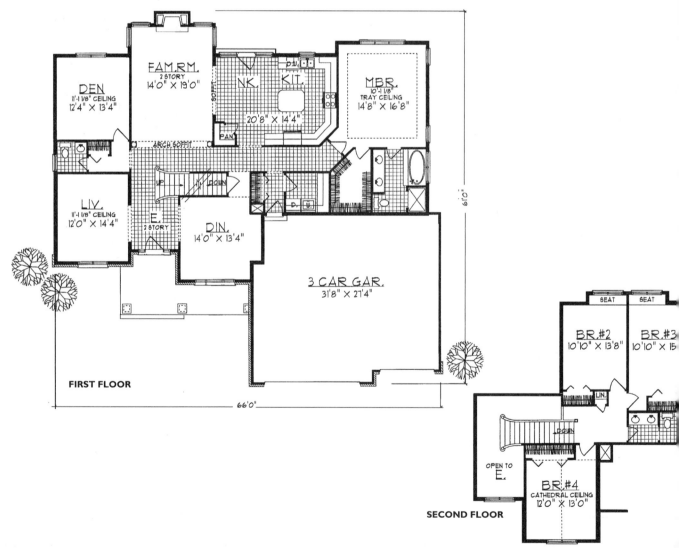

FIRST FLOOR

SECOND FLOOR

Merillat.   Visit us at www.merillat.com

Design 97140

BL

See Order Pages and Index for Info

Units	Single
Price Code	G
Total Finished	2,832 sq. ft.
First Finished	2,032 sq. ft.
Second Finished	800 sq. ft.
Bonus Unfinished	405 sq. ft.
Dimensions	74'x57'
Foundation	Basement
Bedrooms	4
Full Baths	2
Primary Roof Pitch	8:12
Secondary Roof Pitch	10:12
Max Ridge Height	31'
Roof Framing	Truss
Exterior Walls	2x6

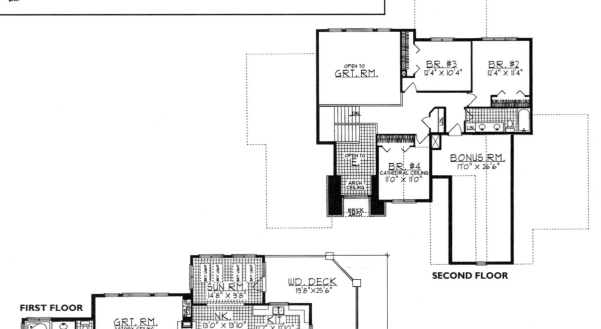

SECOND FLOOR

FIRST FLOOR

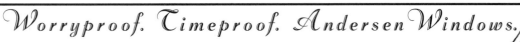

199

Design 96403

BL/ML/RRR

See Order Pages and Index for Info

© Donald A. Gardner Architects, Inc.

B. NATHAN

Units	Single
Price Code	I
Total Finished	2,832 sq. ft.
First Finished	1,483 sq. ft.
Second Finished	1,349 sq. ft.
Bonus Unfinished	486 sq. ft.
Garage Unfinished	738 sq. ft.
Dimensions	66'10"×47'8"
Foundation	Crawl space
Bedrooms	4
Full Baths	2
Half Baths	1
First Ceiling	9'
Second Ceiling	8'
Primary Roof Pitch	12:9.5
Secondary Roof Pitch	12:12
Max Ridge Height	24'10"
Roof Framing	Stick
Exterior Walls	2×4

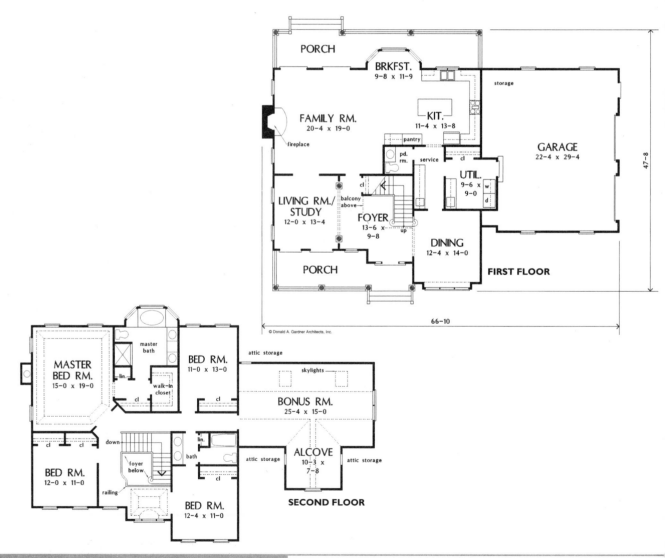

PORCH

BRKFST.
9-8 x 11-9

storage

FAMILY RM.
20-4 x 19-0

KIT.
11-4 x 13-8

fireplace

pantry

GARAGE
22-4 x 29-4

pd. rm.

service

cl

UTIL.
9-6 x 9-0

w d

LIVING RM./STUDY
12-0 x 13-4

balcony above

cl

FOYER
13-6 x 9-8

up

DINING
12-4 x 14-0

PORCH

FIRST FLOOR

47-8

66-10

© Donald A. Gardner Architects, Inc.

master bath

lin.

MASTER BED RM.
15-0 x 19-0

walk-in closet

cl

BED RM.
11-0 x 13-0

attic storage

skylights

cl

BONUS RM.
25-4 x 15-0

cl cl

down

lin.

bath

BED RM.
12-0 x 11-0

foyer below

cl

attic storage

ALCOVE
10-3 x 7-8

attic storage

railing

BED RM.
12-4 x 11-0

SECOND FLOOR

Design 97118

BL

See Order Pages and Index for Info

Units	Single
Price Code	G
Total Finished	2,838 sq. ft.
First Finished	1,542 sq. ft.
Second Finished	1,296 sq. ft.
Dimensions	59'x56'
Foundation	Basement
Bedrooms	4
Full Baths	3
Half Baths	1
Primary Roof Pitch	7:12
Secondary Roof Pitch	9:12
Max Ridge Height	31'
Roof Framing	Truss
Exterior Walls	2x6

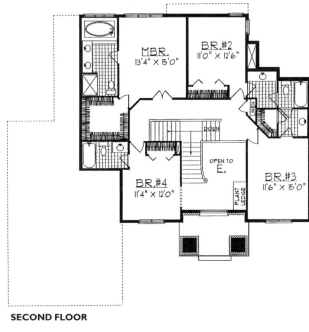

SECOND FLOOR

FIRST FLOOR

Design 94273

BL

See Order Pages and Index for Info

Units	Single
Price Code	H
Total Finished	2,850 sq. ft.
Main Finished	2,850 sq. ft.
Garage Unfinished	588 sq. ft.
Dimensions	63'4"x86'
Foundation	Slab
Bedrooms	3
Full Baths	2
Half Baths	1
Main Ceiling	10'
Primary Roof Pitch	10:12
Max Ridge Height	33'6"
Exterior Walls	2x4

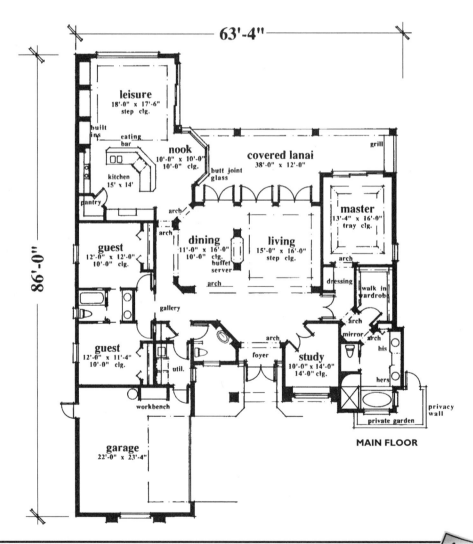

MAIN FLOOR

Design 94630

BL

See Order Pages and Index for Info

Units	Single
Price Code	G
Total Finished	2,852 sq. ft.
First Finished	1,730 sq. ft.
Second Finished	1,122 sq. ft.
Bonus Unfinished	270 sq. ft.
Porch Unfinished	553 sq. ft.
Dimensions	60'x67'6''
Foundation	Crawl space
	Slab
Bedrooms	4
Full Baths	2
Half Baths	1
Primary Roof Pitch	10:12
Secondary Roof Pitch	8:12
Max Ridge Height	32'10''
Roof Framing	Stick
Exterior Walls	2x4

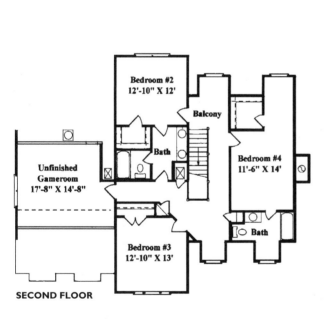

SECOND FLOOR

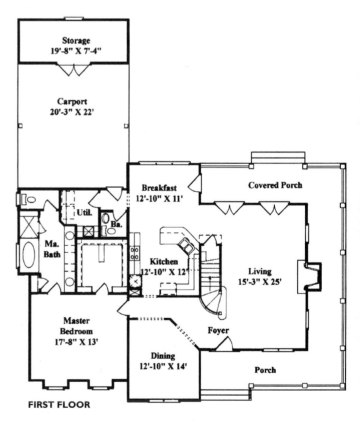

FIRST FLOOR

Design 93612

BL

See Order Pages and Index for Info

Units	Single
Price Code	G
Total Finished	2,864 sq. ft.
First Finished	2,062 sq. ft.
Second Finished	802 sq. ft.
Garage Unfinished	400 sq. ft.
Dimensions	50'x53'
Foundation	Slab
Bedrooms	4
Full Baths	2
Half Baths	1
Primary Roof Pitch	9:12
Secondary Roof Pitch	12:12
Max Ridge Height	32'
Roof Framing	Stick
Exterior Walls	2x4

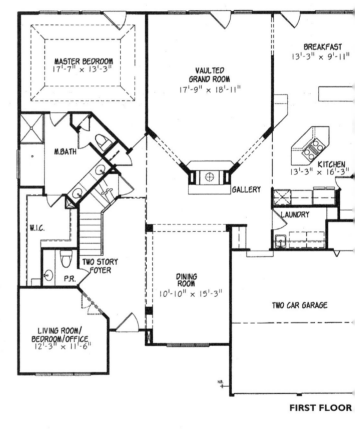

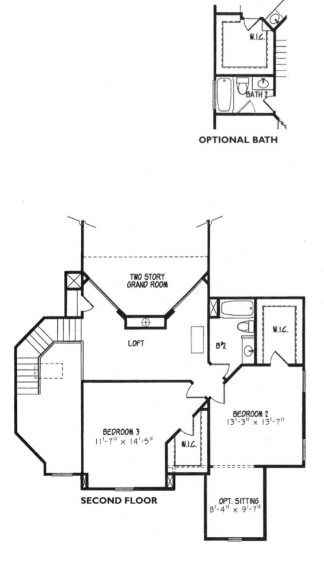

Design 94125

BL   See Order Pages and Index for Info

Units	Single
Price Code	G
Total Finished	2,875 sq. ft.
First Finished	1,657 sq. ft.
Second Finished	1,218 sq. ft.
Basement Unfinished	1,643 sq. ft.
Garage Unfinished	776 sq. ft.
Dimensions	81'4"x43'
Foundation	Basement
Bedrooms	4
Full Baths	2
3/4 Baths	1
Primary Roof Pitch	9:12
Secondary Roof Pitch	12:12
Max Ridge Height	31'
Roof Framing	Stick/Truss
Exterior Walls	2×6

SECOND FLOOR

- MBATH
- WI Closet
- cath cl'g **MBR** 15' x 13'10
- FLAT CL'G FLAT CL'G
- 33'
- **BR2** 10'4 x 11'8
- **BR3** 10'4 x 11'8
- Fam Rm Below
- Balcony
- Balcony
- Foyer Below
- **BATH 2**
- **BR4/LOFT** 12' x 13'2
- 55'4

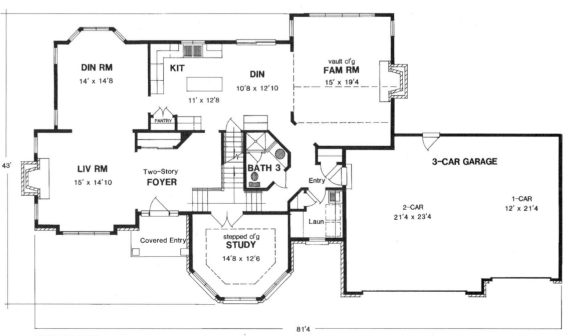

FIRST FLOOR

- **DIN RM** 14' x 14'8
- **KIT** 11' x 12'8
- **DIN** 10'8 x 12'10
- vault cl'g **FAM RM** 15' x 19'4
- PANTRY
- **LIV RM** 15' x 14'10
- Two-Story **FOYER**
- **BATH 3**
- Entry
- **3-CAR GARAGE**
- Laun
- Covered Entry
- stepped cl'g **STUDY** 14'8 x 12'6
- 2-CAR 21'4 x 23'4
- 1-CAR 12' x 21'4
- 43'
- 81'4

Design 97119

BL   See Order Pages and Index for Info

Units	Single
Price Code	G
Total Finished	2,896 sq. ft.
Main Finished	2,896 sq. ft.
Dimensions	80'8"×69'
Foundation	Basement
Bedrooms	3
Full Baths	3
Half Baths	1
Primary Roof Pitch	10:12
Secondary Roof Pitch	10:12
Max Ridge Height	27'
Exterior Walls	2x6

MAIN FLOOR

Design 93055

BL

See Order Pages and Index for Info

Units	Single
Price Code	G
Total Finished	2,924 sq. ft.
First Finished	1,788 sq. ft.
Second Finished	1,136 sq. ft.
Garage Unfinished	552 sq. ft.
Dimensions	67'7"x72'7"
Foundation	Crawl space
	Slab
Bedrooms	4
Full Baths	3
Half Baths	1
Primary Roof Pitch	12:12
Secondary Roof Pitch	10:12
Max Ridge Height	32'
Roof Framing	Stick
Exterior Walls	2x4

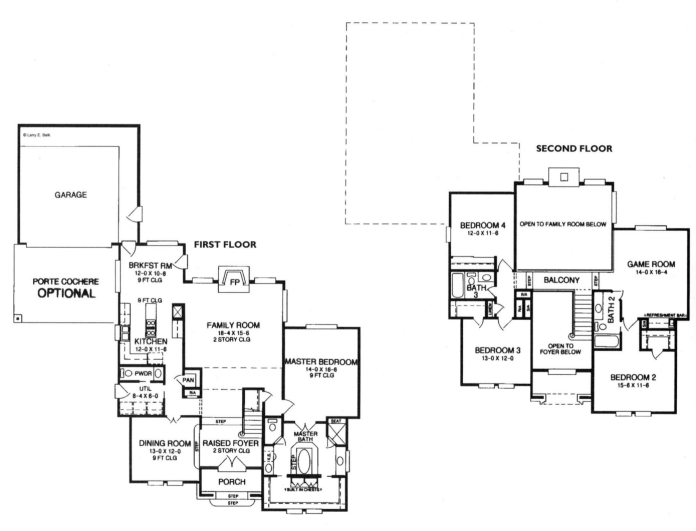

SECOND FLOOR

FIRST FLOOR

© Larry E. Belk

GARAGE

PORTE COCHERE OPTIONAL

BRKFST RM 12-0 X 10-8 9 FT CLG

FP

KITCHEN 12-0 X 11-6

FAMILY ROOM 18-4 X 15-6 2 STORY CLG

MASTER BEDROOM 14-0 X 16-6 9 FT CLG

PWDR

UTIL 8-4 X 6-0

PAN

DINING ROOM 13-0 X 12-0 9 FT CLG

RAISED FOYER 2 STORY CLG

MASTER BATH

PORCH

BEDROOM 4 12-0 X 11-6

OPEN TO FAMILY ROOM BELOW

BATH 3

BALCONY

GAME ROOM 14-0 X 16-4

BATH 2

BEDROOM 3 13-0 X 12-0

OPEN TO FOYER BELOW

REFRESHMENT BAR

BEDROOM 2 15-6 X 11-6

Design 91208

BL   See Order Pages and Index for Info

Units	Single
Price Code	G
Total Finished	2,933 sq. ft.
First Finished	1,598 sq. ft.
Second Finished	1,335 sq. ft.
Garage Unfinished	562 sq. ft.
Dimensions	52'10''x52'10''
Foundation	Slab
Bedrooms	3
Full Baths	2
Half Baths	1

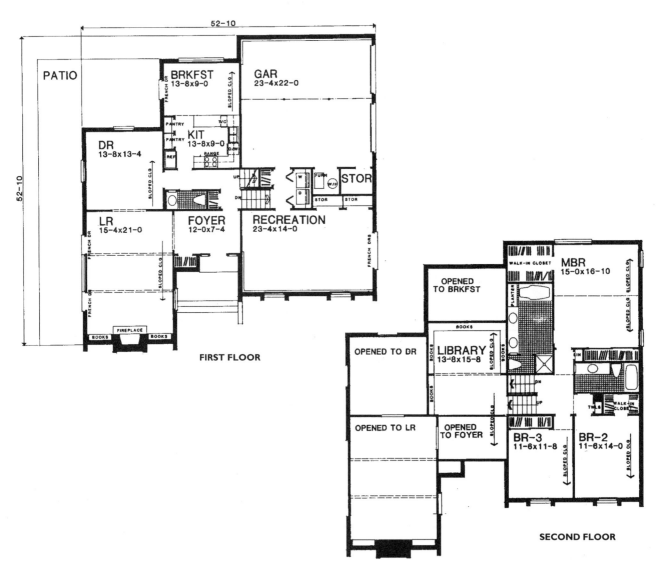

FIRST FLOOR

SECOND FLOOR

Design 92578

BL/ML

See Order Pages and Index for Info

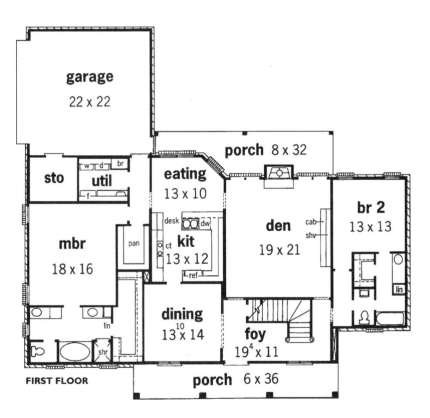

Units	Single
Price Code	G
Total Finished	2,992 sq. ft.
First Finished	2,209 sq. ft.
Second Finished	783 sq. ft.
Garage Unfinished	556 sq. ft.
Porch Unfinished	636 sq. ft.
Dimensions	67'10''x64'5''
Foundation	Crawl space
	Slab
Bedrooms	4
Full Baths	3
First Ceiling	9'
Second Ceiling	8'
Primary Roof Pitch	8:12
Secondary Roof Pitch	12:12
Max Ridge Height	30'6''
Roof Framing	Stick
Exterior Walls	2x4

garage 22 x 22

sto

util w / d / br / f

mbr 18 x 16

pan

eating 13 x 10

desk

kit 13 x 12 ct / dw / ref

dining 13 x 14 10

foy 19⁴ x 11

porch 8 x 32

den 19 x 21 cab / shv

br 2 13 x 13

lin

FIRST FLOOR

porch 6 x 36

br 4 13 x 13

br 3 12 x 13

tic

lin

ra

lin

attic

children's den 15 x 15⁶

down

open to foyer

porch 6 x 36

SECOND FLOOR

Design 98596

BL

See Order Pages and Index for Info

Units	Single
Price Code	H
Total Finished	3,062 sq. ft.
Lower Finished	2,115 sq. ft.
Upper Finished	947 sq. ft.
Bonus Unfinished	195 sq. ft.
Garage Unfinished	635 sq. ft.
Deck Unfinished	210 sq. ft.
Porch Unfinished	32 sq. ft.
Dimensions	68'10''x58'1''
Foundation	Basement
	Crawl space
	Slab
Bedrooms	4
Full Baths	3
Half Baths	1
First Ceiling	10'
Second Ceiling	8'
Primary Roof Pitch	12:12
Max Ridge Height	32'6''
Roof Framing	Stick
Exterior Walls	2x4

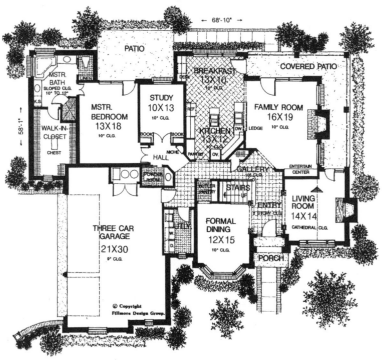

LOWER LEVEL

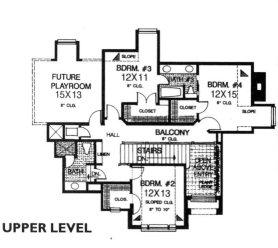

UPPER LEVEL

Design 63067

BL

See Order Pages and Index for Info

Units	Single
Price Code	I
Total Finished	3,064 sq. ft.
Main Finished	3,064 sq. ft.
Bonus Unfinished	366 sq. ft.
Garage Unfinished	716 sq. ft.
Dimensions	79'6''x91'
Foundation	Slab
Bedrooms	4
Full Baths	4
Main Ceiling	10'-12
Second Ceiling	8'
Primary Roof Pitch	6:12
Max Ridge Height	24'4''
Roof Framing	Truss

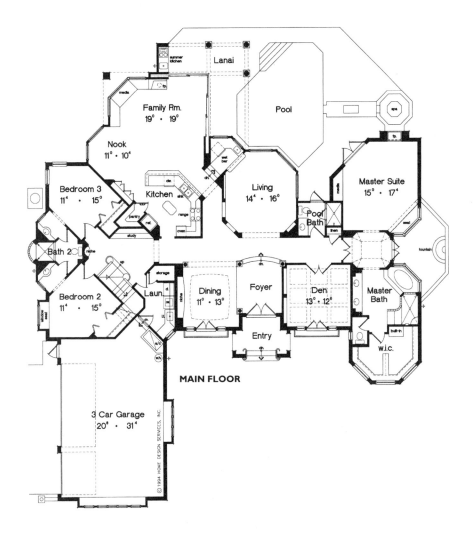

MAIN FLOOR

BONUS SPACE

Design 97400

BL/RRR   See Order Pages and Index for Info

Units	Single
Price Code	H
Total Finished	3,094 sq. ft.
First Finished	2,112 sq. ft.
Second Finished	982 sq. ft.
Basement Unfinished	2,112 sq. ft.
Garage Unfinished	650 sq. ft.
Dimensions	67'1"x65'10.1
Foundation	Basement
	Slab
Bedrooms	4
Full Baths	3
Half Baths	1
First Ceiling	9'
Primary Roof Pitch	9:12
Secondary Roof Pitch	12:12
Max Ridge Height	30'4"
Roof Framing	Stick
Exterior Walls	2x4

SECOND FLOOR

FIRST FLOOR

65'-10 1

67'-1"

© Design Basics, Inc.

Design 92277

BL/ZIP

See Order Pages and Index for Info

Units	Single
Price Code	H
Total Finished	3,110 sq. ft.
First Finished	2,190 sq. ft.
Second Finished	920 sq. ft.
Garage Unfinished	624 sq. ft.
Dimensions	9'x53'10''
Foundation	Basement
	Slab
Bedrooms	4
Full Baths	3
Half Baths	1
First Ceiling	10'
Second Ceiling	8'
Primary Roof Pitch	12:12
Max Ridge Height	29'
Roof Framing	Stick
Exterior Walls	2x4

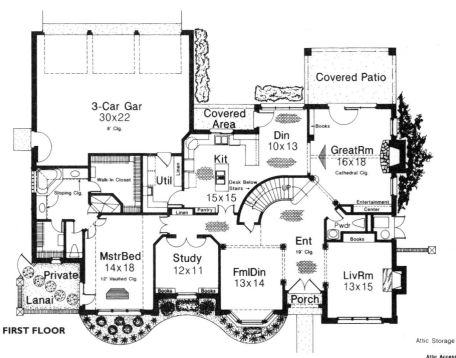

FIRST FLOOR

SECOND FLOOR

Design 98570

BL   See Order Pages and Index for Info

Units	Single
Price Code	H
Total Finished	3,115 sq. ft.
First Finished	2,132 sq. ft.
Second Finished	983 sq. ft.
Garage Unfinished	660 sq. ft.
Deck Unfinished	240 sq. ft.
Porch Unfinished	48 sq. ft.
Dimensions	69'x34'4''
Foundation	Slab
Bedrooms	3
Full Baths	2
Half Baths	1
Primary Roof Pitch	12:12
Max Ridge Height	30'
Roof Framing	Stick
Exterior Walls	2x4

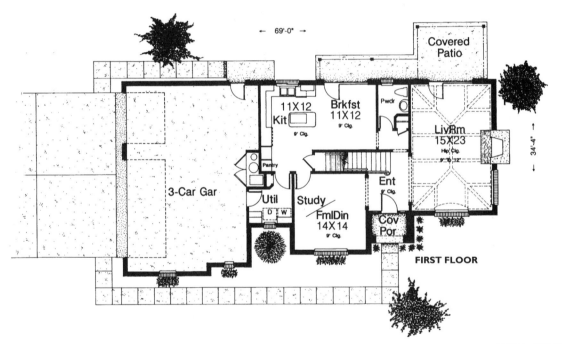

FIRST FLOOR

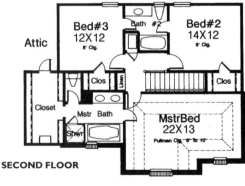

SECOND FLOOR

Design 99134

BL

See Order Pages and Index for Info

Units	Single
Price Code	H
Total Finished	3,124 sq. ft.
First Finished	1,632 sq. ft.
Second Finished	1,492 sq. ft.
Basement Unfinished	1,632 sq. ft.
Dimensions	72'8''x46'6''
Foundation	Basement
Bedrooms	4
Full Baths	2
Half Baths	1
Primary Roof Pitch	10:12
Secondary Roof Pitch	8:12
Max Ridge Height	31'
Roof Framing	Truss
Exterior Walls	2x4

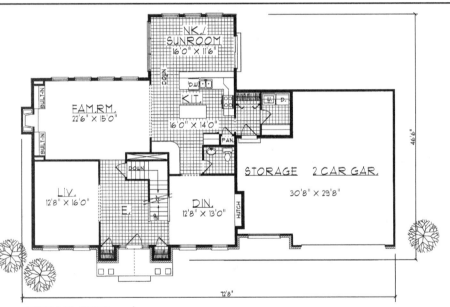

NK./SUNROOM 16'0" X 11'6"

FAM. RM. 22'6" X 15'0"

KIT. 16'0" X 14'0"

STORAGE   2 CAR GAR. 30'8" X 29'8"

LIV. 12'8" X 16'0"

DIN. 12'8" X 13'0"

PAN

DOWN

46'6"

72'8"

MAIN FLOOR

BR #3 14'0" X 13'4"

BR #2 11'8" X 13'4"

LINEN

SHELVES

LINEN

BR #4 14'0" X 13'4"

DOWN

M.B.R. 12'6" X 18'8"

LIN.

SECOND FLOOR

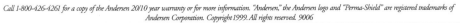

Design 98929

BL

See Order Pages and Index for Info

Units	Single
Price Code	H
Total Finished	3,140 sq. ft.
First Finished	1,553 sq. ft.
Second Finished	1,587 sq. ft.
Basement Unfinished	1,553 sq. ft.
Garage Unfinished	485 sq. ft.
Deck Unfinished	216 sq. ft.
Porch Unfinished	73 sq. ft.
Dimensions	58'x40'4''
Foundation	Basement
Bedrooms	5
Full Baths	4
First Ceiling	9'
Second Ceiling	8'
Primary Roof Pitch	12:12
Max Ridge Height	34'
Roof Framing	Stick
Exterior Walls	2x4

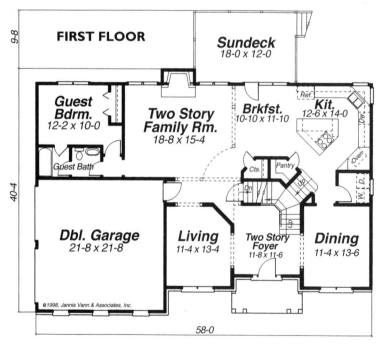

FIRST FLOOR

Sundeck
18-0 x 12-0

Guest Bdrm.
12-2 x 10-0

Two Story Family Rm.
18-8 x 15-4

Brkfst.
10-10 x 11-10

Kit.
12-6 x 14-0

Ref.

Guest Bath

Cts.

Pantry

Dn.

Up.

W.D.

Oven

Dbl. Garage
21-8 x 21-8

Living
11-4 x 13-4

Two Story Foyer
11-8 x 11-6

Dining
11-4 x 13-6

© 1998, Jannis Vann & Associates, Inc.

58-0

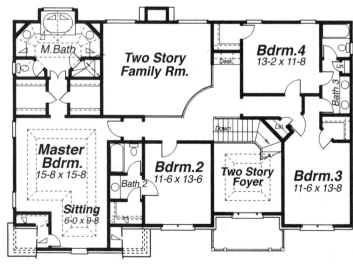

SECOND FLOOR

M. Bath

Two Story Family Rm.

Bdrm. 4
13-2 x 11-8

Desk

Lin.

Bath 3

Master Bdrm.
15-8 x 15-8

Bath 2

Bdrm. 2
11-6 x 13-6

Down

Dn.

Two Story Foyer

Bdrm. 3
11-6 x 13-8

Sitting
6-0 x 9-8

DESIGN **63064**   BL   See Order Pages and Index for Info

Units	Single
Price Code	H
Total Finished	3,164 sq. ft.
First Finished	2,624 sq. ft.
Second Finished	540 sq. ft.
Garage Unfinished	802 sq. ft.
Dimensions	66'x83'
Foundation	Slab
Bedrooms	5
Full Baths	3
3/4 Baths	1
Primary Roof Pitch	8:12
Max Ridge Height	27'
Roof Framing	Truss
Exterior Walls	2x4

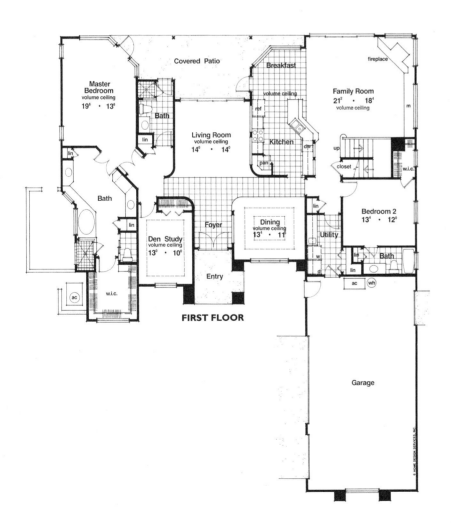

FIRST FLOOR

SECOND FLOOR

Design 63066

BL

See Order Pages and Index for Info

Units	Single
Price Code	H
Total Finished	3,200 sq. ft.
First Finished	2,531 sq. ft.
Second Finished	669 sq. ft.
Garage Unfinished	656 sq. ft.
Dimensions	70'x82'4''
Foundation	Slab
Bedrooms	4
Full Baths	3
Half Baths	2
Primary Roof Pitch	6:12
Max Ridge Height	26'10''

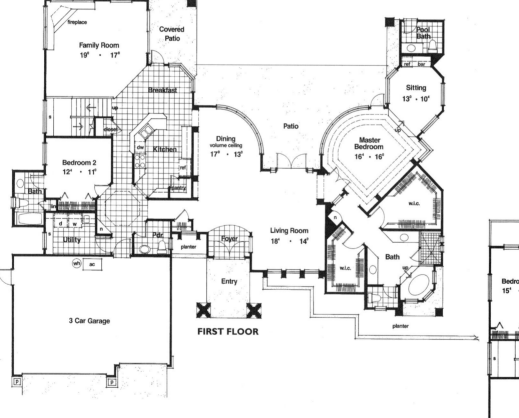

FIRST FLOOR

SECOND FLOOR

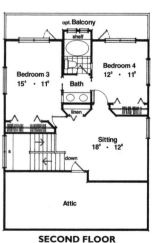

Design 92581

BL/ML

See Order Pages and Index for Info

© Donald A. Gardner Architects, Inc.

Units	Single
Price Code	H
Total Finished	3,213 sq. ft.
First Finished	1,488 sq. ft.
Second Finished	1,725 sq. ft.
Garage Unfinished	580 sq. ft.
Porch Unfinished	605 sq. ft.
Dimensions	64'11"x45'5"
Foundation	Crawl space
	Slab
Bedrooms	4
Full Baths	3
Half Baths	1
Primary Roof Pitch	8:12
Secondary Roof Pitch	12:12
Max Ridge Height	30'
Roof Framing	Stick
Exterior Walls	2x4

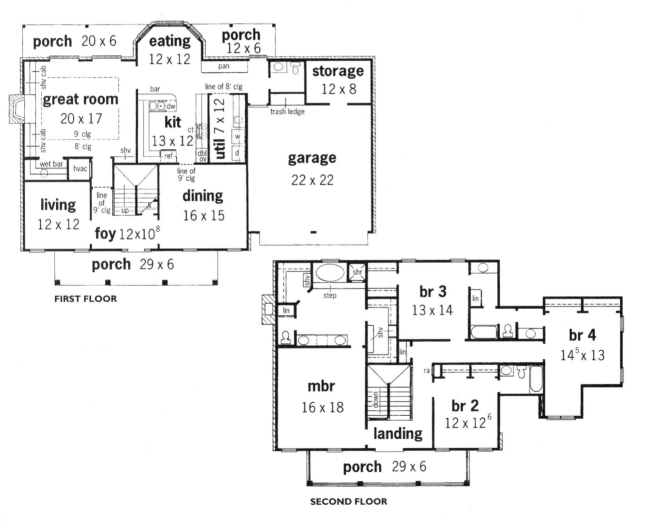

FIRST FLOOR

porch 20 x 6

eating 12 x 12

porch 12 x 6

pan

great room 20 x 17

9' clg

8' clg

shv cab

bar

dw

line of 8' clg

storage 12 x 8

trash ledge

w

kit 13 x 12

ct

shv

ref

dbl ov

util 7 x 12

d

wet bar

hvac

line of 9' clg

up

line of 9' clg

dining 16 x 15

garage 22 x 22

living 12 x 12

foy 12x10⁸

porch 29 x 6

SECOND FLOOR

br 3 13 x 14

lin

step

shr

lin

lin

shv

lin

br 4 14⁵ x 13

mbr 16 x 18

down

rail

br 2 12 x 12⁶

landing

porch 29 x 6

Design 98038

BL/ML   See Order Pages and Index for Info

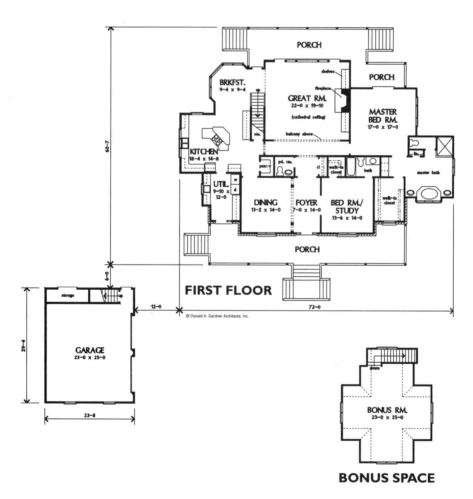

© Donald A. Gardner Architects, Inc.

B. NATHAN.

Units	Single
Price Code	J
Total Finished	3,238 sq. ft.
First Finished	2,516 sq. ft.
Second Finished	722 sq. ft.
Bonus Unfinished	513 sq. ft.
Dimensions	72'×60'7''
Foundation	Crawl space
Bedrooms	4
Full Baths	3
Half Baths	1
First Ceiling	9'
Second Ceiling	8'
Primary Roof Pitch	4:12
Secondary Roof Pitch	9:12
Max Ridge Height	28'
Roof Framing	Stick
Exterior Walls	2x4

FIRST FLOOR

© Donald A. Gardner Architects, Inc.

PORCH

BRKFST.
9-4 x 9-4

PORCH

GREAT RM.
22-0 x 19-10
(cathedral ceiling)

shelves

fireplace

MASTER
BED RM.
17-0 x 17-0

balcony above

KITCHEN
18-4 x 14-8

pantry

pd. rm.

cl

walk-in
closet

bath

master bath

UTIL
9-10 x
12-0

DINING
13-2 x 14-0

FOYER
7-0 x 14-0

BED RM./
STUDY
13-6 x 14-0

walk-in
closet

PORCH

GARAGE
23-0 x 25-0

storage

up

23-8

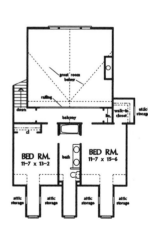

BONUS SPACE

BONUS RM.
23-0 x 25-0

down

SECOND FLOOR

great room
below

railing

walk-in
closet

attic
storage

down

balcony

BED RM.
11-7 x 13-2

bath

BED RM.
11-7 x 15-6

attic
storage

attic
storage

attic
storage

attic
storage

220

Design 94269

BL   See Order Pages and Index for Info

Units	Single
Price Code	I
Total Finished	3,250 sq. ft.
Main Finished	3,250 sq. ft.
Dimensions	65'x88'
Foundation	Slab
Bedrooms	3
Full Baths	3
Half Baths	I
Main Ceiling	10'
Roof Framing	Truss
Exterior Walls	2x8

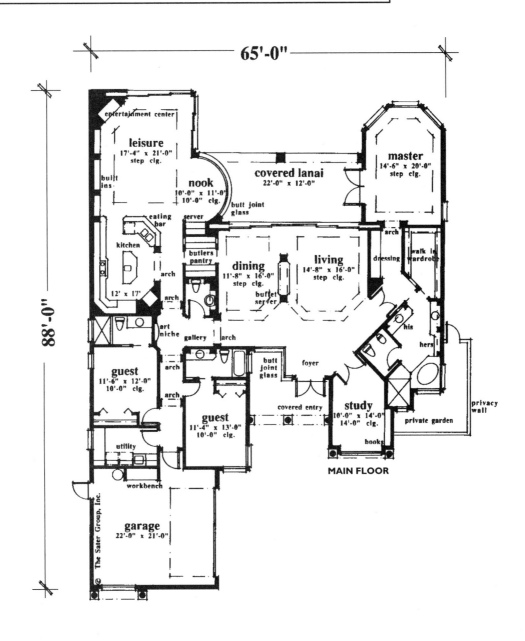

65'-0"

88'-0"

entertainment center

leisure
17'-4" x 21'-0"
step clg.

built ins

nook
10'-0" x 11'-0"
10'-0" clg.

covered lanai
22'-0" x 12'-0"

master
14'-6" x 20'-0"
step clg.

eating bar

server

butt joint glass

arch

walk in wardrobe

kitchen

butlers pantry

dining
11'-8" x 16'-0"
step clg.

living
14'-8" x 16'-0"
step clg.

dressing

12' x 17'

buffet server

arch

arch

his

hers

art niche

gallery

arch

foyer

guest
11'-6" x 12'-0"
10'-0" clg.

arch

butt joint glass

covered entry

study
10'-0" x 14'-0"
14'-0" clg.

privacy wall

arch

guest
11'-4" x 13'-0"
10'-0" clg.

private garden

utility

books

MAIN FLOOR

workbench

garage
22'-0" x 21'-0"

The Sater Group, Inc.

Design 98124

BL

See Order Pages and Index for Info

© Donald A. Gardner Architects, Inc.

Units	Single
Price Code	K
Total Finished	3,296 sq. ft.
First Finished	2,477 sq. ft.
Second Finished	819 sq. ft.
Bonus Unfinished	360 sq. ft.
Garage Unfinished	556 sq. ft.
Porch Unfinished	483 sq. ft.
Dimensions	100'x66'2''
Foundation	Crawl space
Bedrooms	4
Full Baths	4
First Ceiling	9'
Second Ceiling	9'
Primary Roof Pitch	10:12
Secondary Roof Pitch	12:12
Max Ridge Height	27'
Roof Framing	Stick
Exterior Walls	2x4

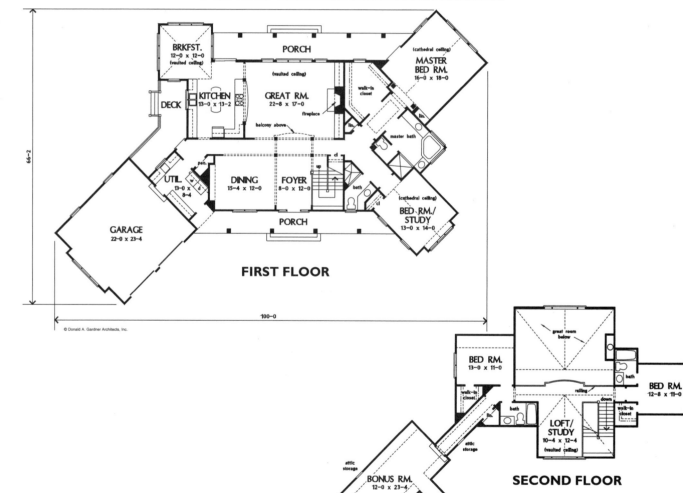

FIRST FLOOR

© Donald A. Gardner Architects, Inc.

SECOND FLOOR

Design 93324

BL

See Order Pages and Index for Info

Units	Single
Price Code	I
Total Finished	3,345 sq. ft.
First Finished	1,880 sq. ft.
Second Finished	1,465 sq. ft.
Basement Unfinished	1,880 sq. ft.
Garage Unfinished	900 sq. ft.
Dimensions	84'6"x54'4"
Foundation	Basement
Bedrooms	4
Full Baths	2
Half Baths	I
Primary Roof Pitch	10:12
Secondary Roof Pitch	12:12
Max Ridge Height	31'
Roof Framing	Stick
Exterior Walls	2x4

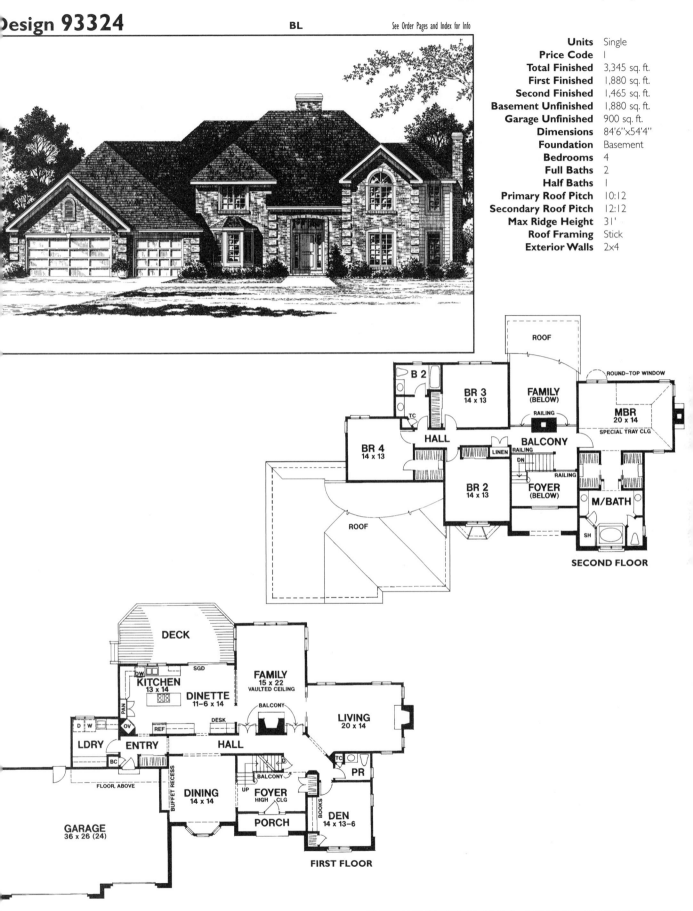

SECOND FLOOR

FIRST FLOOR

Design 98490

BL

See Order Pages and Index for Info

Units	Single
Price Code	J
Total Finished	3,559 sq. ft.
First Finished	1,865 sq. ft.
Second Finished	1,694 sq. ft.
Basement Unfinished	1,865 sq. ft.
Garage Unfinished	481 sq. ft.
Dimensions	59'x50'
Foundation	Basement
	Crawl space
Bedrooms	5
Full Baths	3
First Ceiling	9'
Second Ceiling	8'
Primary Roof Pitch	10:12
Max Ridge Height	34'
Roof Framing	Stick
Exterior Walls	2x4

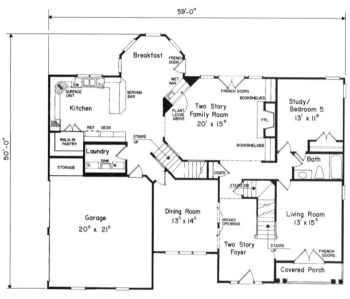

FIRST FLOOR

SECOND FLOOR

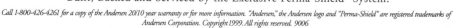

Welcome to our Neighborhood...

We know what builders want. For more than 15 years, Nelson Design Group, LLC has been designing *superior* homes for builders and *custom* plans for clients throughout the country. We are constantly adding to our collection of fine designs, resulting in several hundred new home designs per year. We offer *unique* and diversified designs, as well as southern traditionals, vacation homes, country styles and modern classics. Our advanced technology can modify any of our plans to suit your needs—saving time and guaranteeing customer *satisfaction*.

We offer numerous services which will assist in making your building experience as *easy* and *rewarding* as possible including: Stock Plans, Modified Plans, Custom Plans, Master-Planned Communities, Multi-Family Plans and Marketing Materials.

Join us today at *www.nelsondesigngroup.com*.

100 E. Huntington, Suite C • Jonesboro, AR 72401
Fax: 870-931-5792 • Toll Free: 800-590-AIBD(2423)
info@nelsondesigngroup.com

Nelson Design Group wants to ensure that our customers have the most current and helpful designs available. Hence, we have created a full color plan book complete with more than 135 renderings and floor plans. We also offer 2 Builder Edition plan books. Volume I features renderings and specs on more than 150 plans. Volume II includes over 140 home designs.

Color Plan Book.....................$30
Builder Edition - Volume I..........$20
Builder Edition - Volume II.........$20
All Three..............................$50

Collections of Narrow Lot, Duplexes & Cottage Cabin Designs

Create Your Own Development!

Three collections for narrow lot configurations in Traditional Neighborhood, French Country and European Traditional styles.
Our Duplex Collection I features over 40 designs that represent actual homes.
Our River Bend Collection of cottage cabins are perfect for weekend or second residences.

Preview Portfolios......$20   All Five......$75

Marketing Materials

Choose from 8.5" x 11" color feature sheets, $50/per 100; 16" x 20" framed and matted color renderings, $89; 24" x 36" outdoor, black and white laminated prints, $179; and 24" x 36" outdoor, color laminated prints, $195.
To order call: **1-800-590-2423**. *We accept check, money order, Mastercard, Visa, Discover and American Express with next day service available.*

Nelson Design Group LLC

RESIDENTIAL PLANNERS - DESIGNERS

225

Design 93154

BL

See Order Pages and Index for Info

Units	Single
Price Code	J
Total Finished	3,578 sq. ft.
Main Finished	2,443 sq. ft.
Lower Finished	1,135 sq. ft.
Basement Unfinished	1,308 sq. ft.
Porch Unfinished	196 sq. ft.
Dimensions	82'4"x71'
Foundation	Basement
Bedrooms	3
Full Baths	3
Primary Roof Pitch	9:12
Secondary Roof Pitch	9:12
Max Ridge Height	23'
Roof Framing	Stick
Exterior Walls	2x6

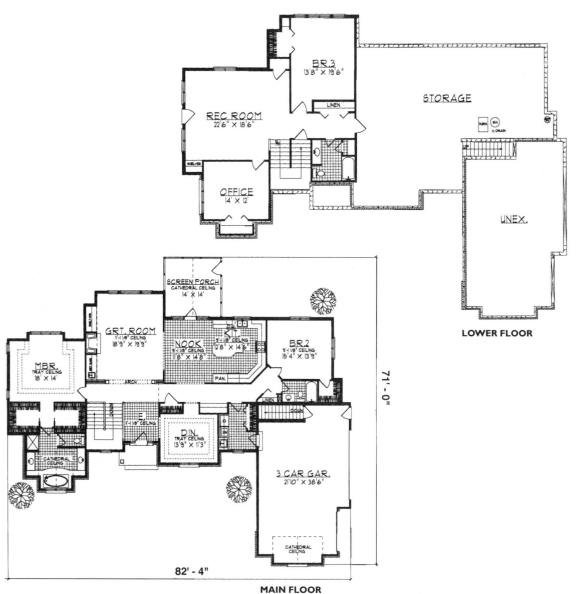

LOWER FLOOR

MAIN FLOOR

Design 90482

BL/ML

See Order Pages and Index for Info

Units	Single
Price Code	J
Total Finished	3,591 sq. ft.
First Finished	1,711 sq. ft.
Second Finished	1,880 sq. ft.
Basement Unfinished	1,705 sq. ft.
Garage Unfinished	441 sq. ft.
Deck Unfinished	252 sq. ft.
Dimensions	58'4"x39'10"
Foundation	Basement
	Crawl space
Bedrooms	3
Full Baths	2
Half Baths	1
Primary Roof Pitch	12:12
Max Ridge Height	35'10"
Roof Framing	Stick
Exterior Walls	2x4

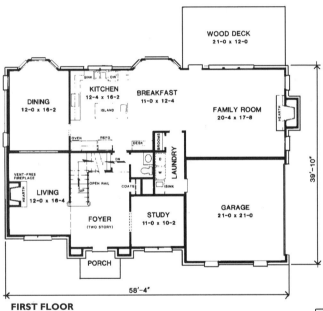

FIRST FLOOR

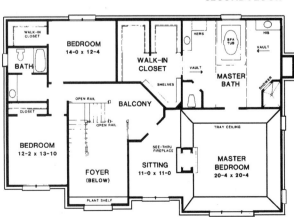

SECOND FLOOR

Design 98123

BL/ML

See Order Pages and Index for Info

© Donald A. Gardner Architects, Inc.

Units	Single
Price Code	L
Total Finished	3,613 sq. ft.
First Finished	3,613 sq. ft.
Bonus Unfinished	590 sq. ft.
Garage Unfinished	891 sq. ft.
Deck Unfinished	168 sq. ft.
Porch Unfinished	327 sq. ft.
Dimensions	99'7''×67'10''
Foundation	Crawl space
Bedrooms	4
Full Baths	3
Half Baths	1
First Ceiling	9'
Primary Roof Pitch	9:12
Secondary Roof Pitch	12:12
Max Ridge Height	29'3''
Exterior Walls	2x4

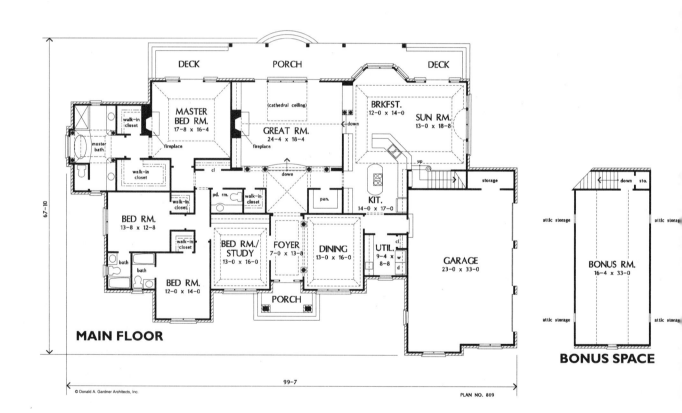

MAIN FLOOR

© Donald A. Gardner Architects, Inc.

PLAN NO. 809

BONUS SPACE

Design 97139

BL

See Order Pages and Index for Info

Units	Single
Price Code	J
Total Finished	3,622 sq. ft.
First Finished	2,646 sq. ft.
Second Finished	976 sq. ft.
Basement Unfinished	2,646 sq. ft.
Deck Unfinished	150 sq. ft.
Dimensions	93'x59'2''
Foundation	Basement
Bedrooms	4
Full Baths	3
Half Baths	1
Primary Roof Pitch	10:12
Secondary Roof Pitch	12:12
Max Ridge Height	33'
Roof Framing	Truss
Exterior Walls	2x6

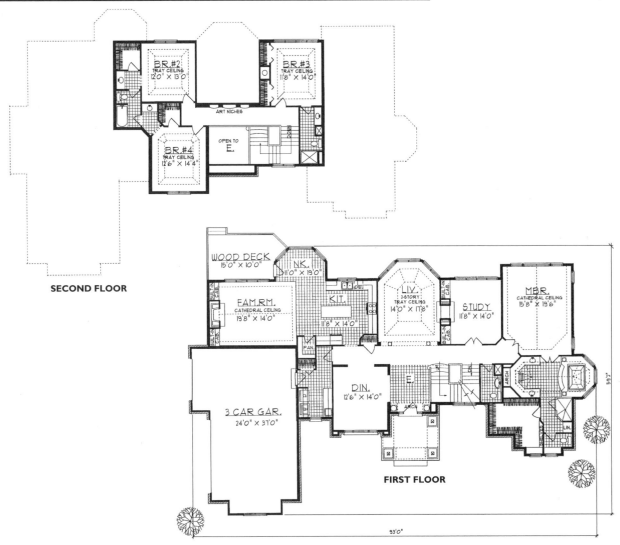

SECOND FLOOR

BR. #2
TRAY CEILING
12'0" x 13'0"

BR. #3
TRAY CEILING
11'8" x 14'0"

ART NICHES

BR. #4
TRAY CEILING
12'6" x 14'4"

OPEN TO E.

FIRST FLOOR

WOOD DECK
15'0" x 10'0"

NK.
11'0" x 19'0"

FAM. RM.
CATHEDRAL CEILING
19'8" x 14'0"

KIT.
11'8" x 14'0"

LIV.
2-STORY
TRAY CEILING
14'0" x 17'8"

STUDY
11'8" x 14'0"

MBR.
CATHEDRAL CEILING
15'8" x 19'6"

3 CAR GAR.
24'0" x 31'0"

DIN.
12'6" x 14'0"

E.

93'0"

59'2"

Design 60034

BL

See Order Pages and Index for Info

Units	Single
Price Code	J
Total Finished	3,698 sq. ft.
First Finished	1,802 sq. ft.
Second Finished	1,896 sq. ft.
Dimensions	68'x45'4''
Foundation	Basement
	Crawl space
Bedrooms	5
Full Baths	5
Half Baths	1
First Ceiling	9'
Second Ceiling	9'
Primary Roof Pitch	9:12
Max Ridge Height	36'8''
Roof Framing	Stick
Exterior Walls	2x4

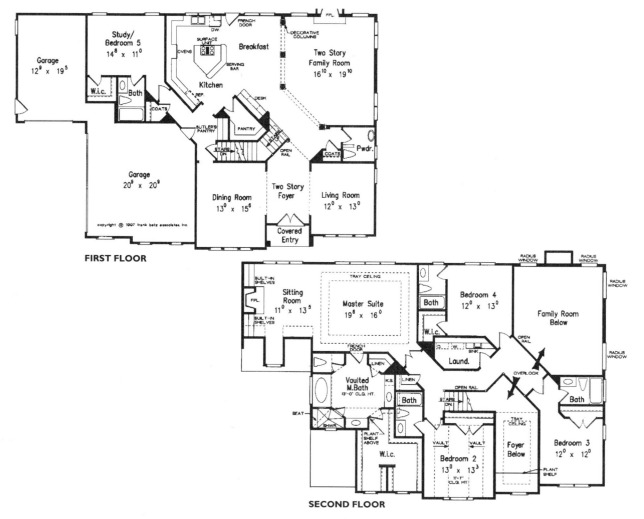

FIRST FLOOR

SECOND FLOOR

Design 63069

BL

See Order Pages and Index for Info

Units	Single
Price Code	J
Total Finished	3,730 sq. ft.
First Finished	3,236 sq. ft.
Second Finished	494 sq. ft.
Garage Unfinished	572 sq. ft.
Dimensions	80'x89'10"
Foundation	Slab
Bedrooms	4
Full Baths	3
Half Baths	1
Primary Roof Pitch	6:12
Max Ridge Height	32'5"
Roof Framing	Truss

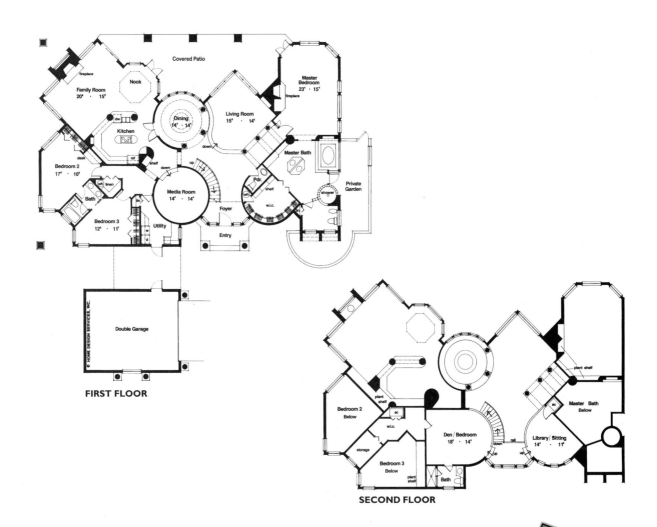

FIRST FLOOR

SECOND FLOOR

Design 63071

BL

See Order Pages and Index for Info

Units	Single
Price Code	K
Total Finished	3,800 sq. ft.
First Finished	2,530 sq. ft.
Second Finished	1,270 sq. ft.
Garage Unfinished	818 sq. ft.
Dimensions	90'6"x98'6"
Foundation	Slab
Bedrooms	4
Full Baths	3
Half Baths	1
First Ceiling	10'-12'
Primary Roof Pitch	8.75:12
Max Ridge Height	29'5"
Roof Framing	Stick/ Truss
Exterior Walls	2x6

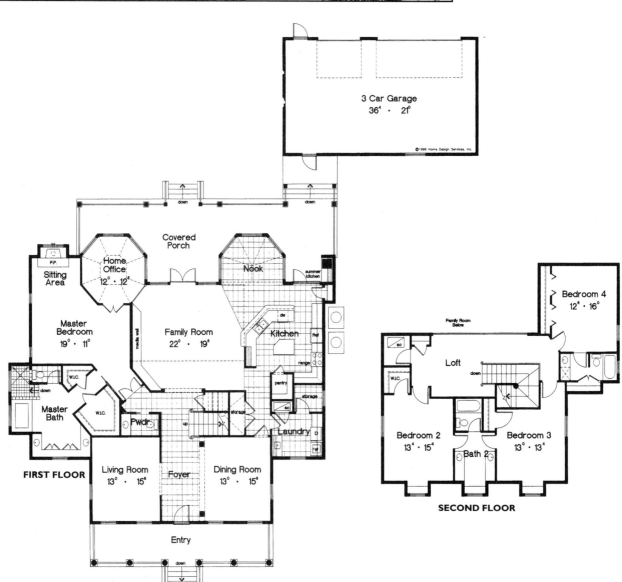

3 Car Garage
36⁴ · 21⁰

©1998 Home Design Services, Inc.

Covered Porch

Home Office
12⁰ · 12⁶

Nook

summer kitchen

Sitting Area

F.P.

Master Bedroom
19⁰ · 11⁰

Family Room
22⁰ · 19⁸

Kitchen

dw

Ref

range

W.I.C.

pantry

storage

ac

Master Bath

W.I.C.

Pwdr

up

storage

Laundry

FIRST FLOOR

Living Room
13⁰ · 15⁸

Foyer

Dining Room
13⁰ · 15⁸

Entry

Bedroom 4
12⁸ · 16⁰

Family Room Below

Loft

ac

W.I.C.

down

Bedroom 2
13⁴ · 15⁴

Bath 2

Bedroom 3
13⁰ · 13⁴

SECOND FLOOR

Design 92504

BL/ML

See Order Pages and Index for Info

Units	Single
Price Code	K
Total Finished	3,813 sq. ft.
First Finished	2,553 sq. ft.
Second Finished	1,260 sq. ft.
Garage Unfinished	714 sq. ft.
Dimensions	82'x52'
Foundation	Crawl space
	Slab
Bedrooms	4
Full Baths	3
Half Baths	1
First Ceiling	9'
Second Ceiling	9'
Primary Roof Pitch	10:12
Max Ridge Height	36'
Roof Framing	Stick
Exterior Walls	2x4

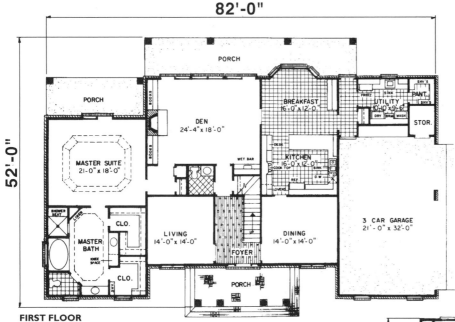

82'-0"

52'-0"

FIRST FLOOR

PORCH

PORCH

DEN
24'-4" x 18'-0"

MASTER SUITE
21'-0" x 18'-0"

BREAKFAST
16'-0" x 12'-0"

UTILITY
10'-0" x 9'-6"

PANT.

STOR.

KITCHEN
16'-0" x 12'-0"

WET BAR

SHOWER SEAT

MASTER BATH

KNEE SPACE

CLO.

CLO.

LIVING
14'-0" x 14'-0"

FOYER
UP

DINING
14'-0" x 14'-0"

3 CAR GARAGE
21'-0" x 32'-0"

PORCH

SECOND FLOOR

34'-0"

CHILDRENS DEN
18'-8" x 12'-0"

BEDROOM 3
14'-0" x 12'-0"

CLO.

BATH 4

LIN

HALL

HVAC

BATH 3

CLO.

CLO.

CLO.

BEDROOM 4
14'-4" x 12'-0"

OPEN TO FOYER
DOWN

BEDROOM 2
16'-4" x 12'-0"

40'-8"

Design 63072

BL/ML

See Order Pages and Index for Info

Units	Single
Price Code	K
Total Finished	3,891 sq. ft.
Main Finished	3,891 sq. ft.
Garage Unfinished	813 sq. ft.
Dimensions	86'8''x96'4''
Foundation	Slab
Bedrooms	4
Full Baths	3
Half Baths	1
Main Ceiling	10'-21'
Primary Roof Pitch	6:12
Max Ridge Height	24'8''
Roof Framing	Truss
Exterior Walls	2x4

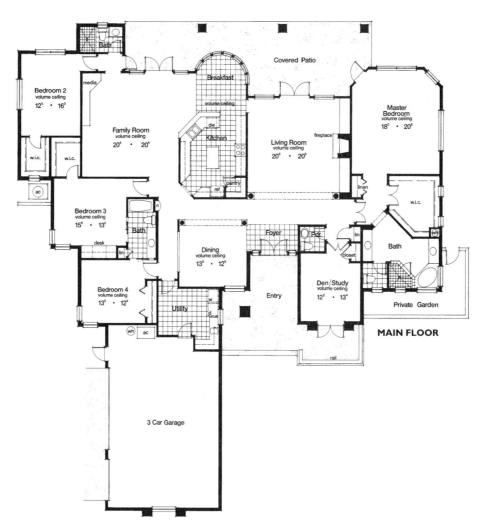

MAIN FLOOR

Design 32146

BL/ZIP   See Order Pages and Index for Info

Photography supplied by the Meredith Corporation

Units	Single
Price Code	K
Total Finished	3,895 sq. ft.
First Finished	2,727 sq. ft.
Second Finished	1,168 sq. ft.
Bonus Unfinished	213 sq. ft.
Basement Unfinished	2,250 sq. ft.
Garage Unfinished	984 sq. ft.
Deck Unfinished	230 sq. ft.
Porch Unfinished	402 sq. ft.
Dimensions	73'8"×72'2"
Foundation	Basement
Bedrooms	4
Full Baths	4
Half Baths	1
First Ceiling	9'
Second Ceiling	8'
Vaulted Ceiling	22'
Primary Roof Pitch	12:12
Secondary Roof Pitch	8:12
Max Ridge Height	43'
Roof Framing	Stick
Exterior Walls	2×6

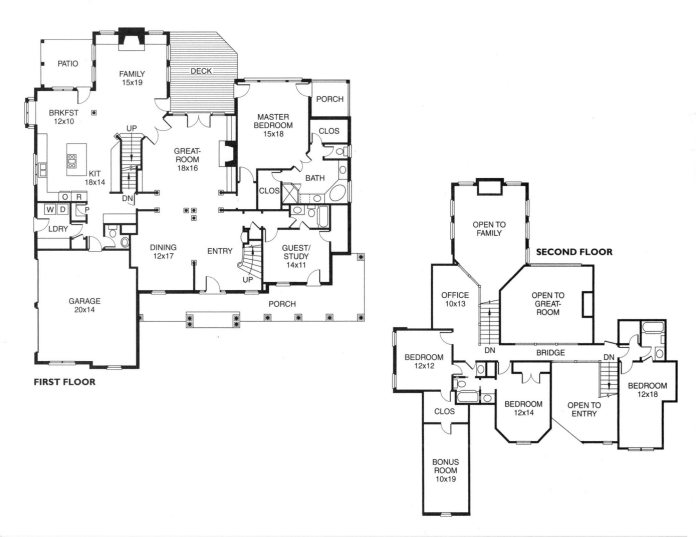

FIRST FLOOR

PATIO

FAMILY 15x19

DECK

BRKFST 12x10

UP

PORCH

MASTER BEDROOM 15x18

CLOS

KIT 18x14

GREAT-ROOM 18x16

DN

BATH

CLOS

O R

W D R

P

LDRY

DINING 12x17

ENTRY

GUEST/ STUDY 14x11

UP

GARAGE 20x14

PORCH

SECOND FLOOR

OPEN TO FAMILY

OFFICE 10x13

OPEN TO GREAT-ROOM

DN

BEDROOM 12x12

BRIDGE

DN

BEDROOM 12x18

CLOS

BEDROOM 12x14

OPEN TO ENTRY

BONUS ROOM 10x19

Design 98539

BL/ZIP   See Order Pages and Index for Info

Units	Single
Price Code	K
Total Finished	3,936 sq. ft.
First Finished	2,751 sq. ft.
Second Finished	1,185 sq. ft.
Bonus Unfinished	343 sq. ft.
Garage Unfinished	790 sq. ft.
Deck Unfinished	242 sq. ft.
Porch Unfinished	36 sq. ft.
Dimensions	79'×66'4''
Foundation	Basement
	Slab
Bedrooms	4
Full Baths	3
Half Baths	1
First Ceiling	10'
Primary Roof Pitch	12:12
Max Ridge Height	35'
Roof Framing	Stick
Exterior Walls	2x4

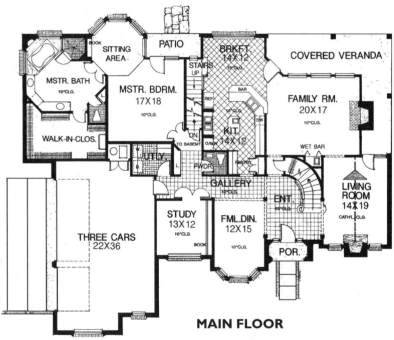

MAIN FLOOR

UPPER FLOOR

Design 93711

BL See Order Pages and Index for Info

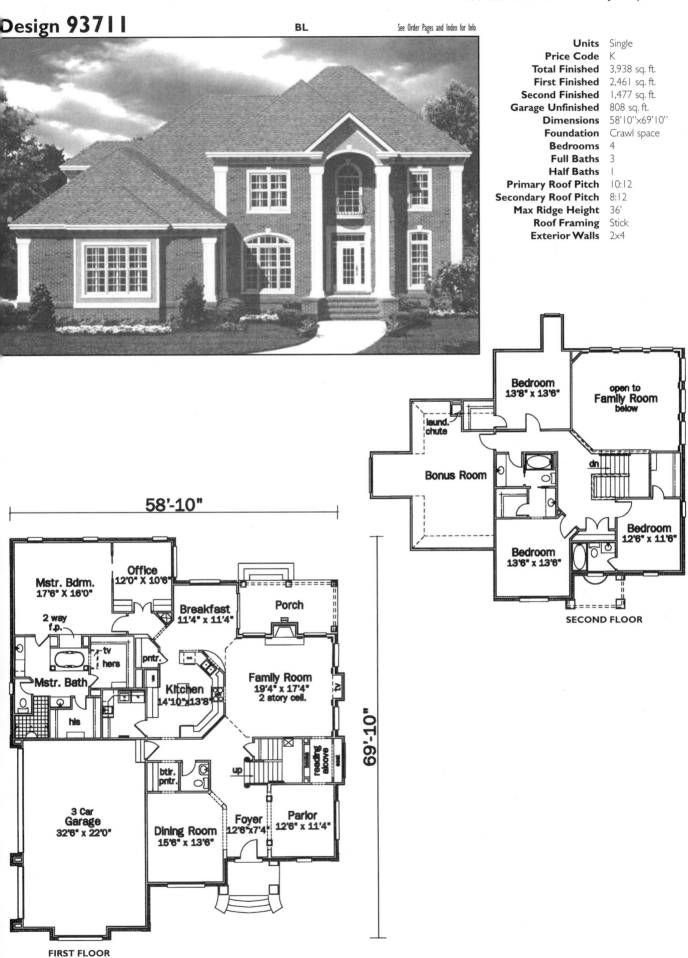

Units	Single
Price Code	K
Total Finished	3,938 sq. ft.
First Finished	2,461 sq. ft.
Second Finished	1,477 sq. ft.
Garage Unfinished	808 sq. ft.
Dimensions	58'10''x69'10''
Foundation	Crawl space
Bedrooms	4
Full Baths	3
Half Baths	1
Primary Roof Pitch	10:12
Secondary Roof Pitch	8:12
Max Ridge Height	36'
Roof Framing	Stick
Exterior Walls	2x4

DESIGN 62019

BL   See Order Pages and Index for Info

Units	Single
Price Code	K
Total Finished	3,947 sq. ft.
First Finished	2,777 sq. ft.
Second Finished	1,170 sq. ft.
Lower Unfinished	1,616 sq. ft.
Garage Unfinished	794 sq. ft.
Porch Unfinished	704 sq. ft.
Dimensions	70'x75'10''
Foundation	Basement
	Crawl space
	Slab
Bedrooms	3
Full Baths	3
Half Baths	2
First Ceiling	10'
Second Ceiling	9'
Primary Roof Pitch	10:12
Roof Framing	Stick
Exterior Walls	2x4

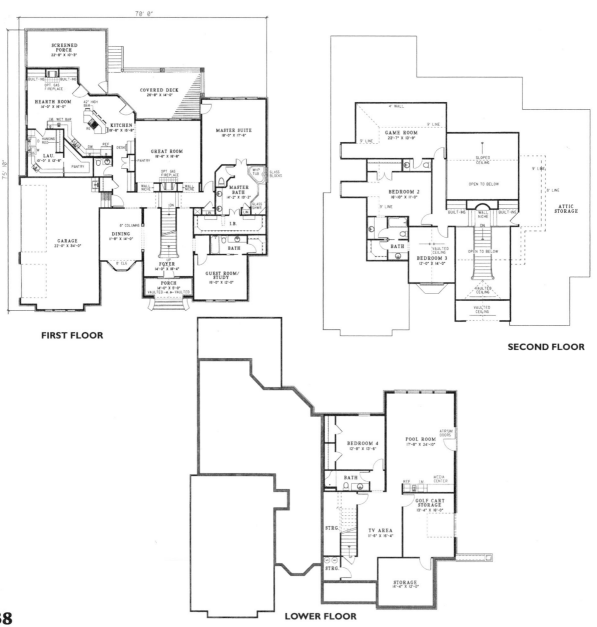

FIRST FLOOR

SECOND FLOOR

LOWER FLOOR

Design 94239

ML

See Order Pages and Index for Info

Units	Single
Price Code	L
Total Finished	4,106 sq. ft.
First Finished	3,027 sq. ft.
Second Finished	1,079 sq. ft.
Basement Unfinished	3,027 sq. ft.
Garage Unfinished	802 sq. ft.
Deck Unfinished	245 sq. ft.
Porch Unfinished	884 sq. ft.
Dimensions	87'4"x80'4"
Foundation	Basement Slab
Bedrooms	4
Full Baths	1
Half Baths	1
3/4 Baths	2
Primary Roof Pitch	10:12
Max Ridge Height	38'
Roof Framing	Truss
Exterior Walls	2x6

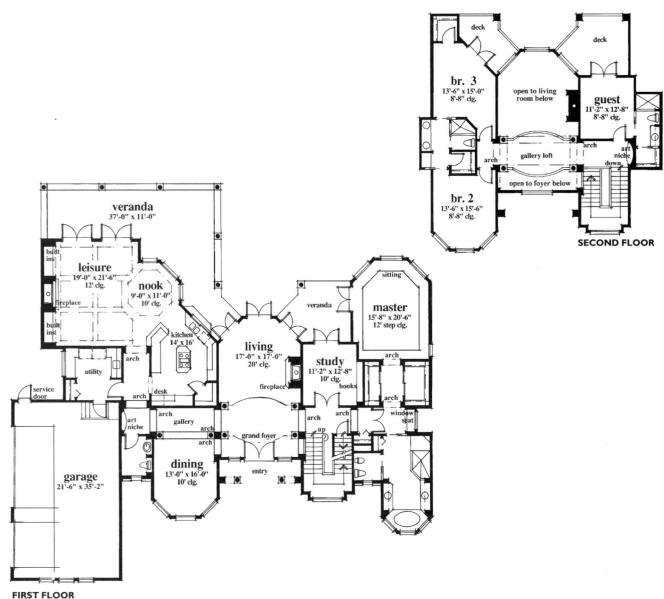

SECOND FLOOR

FIRST FLOOR

Design 97749

See Order Pages and Index for Info

Units	Single
Price Code	L
Total Finished	4,124 sq. ft.
First Finished	3,087 sq. ft.
Second Finished	1,037 sq. ft.
Garage Unfinished	691 sq. ft.
Deck Unfinished	489 sq. ft.
Porch Unfinished	255 sq. ft.
Dimensions	92'2"x70'10"
Foundation	Basement
Bedrooms	4
Full Baths	3
Half Baths	1
First Ceiling	9'
Second Ceiling	8'
Primary Roof Pitch	12:12
Secondary Roof Pitch	10:12
Max Ridge Height	28'6"
Roof Framing	Truss
Exterior Walls	2x6,2x8

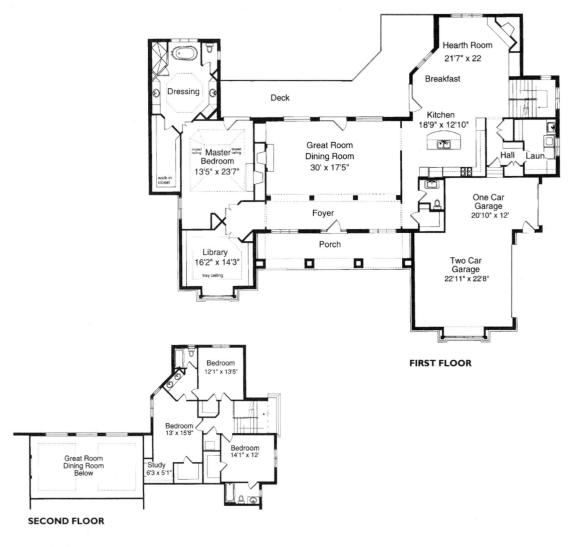

FIRST FLOOR

SECOND FLOOR

Design 98590

See Order Pages and Index for Info

Units	Single
Price Code	L
Total Finished	4,166 sq. ft.
Lower Finished	3,168 sq. ft.
Upper Finished	998 sq. ft.
Bonus Unfinished	320 sq. ft.
Garage Unfinished	810 sq. ft.
Deck Unfinished	290 sq. ft.
Porch Unfinished	180 sq. ft.
Dimensions	90'x63'5''
Foundation	Basement
	Crawl space
	Slab
Bedrooms	4
Full Baths	3
Half Baths	I
First Ceiling	10'
Second Ceiling	9'
Primary Roof Pitch	12:12
Secondary Roof Pitch	16:12
Max Ridge Height	36'
Roof Framing	Stick
Exterior Walls	2x4

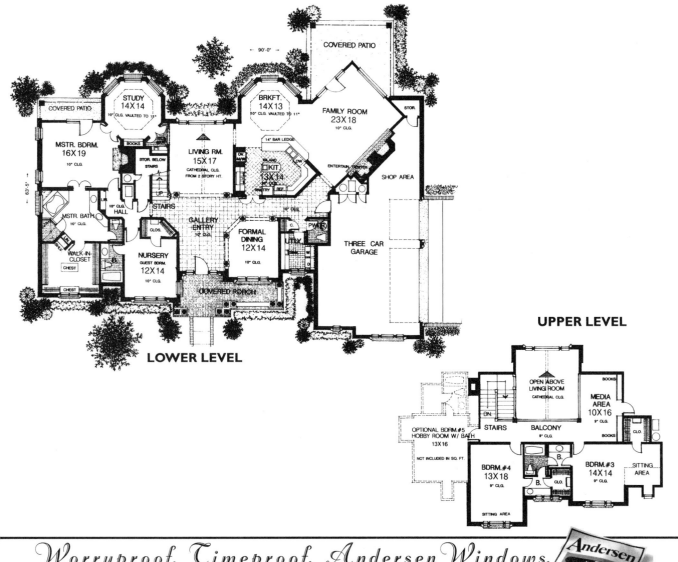

LOWER LEVEL

UPPER LEVEL

Design 93714

See Order Pages and Index for Info

Units	Single
Price Code	L
Total Finished	4,224 sq. ft.
First Finished	2,180 sq. ft.
Second Finished	672 sq. ft.
Lower Finished	1,372 sq. ft.
Garage Unfinished	578 sq. ft.
Porch Unfinished	357 sq. ft.
Dimensions	60'10''x58'2''
Foundation	Basement
Bedrooms	4
Full Baths	3
Half Baths	1
Primary Roof Pitch	10:12
Max Ridge Height	29'
Roof Framing	Stick
Exterior Walls	2x4

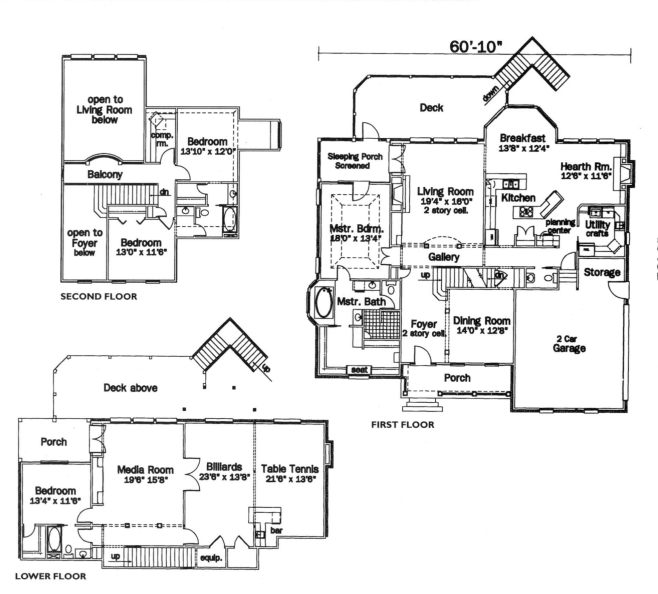

SECOND FLOOR

open to Living Room below

comp. rm.

Bedroom 13'10" x 12'0"

Balcony

dn

open to Foyer below

Bedroom 13'0" x 11'6"

FIRST FLOOR

60'-10"

58'2"

Deck

down

Breakfast 13'8" x 12'4"

Hearth Rm. 12'6" x 11'6"

Sleeping Porch Screened

Living Room 19'4" x 16'0" 2 story ceil.

Kitchen

planning center

Utility crafts

Mstr. Bdrm. 18'0" x 13'4"

Gallery

up

Storage

Mstr. Bath

Foyer 2 story ceil.

Dining Room 14'0" x 12'8"

2 Car Garage

dn

seat

Porch

LOWER FLOOR

Deck above

Porch

Bedroom 13'4" x 11'6"

Media Room 19'6" 15'8"

Billiards 23'6" x 13'8"

Table Tennis 21'6" x 13'6"

bar

up

equip.

Design 32063

BL/ML/ZIP/RRR   See Order Pages and Index for Info

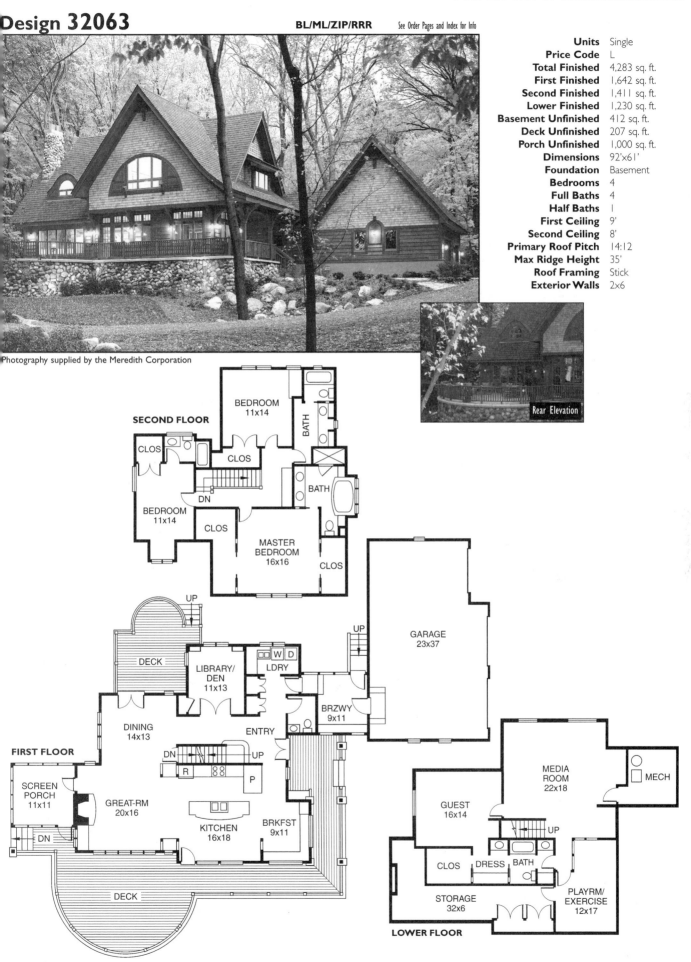

Photography supplied by the Meredith Corporation

Rear Elevation

Units	Single
Price Code	L
Total Finished	4,283 sq. ft.
First Finished	1,642 sq. ft.
Second Finished	1,411 sq. ft.
Lower Finished	1,230 sq. ft.
Basement Unfinished	412 sq. ft.
Deck Unfinished	207 sq. ft.
Porch Unfinished	1,000 sq. ft.
Dimensions	92'x61'
Foundation	Basement
Bedrooms	4
Full Baths	4
Half Baths	1
First Ceiling	9'
Second Ceiling	8'
Primary Roof Pitch	14:12
Max Ridge Height	35'
Roof Framing	Stick
Exterior Walls	2x6

SECOND FLOOR

BEDROOM 11x14
CLOS
CLOS
BATH
BATH
DN
BEDROOM 11x14
CLOS
MASTER BEDROOM 16x16
CLOS

FIRST FLOOR

UP
DECK
LIBRARY/ DEN 11x13
W D
LDRY
GARAGE 23x37
UP
BRZWY 9x11
DINING 14x13
ENTRY
SCREEN PORCH 11x11
DN   UP
R   P
DN
GREAT-RM 20x16
KITCHEN 16x18
BRKFST 9x11
DECK

LOWER FLOOR

MEDIA ROOM 22x18
MECH
GUEST 16x14
UP
CLOS   DRESS   BATH
STORAGE 32x6
PLAYRM/ EXERCISE 12x17

Design 63075

See Order Pages and Index for Info

Units	Single
Price Code	L
Total Finished	4,517 sq. ft.
First Finished	3,739 sq. ft.
Second Finished	778 sq. ft.
Garage Unfinished	844 sq. ft.
Dimensions	105'×84'
Foundation	Slab
Bedrooms	5
Full Baths	3
Half Baths	2
3/4 Baths	2
Primary Roof Pitch	8:12
Max Ridge Height	33'5"
Roof Framing	Truss
Exterior Walls	2x6

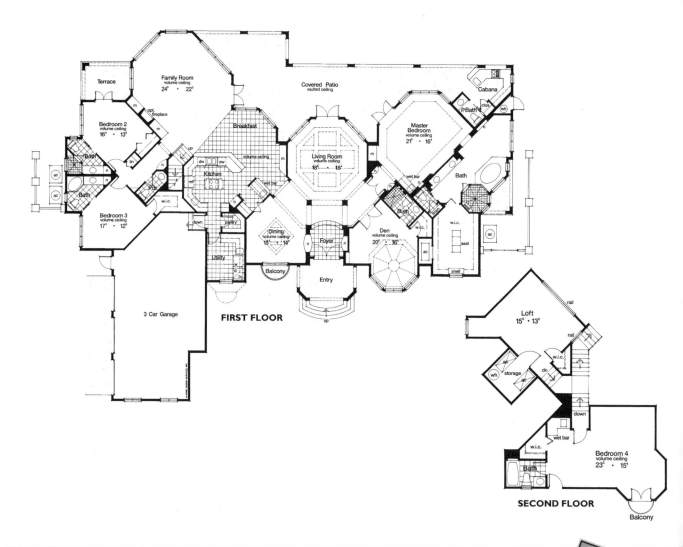

FIRST FLOOR

SECOND FLOOR

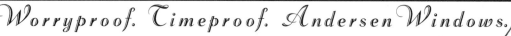

Design 63077

See Order Pages and Index for Info

Units	Single
Price Code	L
Total Finished	4,698 sq. ft.
First Finished	2,936 sq. ft.
Second Finished	1,762 sq. ft.
Bonus Unfinished	656 sq. ft.
Garage Unfinished	1,049 sq. ft.
Dimensions	77'x100'10''
Foundation	Slab
Bedrooms	4
Full Baths	4
First Ceiling	10'
Primary Roof Pitch	12:12
Max Ridge Height	37'
Roof Framing	Truss
Exterior Walls	2x4

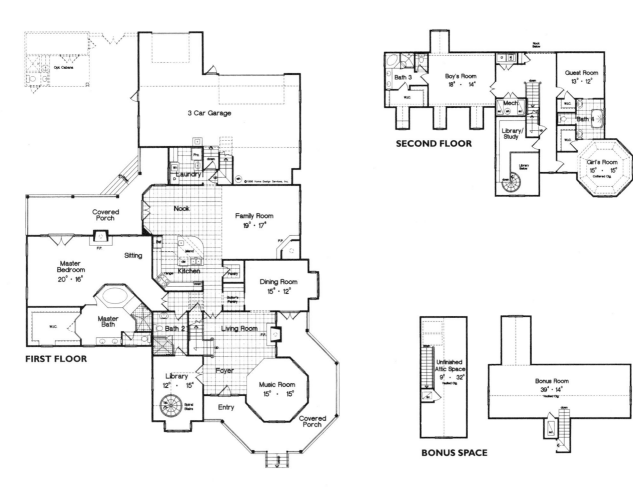

Design 94815

ML   See Order Pages and Index for Info

Units	Single
Price Code	L
Total Finished	4,986 sq. ft.
First Finished	3,687 sq. ft.
Second Finished	1,299 sq. ft.
Bonus Unfinished	233 sq. ft.
Basement Unfinished	3,036 sq. ft.
Garage Unfinished	683 sq. ft.
Deck Unfinished	334 sq. ft.
Dimensions	83'11"x73'
Foundation	Basement
Bedrooms	4
Full Baths	3
Half Baths	1
First Ceiling	10'
Second Ceiling	9'
Primary Roof Pitch	10:12
Max Ridge Height	39'
Roof Framing	Stick
Exterior Walls	2x4

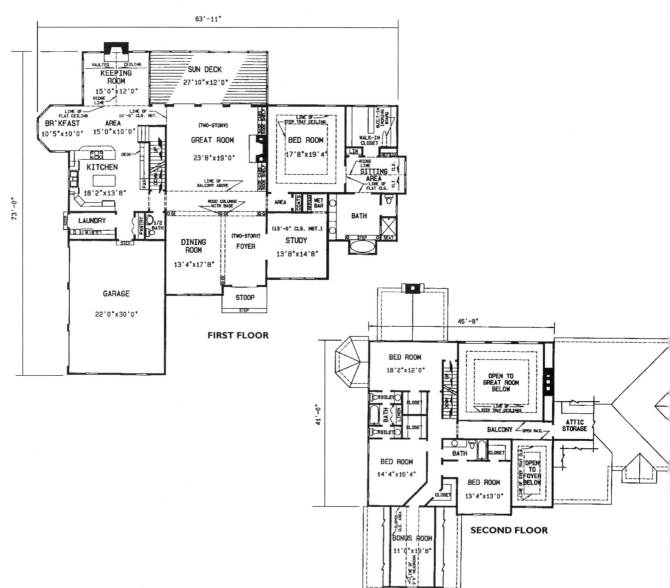

FIRST FLOOR

SECOND FLOOR

Design 63076

See Order Pages and Index for Info

Units	Single
Price Code	L
Total Finished	5,300 sq. ft.
First Finished	4,535 sq. ft.
Second Finished	765 sq. ft.
Garage Unfinished	834 sq. ft.
Dimensions	87'x97'6"
Foundation	Slab
Bedrooms	4
Full Baths	3
Half Baths	1
Primary Roof Pitch	6:12
Max Ridge Height	35'
Roof Framing	Truss
Exterior Walls	2x4

© HOME DESIGN SERVICES, INC.

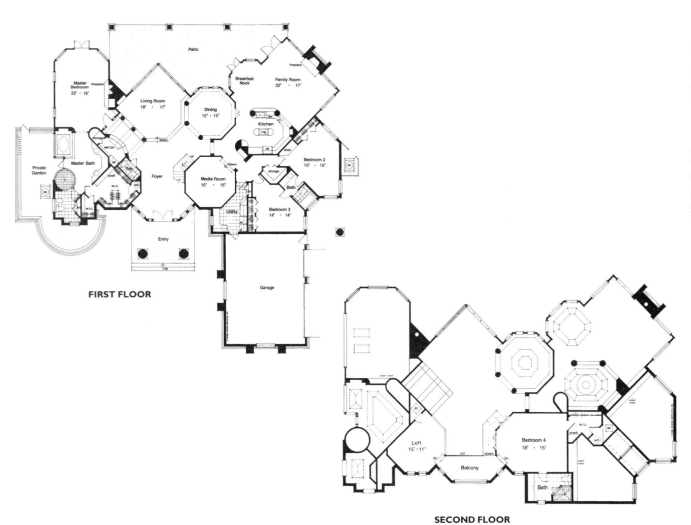

FIRST FLOOR

Patio

Master Bedroom 23' · 16' — fireplace

Living Room 18' · 17⁴

Breakfast Nook

Family Room 22⁰ · 17¹ — fireplace

Dining 15⁵ · 15⁵

Kitchen

Private Garden

Master Bath

Foyer

Media Room 15⁵ · 15⁵

Bedroom 2 15⁵ · 15⁵

Bath

Bedroom 3 14⁸ · 14⁸

Utility

Entry

Garage

SECOND FLOOR

Loft 15⁵ · 11⁰

Balcony

Bedroom 4 18⁰ · 15⁵

Bath

Design 63081

Units	Single
Price Code	L
Total Finished	5,603 sq. ft.
First Finished	4,284 sq. ft.
Second Finished	1,319 sq. ft.
Garage Unfinished	800 sq. ft.
Dimensions	109'4''x73'2''
Foundation	Slab
Bedrooms	4
Full Baths	5
Primary Roof Pitch	6:12
Max Ridge Height	32'9''
Roof Framing	Truss

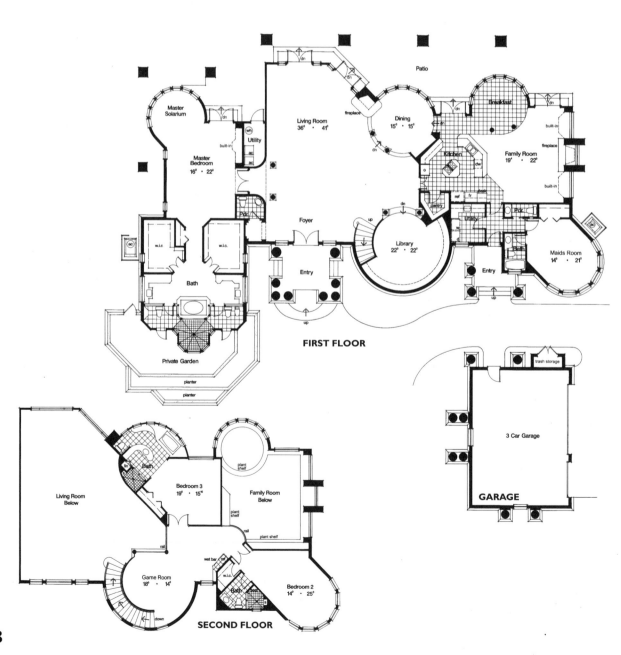

FIRST FLOOR

SECOND FLOOR

GARAGE

Design 63082

Units	Single
Price Code	L
Total Finished	6,462 sq. ft.
First Finished	3,874 sq. ft.
Second Finished	2,588 sq. ft.
Garage Unfinished	1,000 sq. ft.
Dimensions	137'8"x91'7"
Foundation	Slab
Bedrooms	5
Full Baths	8
Primary Roof Pitch	12:16
Max Ridge Height	44'6"
Roof Framing	Truss

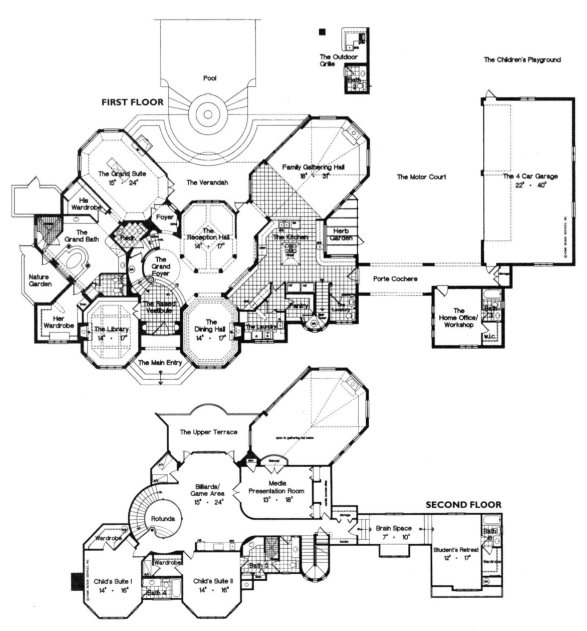

249

Exterior Elevations

Scaled drawings of the front, rear, sides of the home. Information pertaining to the exterior finish materials, roof pitches and exterior height dimensions.

Cabinet Plans

These plans, or in some cases elevations, will detail the layout of the kitchen and bathroom cabinets at a larger scale. Available for most plans.

Typical Wall Section

This section will address insulation, roof components, and interior and exterior wall finishes. Your plans will be designed with either 2x4 or 2x6 exterior walls, but most professional contractors can easily adapt the plans to the wall thickness you require.

Fireplace Details

If the home you have chosen includes a fireplace, the fireplace detail will show typical methods to construct the firebox, hearth and flue chase for masonry units, or a wood frame chase for a zero-clearance unit. Available for most plans.

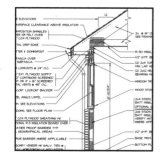

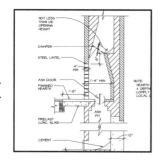

Foundation Plan

These plans will accurately dimension the footprint of your home including load bearing points and beam placement if applicable. The foundation style will vary from plan to plan.

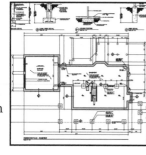

Roof Plan

The information necessary to construct the roof will be included with your home plans. Some plans will reference roof trusses, while many others contain schematic framing plans. These framing plans will indicate the lumber sizes necessary for the rafters and ridgeboards based on the designated roof loads.

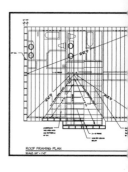

Typical Cross Section

A cut-away cross-section through the entire home shows your building contractor the exact correlation of construction components at all levels of the house. It will help to clarify the load bearing points from the roof all the way down to the basement. Available for most plans.

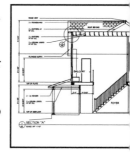

Detailed Floor Plans

The floor plans of your home accurately dimension the positioning of all walls, doors, windows, stairs and permanent fixtures. They will show you the relationship and dimensions of rooms, closets and traffic patterns. The schematic of the electrical layout may be included in the plan.

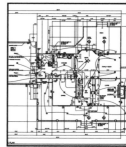

Stair Details

If stairs are an element of the design you have chosen, the plans will show the necessary information to build these, either through a stair cross section, or on the floor plans.

Reversed Plans Can Make Your Dream Home Just Right!

You could have exactly the home you want by flipping it end-for-end. Simply order your plans "reversed." We'll send you one full set of mirror-image plans (with the writing backwards) as a master guide for you and your builder.

The remaining sets of your order will come as shown in this book so the dimensions and specifications are easily read on the job site...but most plans in our collection come stamped "reversed" so there is no confusion.

As Shown   Reversed

We can only send reversed plans with multiple-set orders. There is a $50 charge for this service.

Some plans in our collection are available in Right Reading Reverse. Right Reading Reverse plans will show your home in reverse, with the writing on the plan being readable. This easy-to-read format will save you valuable time and money. Please contact our Customer Service Department to check for Right Reading Reverse availability. There is a $135 charge for Right Reading Reverse. **RRR**

Remember To Order Your Materials List

Available at a modest additional charge, the Materials List gives the quantity, dimensions, and specifications for the major materials needed to build your home. You will get faster, more accurate bids from your contractors and building suppliers — and avoid paying for unused materials and waste. Materials Lists are available for all home plans except as otherwise indicated, but can only be ordered with a set of home plans. Due to differences in regional requirements and homeowner or builder preferences... electrical, plumbing and heating/air conditioning equipment specifications are not designed specifically for each plan. **ML**

What Garlinghouse Offers

Home Plan Blueprint Package

By purchasing a multiple set package of blueprints or a vellum from Garlinghouse, you not only receive the physical blueprint documents necessary for construction, but you are also granted a license to build one, and only one, home. You can also make simple modifications, including minor non-structural changes and material substitutions, to our design, as long as these changes are made directly on the blueprints purchased from Garlinghouse and no additional copies are made.

Home Plan Vellums

By purchasing vellums for one of our home plans, you receive the same construction drawings found in the blueprints, but printed on vellum paper. Vellums can be erased and are perfect for making design changes. They are also semi-transparent making them easy to duplicate. But most importantly, the purchase of home plan vellums comes with a broader license that allows you to make changes to the design (ie, create a hand drawn or CAD derivative work), to make copies of the plan, and to build one home from the plan.

License To Build Additional Homes

With the purchase of a blueprint package or vellums you automatically receive a license to build one home and only one home, respectively. If you want to build more homes than you are licensed to build through your purchase of a plan, then additional licenses may be purchased at reasonable costs from Garlinghouse. Inquire for more information.

Modify Your Favorite Design, Made Easy

Questions?

Call our customer service department at 1.860.659.5667

#1 Modifying Your Garlinghouse Home Plan

Simple modifications to your dream home, including minor non-structural changes and mate substitutions, can be made between you and your builder by marking the changes directly on yo blueprints. However, if you are considering making significant changes to your chosen design, recommend that you use the services of The Garlinghouse Design Staff. We will help take you ideas and turn them into a reality, just the way you want. Here's our procedure!

When you place your Vellum order, you may also request a free Garlinghouse Modification K In this kit, you will receive a red marking pencil, furniture cut-out sheet, ruler, a self addressed mailing label and a form for specifying any additional notes or drawings that will help us under stand your design ideas. Mark your desired changes directly on the Vellum drawings. NOTE: Please use only a **red pencil** to mark your desired changes on the Vellum. Then, return the red lined Vellum set in the original box to us.

Important: Please roll the Vellums for shipping, *do not fold*.

We also offer modification estimates. We will provide you with an estimate to draft your changes based on your specific modifications before you purchase the vellums, for a $50 fee. A you receive your estimate, if you decide to have us do the changes, the $50 estimate fee will be deducted from the cost of your modifications. If, however, you choose to use a different service the $50 estimate fee is non-refundable. (Note: Personal checks cannot be accepted for the esti mate.)

Within 5 days of receipt of your plans, you will be contacted by a member of the design staff with an estimate for the design services to draw those changes. A 50% deposit is required befor we begin making the actual modifications to your plans.

Once the design changes have been completed to your vellum plan, a representative will call inform you that your modified Vellum plan is complete and will be shipped as soon as the final payment has been made. For additional information call us at 1-860-659-5667. Please refer to Modification Pricing Guide for estimated modification costs.

#2 Reproducible Vellums for Local Modification Ease

If you decide not to use Garlinghouse for your modifications, we recommend that you follow same procedure of purchasing Vellums. You then have the option of using the services of the or inal designer of the plan, a local professional designer, or architect to make the modifications.

With a Vellum copy of our plans, a design professional can alter the drawings just the way yo want, then you can print as many copies of the modified plans as you need to build your house. And, since you have already started with our complete detailed plans, the cost of those expensi professional services will be significantly less than starting from scratch. Refer to the price sche ule for Vellum costs.

Important Exchange policy: Reproducible Vellum copies of our home plans are co right protected and only sold under the terms of a license agreement that you will receive with your order. Should you not agree to the terms, then the Vellums may be exchanged. A 20% exchange fee will be charged. For any additional information, please call us at 1-860-659-5667